Problem Solving and Programming

MCS-011

For

Master In Computer Applications [MCA]

Dinesh Verma

MCA, BCA, 'A' & 'O' Level, SCJP(USA), JP

S.Roy

MCA, B.SC., DECM, DCPA, DECOM

Academic Consultant - Indira Gandhi National Open University

Visiting Faculty - Punjab Technical University

Guest Lecturer - Delhi College, Delhi University

Academic Counsellor - ST. Xavier's College, Kolkata University

Useful For

IGNOU, KSOU (Karnataka), Bihar University (Muzaffarpur), Nalanda University, Jamia Millia Islamia, Vardhman Mahaveer Open University (Kota), Uttarakhand Open University, Kurukshetra University, Seva Sadan's College of Education (Maharashtra), Lalit Narayan Mithila University, Andhra University, Pt. Sunderlal Sharma (Open) University (Bilaspur), Annamalai University, Bangalore University, Bharathiar University, Bharathidasan University, HP University, Centre for distance and open learning, Kakatiya University (Andhra Pradesh), KOU (Rajasthan), MPBOU (MP), MDU (Haryana), Punjab University, Tamilnadu Open University, Sri Padmavati Mahila Visvavidyalayam (Andhra Pradesh), Sri Venkateswara University (Andhra Pradesh), UCSDE (Kerala), University of Jammu, YCMOU, Rajasthan University, UPRTOU, Kalyani University, Banaras Hindu University (BHU) and all other Indian Universities.

Closer to Nature We use Recycled Paper

GULLYBABA PUBLISHING HOUSE PVT. LTD.

ISO 9001 & ISO 14001 CERTIFIED CO.

Published by:
GullyBaba Publishing House Pvt. Ltd.

Regd. Office:
2525/193, 1st Floor, Onkar Nagar-A,
Tri Nagar, Delhi-110035
(From Kanhaiya Nagar Metro Station Towards Old Bus Stand)
Ph. 011-27387998, 27384836, 27385249

Branch Office:
1A/2A, 20, Hari Sadan,
Ansari Road, Daryaganj,
New Delhi-110002
Ph. 011-23289034
011-45794768

E-mail: hello@gullybaba.com, Website: GullyBaba.com

New Edition

ISBN: 978-81-89086-42-8

Preface

This book is mainly targeted for MCA (New Course) exam of Problem Solving And Programming. It has been introduced in market after seeing the huge demand of ready to grasp material for exams with high level of quality, and its un-availability in market. We the GullyBaba Publishing House took a step ahead to publish the quality material focusing on exams at the same time giving you indepth knowledge about the subject.

GPH Book is the pioneer effort that provides a unique methodology so as to perform better in exams. If your goal is to attain higher grade use this powerful study tool independently or along with your text.

*On the Web : **www.gullybaba.com** is the vital resource for your exams acting as catalyst to boost up your preparation. Now you can access us on the net through **www.doctorignou.com, www.doeacconline.com, www.ignouonline.com, and www.astrologyeverywhere.com.***

Feedback about the book can be sent at **mcs014writers@gullybaba.com.**

Acknowledgments :

We appreciate the staff and facility support provided by GullyBaba Publishing House. In particular, we appreciate the encouragement and professional advises received from Mr. Ajay Saini, Mr. Tarun Sharma, H. Faheem Ahmed and many more. We are also thankful to Mr. Arun Bansal(Legal Advisor) for his advises given at various stages of publishing.

Also we would like to thank typesetting and designing team Mrs. Bhawna Verma, Mr. Shravan Vats, Mr. Mukesh.

We gratefully acknowledges the significant contributions of Mr. Mahesh Chand, Mrs. Bimla Devi, Mrs. Bhawna Verma and our experts in bringing out this publication.

New Delhi

Contents

Question Papers

Chapter - 1

INDTRODUCTION TO PROGRAM DEVELOPMENT

How to solve a problem?

Programming is a problem-solving activity. If you are a good problem solver, you could become a good programmer. Problem-solving methods are covered in many subject areas: - Business students learn to solve problems with a **systems approach**

- Engineering and Science students use the **engineering and science methods**
- Programmers use the **Software Development Method**

Software Development Method

To solve a problem using a computer, you need to: Think carefully about the problem & its solution

- Analyze the problem
- Specify the problem requirements

Plan it out beforehand (write an **algorithm**) Check it over to see that it addresses the problem Modify the solution if necessary Use the outlines to write a **program** that you can run on a computer Finally, the program is tested to verify that it behaves as intended.

Introduction to Algorithms

The **algorithm** is the abstract idea of solving a problem.

An **algorithm** is a step-to-step problem solving process in which a solution is arrived at a finite amount of time. The **algorithm** is written in an algorithmic language (or a pseudo code).

Algorithms vis programs

When an **algorithm** is coded using any programming language (e.g. C++), then it is called a **program**.The **program** is a set of instructions that can run by the computer.

Characteristics of Algorithms It should be **accurate**:

- It shouldn't be ambiguous (each step in the **algorithm** should exactly deter-

mine the action to be done).
It should be **effective**:
- It shouldn't include a step which is difficult to follow by a person (or the computer) in order to perform it. e.g. An **algorithm** to find the square root of 2 accurately could be written as
-This number cannot be executed in a finite time & it cannot be stored in a computer. Hence it is not effective.The **algorithm** should be **finite**:
- the **algorithm** has to end up in a point at which the task is complete.

Flowchart
It is another way to display the **algorithm**. It is composed of special geometric symbols connected by lines and contain the instructions. You can follow the lines from one symbol to another, executing the instructions inside it.

Flowchart Symbols
Start / End symbol
Input/Output symbol
Processing symbol
Condition & decision symbol
Continuation (connection symbol)

Problem Solving and Programming Strategy
Programming is a process of problem solving. The problem is solved according to the problem domain (e.g. students, money).To be a good problem solver and hence a good programmer, you must follow good problem solving technique. One common problem solving technique to solve the problem includes
- **analyzing** the problem & outlining the problem's **requirements**,
- **designing** steps (writing an **algorithm**)
- **implementing** the **algorithm** in a programming language (e.g. C++) and verify that the **algorithm** works,
- **maintaining** the program by using and modifying it if the problem domain changes.

(a) Problem Analysis
1- Thoroughly understand the problem
2- Understand the problem **specifications.**
3- If the problem is complex, you need to divide it into **sub-problems** and repeat steps (1& 2). That is, you need to analyze each sub-problem and understand its requirements.
Specifications can include the following:
- Does the problem require interaction with the user?

- Does the problem manipulate data? What is the input data & how it is represented?
- Does the problem produce output? How the results should be generated and formatted.
- What are the required formula for solution
- Is there any constraints on problem solution? An Example for Problem Specifications:

Problem Statement:
Determine the total cost of apples given the number of kilos of apples purchased and the cost per kilo of apples. We can summarize the information contained in the problem statement as follows:

Problem Input:
- Quantity of apples purchased (in kilos)
- Cost per kilo of apples (in dinars per kilo)

Problem Output:
- Total cost of apples (in dinars)

Formula:
Total cost = Number of kilos of apples × Cost per kilo

(b) Algorithm Design
Design an **algorithm** for the problem. If the problem is divided into smaller sub-problems, then design an **algorithm** for each sub-problem.

How to write an Algorithm?
An **algorithm** is a sequence of statements to perform some operations. You can write an **algorithm** with the following layout:

ALGORITHM algorithm_name
statements of **algorithm**
END algorithm_name

The **algorithm** would consist of at least the following tasks:
1- **Input** (Read the data)
2- **Processing** (Perform the computation)
3- **Output** (Display the results)

Structured Design:

Dividing the problem into smaller sub-problems is called "**structured design**", "**top-down design**", "**step-wise refinement**", and "**modular Programming**"

Structured Programming:

In the structured design

- The problem is divided into smaller sub-problems
- Each sub-problem is analyzed
- A solution is obtained to solve the sub-problem
- The solutions of all sub-problems are combined to solve the overall problem.This process of implementing a structured design is called "**structured programming**".

(c) Testing the Algorithm and Coding

Testing the Algorithm:

- You need to check the **algorithm** for correctness
- Use sample data for **algorithm** testing

Coding:

- After verifying that the **algorithm** is correct, you can code it in any high-level programming language
- The **algorithm** is now converted into a **program**

(d) Executing the Program

Compile the program (to check for syntax error) Run the program. If the execution doesn't go well, then reexamine the code, the **algorithm**, or even the problem analysis.

Advantages of Structured Programming Easy to discover errors in a program that is well analyzed and well designed. Easy to modify a program that is thoroughly analyzed and carefully deigned.

Q1. What are the benefits of using flowchart ?

The benefits of using flowcharts are :

○ **Promote process understanding by explaining the steps pictorially.** People may have differing ideas about how a process works. A flowchart can help you gain agreement about the sequence of steps. Flowcharts promote understanding in a way that written procedures cannot do. One good flowchart can replace pages of words.

○ **Provide a tool for training employees.** Because of the way they visually lay out the sequence of steps in a process, flowcharts can be very helpful in training employees to perform the process according to standardized procedures.

o **Identify problem areas and opportunities for process improvement.** Once you break down the process steps and diagram them, problem areas become more visible. It is easy to spot opportunities for simplifying and refining your process by analyzing decision points, redundant steps, and rework loops.

o **Depict customer-supplier relationship,** helping the process workers understand who their customers are, and how they may sometimes act as suppliers, and sometimes as customers in relation to other people.

o They are **self-documenting**.

o **Allow easy review and maintenance** of a software system. This results in less time spent on debugging

o **Helps to develop reusable algorithmic structures** hence they are useful for identifying the logic of generic systems. Hence they help the user to develop concise generalize algorithmic solutions to similar problems.

o Force **careful and concise solution** to the logic of a program problem.

o A simplified **consistent means** for developing program logic

Q2. Draw the various symbols used in flowchart with explanation.

Flow Chart : The program flowchart is a detailed graphical representation of the logical flow of data within that module. It serves as the logical road map that the programmers will use to write programming code. When following structured programming principles, the program flowchart must use the standard symbols as shown in Figure and certain guidelines concerning control structures, which will now be described:

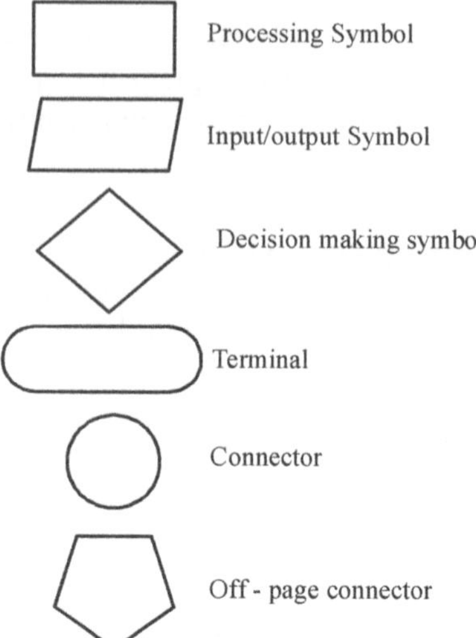

Standard Symbols Used to Construct a Program flowchart

LIMITATIONS OF USING FLOWCHARTS

Q3. What are the limitations of using Flowcharts ?

Complex logic : Sometimes, the program logic is quite complicated. In that case, flowchart becomes complex and clumsy.

Alterations and Modifications: If alterations are required the flowchart may require re-drawing completely.

Reproduction : As the flowchart symbols cannot be typed, reproduction of flowchart becomes a problem.

The essentials of what is done can easily be lost in the technical details of how it is done.

Q4. Write the guidelines in flowcharting.

The following are some guidelines in flowcharting:

a. In drawing a proper flowchart, all necessary requirements should be listed out in logical order.

b. The flowchart should be clear, neat and easy to follow. There should not be any room for ambiguity in understanding the flowchart.

c. The usual direction of the flow of a procedure or system is from left to right or top to bottom.

d. Only one flow line should come out from a process symbol.

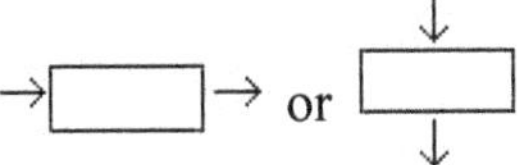

e. Only one flow line should enter a decision symbol, but two or three flow lines, one for each possible answer, should leave the decision symbol.

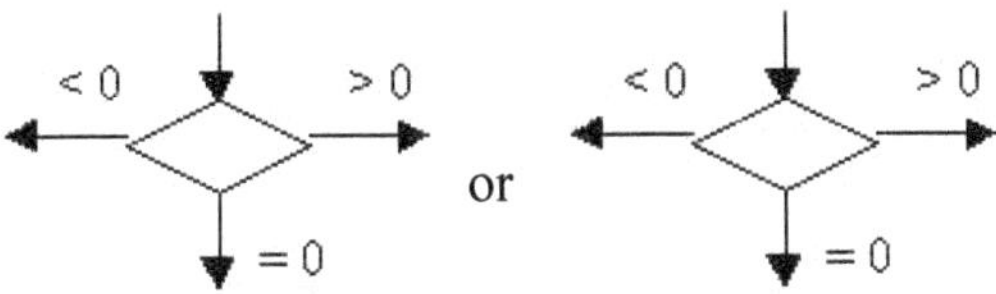

f. Only one flow line is used in conjunction with terminal symbol.

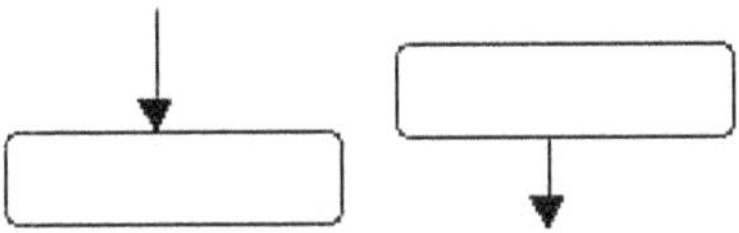

g. Write within standard symbols briefly. As necessary, you can use the annotation symbol to describe data or computational steps more clearly.

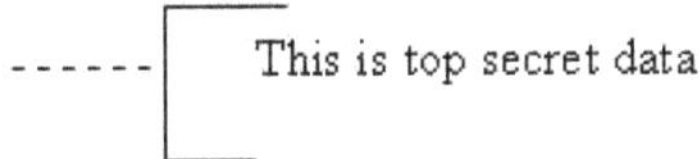

h. If the flowchart becomes complex, it is better to use connector symbols to reduce the number of flow lines. Avoid the intersection of flow lines if you want to make it more effective and better way of communication.
i. Ensure that the flowchart has a logical *start* and *finish.* It is useful j. to test the validity of the flowchart by passing through it with a simple test data.

Example 1
Draw a flowchart to find the sum of first 50 natural numbers.
Answer: The required flowchart is given in Fig.

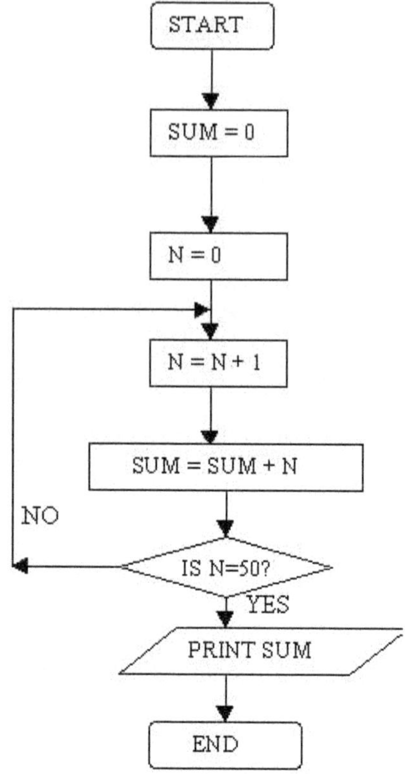

Fig. Sum of first 50 natural numbers

Example 2
Draw a flowchart to find the largest of three numbers A, B, and C.
Answer: The required flowchart is shown in Fig

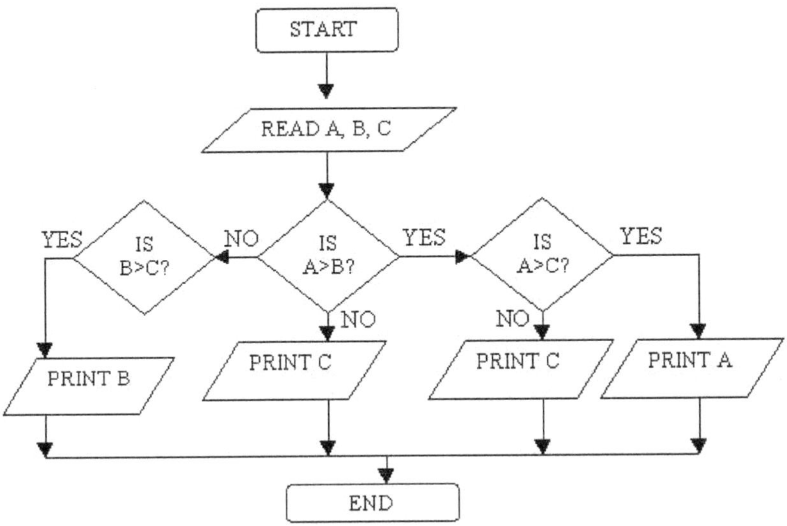

Fig . Flowchart for finding out the largest of three numbers

Example 3

Draw a flowchart for computing factorial N (N!)
Where N! = 1 ´ 2 ´ 3 ´ ...... N .

Answer:

The required flowchart has been shown in fig

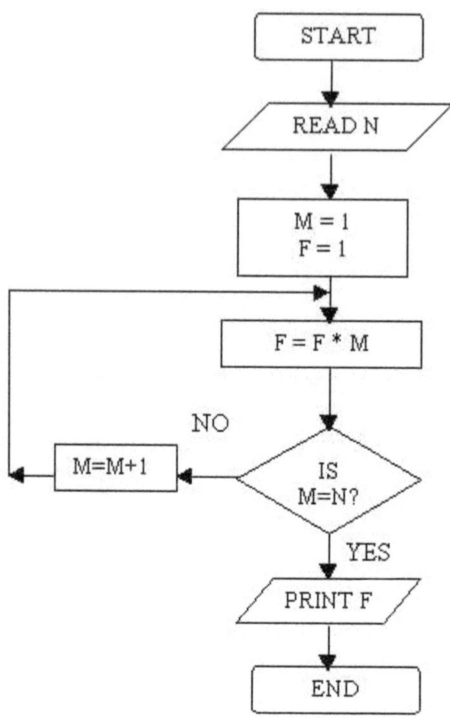

Fig. Flowchart for computing factorial N

When a flowchart describes a process in which a number of different people, departments, or functional areas are involved, it is sometimes difficult to keep track of who is responsible for each step. A useful additional technique for tracking this, and for analysing the number of times a process is 'handed over' to different people, is to divide the flowchart into columns. Head up each column with the name of the person or function involved in the process, and each time they carry out an action show it in their column. This is illustrated in the flowchart below which covers a simple purchasing process. It shows how control of the process passes from the person initiating the purchase, to the Purchasing Dept. and then to the Supplier.

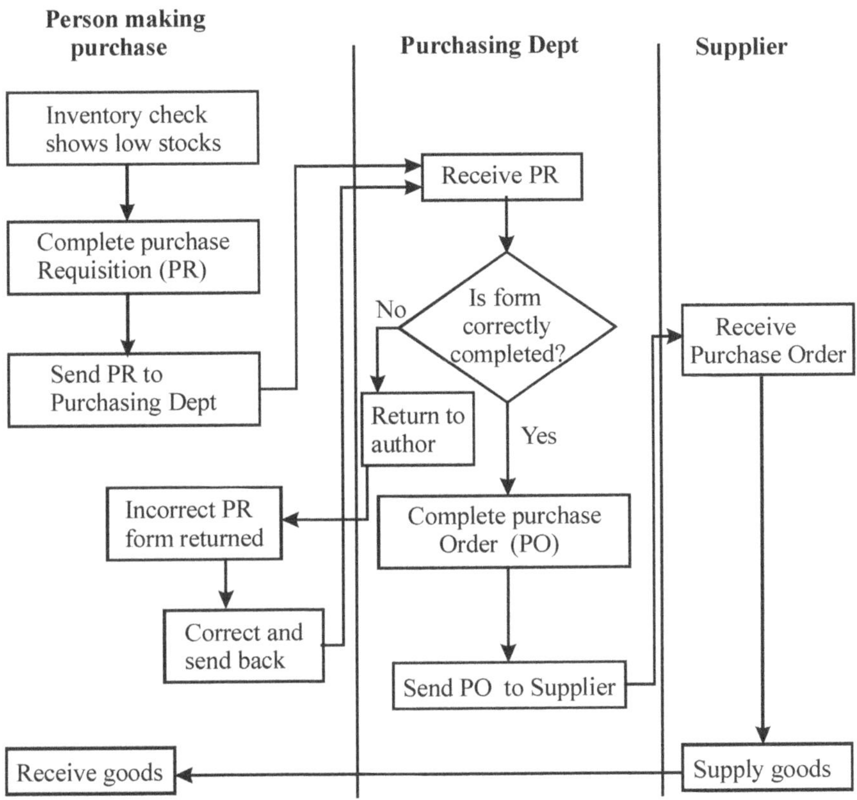
Person making purchase
Purchasing Dept
Supplier
Inventory check shows low stocks
Complete purchase Requisition (PR)
Send PR to Purchasing Dept
Receive PR
Is form correctly completed?
No
Yes
Return to author
Incorrect PR form returned
Correct and send back
Complete purchase Order (PO)
Send PO to Supplier
Receive Purchase Order
Supply goods
Receive goods

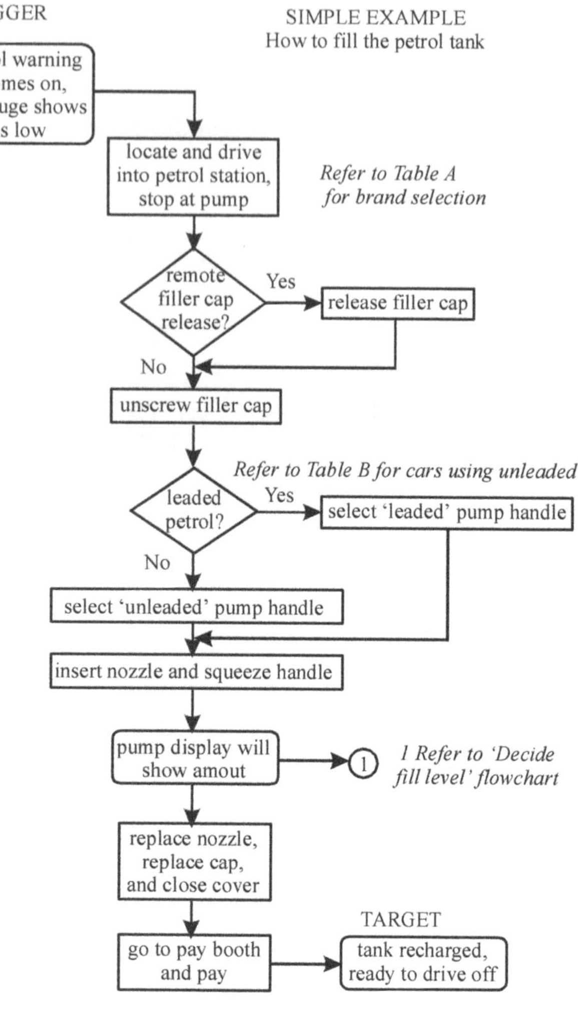

Flowcharts help to identify all the key tasks involved and the finished chart can be used,

- as a springboard for further discussion of the process
- to connect with other flowcharts explaining related activities
- to identify points where data can be usefully collected and analysed
- to isolate possible problem areas
- to communicate the process to those unfamiliar with it.

Q5. Write a program in 'C' to append some characters in an already existing file and also find the number of characters in the resultant file after appending. [DECO5, Q5(a)] [10]

```
#include<conio.h>
#include<stdio.h>
main()
{

FILE *fs,*ft;
int noc=0;
char ch,ch1;
clrscr();
fs=fopen("C:\\file1.c","r");
if(fs==NULL)
{
puts("Could not open source file");
exit();
}
ft= fopen("C:\\file2.c","ar");
if(ft==NULL)
{
puts("Cannot open target file");
fclose(fs);
exit();
}

while(1)
{
ch = fgetc(fs);
if(ch==EOF)
break;
else
fputc(ch,ft);
}


fclose(ft);

ft= fopen("C:\\file2.c","a+");
if(ft==NULL)
{
```

```
puts("Cannot open target file");
fclose(fs);
exit();
}


ch1=fgetc(ft);
while(ch1!=EOF)
{
noc++;
ch1=fgetc(ft);
}

printf("\n The number of characters in the file are :-  %d ",noc);

fclose(fs);
fclose(ft);
getch();
}
```

Chapter - 2
'C' CONCEPTS & PROGRAMMING INVOLVING POINTERS, FUNCTIONS & FILES

1. *Introduction*

C is a programming language developed at AT & T's Bell Laboratories of USA in 1972. It was designed and written by a man named Dennis Ritchie. In the late seventies C began to replace the more familiar languages of that time like PL/I, ALGOL etc. Ritchie seems to have been rather surprised that so many programmers preferred C to older languages like FORTRAN or PL/I, or the newer ones like Pascal and APL.

2. *Constants*

Constants whose value is not change when the program is run.
For example In C old version we declare constant with the help of **#define** statement. But in latest version we use the small keyword to define constant **const**

eg.

```
#define  size 10
const int a=10;
```

3. *Identifiers*

Names, also called *identifiers* or words, denote the variables, arrays, structures, unions, functions in the program, whether defined by the programmer or by the C system. The names that have predefined meaning are known as *reserved words or key words*, and can't be used by the programmer for other purpose. The various reserved words in C are listed in Table. A C name consists of a sequence of alphanumeric characters. The following are valid C names:
Word_count_ax sum lamda1 factorial integer a2345 number serno temp

4. *Variable*

variable whose value is change throughout a program.Declaration of variable e.g

```
int a;        //declaring a int type variable that store int type of data
char  b;      //declaring a char type of variable that store float type of data
float c;      // declaring a float type of variable that store float type of
              // data
```

5. *C data types*

C has a concept of 'data types' which are used to define a variable before its use.

The definition of a variable will assign storage for the variable and define the type of data that will be held in the location.

✓ **Type of data type**

So what data types are available in C? Are two type.

1. Build In
2. User Define

5.1 Build in

The data type that are made at the time design of compiler is know as build in data type.

✓ int
✓ float
✓ double
✓ char
✓ void

5.2 User Define

The data type that is made by the user. According to it need. Is know as user define data type.

✓ **Structure**
✓ **Enum**

KEYWORDS IN C

Auto	double	if	static
Break	else	int	struct
Case	enum	long	switch
Char	extern	near	typedef
Const	float	register	union
Continue	far	return	unsigned
Default	for	short	void
Do	goto	signed	while

Storage Classes :

1) auto - storage class

auto is the default storage class for local variables.

```
{
   int Count;
   auto int Month;
}
```

The example above defines two variables with the same storage class. Auto can only be used within functions, i.e. local variables.

2) register - Storage Class

register is used to define local variables that should be stored in a register instead of RAM. This means that the variable has a maximum size equal to the register size (usually one word) and cant have the unary '&' operator applied to it (as it does not have a memory location).

```
{
  register int  Miles;
}
```

Register should only be used for variables that require quick access - such as counters. It should also be noted that defining 'register' goes not mean that the variable will be stored in a register. It means that it MIGHT be stored in a register - depending on hardware and implementation restrictions.

3) static - Storage Class

static is the default storage class for global variables. The two variables below (count and road) both have a static storage class.

```
static int Count;
int Road;

main()
{
  printf("%d\n", Count);
  printf("%d\n", Road);
}
```

'Static' can also be defined within a function. If this is done, the variable is initialised at compilation time and retains its value between calls. Because it is initialized at compilation time, the initialisation value must be a constant. This is serious stuff - tread with care.

```
void Func(void)
{
  static Count=1;
```

```
}
```

Here is an example

There is one very important use for 'static'. Consider this bit of code.

```
char *Func(void);
main()
{
  char *Text1;
  Text1 = Func();
}
char *Func(void)
{
  char Text2[10]="martin";
  return(Text2);
}
```

'Func' returns a pointer to the memory location where 'Text2' starts BUT Text2 has a storage class of auto and will disappear when we exit the function and could be overwritten by something else. The answer is to specify:

```
static char Text[10]="martin";
```

The storage assigned to 'Text2' will remain reserved for the duration if the program.

4) Extern - storage Class

extern defines a global variable that is visible to ALL object modules. When you use 'extern' the variable cannot be initialized as all it does is point the variable name at a storage location that has been previously defined.

Source 1	**Source 2**
extern int count;	int count=5;
write()	main()
{	{
printf("count is %d\n", count);	write();
}	}

Count in 'source 1' will have a value of 5. If source 1 changes the value of count - source 2 will see the new value.

Type Casting :

In arithmetic expressions, we have seen that if operation is to be performed on operands of different data type with lower rank is converted to a value of higher rank, and then operation takes place. Similarly in an assignment statement, the value on the right hand side of the assignment operator is converted to type of the variable to which it is to be assigned, and then value is stored in that variable.

In addition to these situations, sometimes we need to force the compiler to convert a value to a particular data type. For example, suppose our program uses a variable named *temp* of type *float*, and at some point we want to calculate square root of its value. Turbo C contains a library function *sqrt()*, declared in *math.h* header file, that return the square root, but the argument sent to this function must be of type *double*, otherwise it will return a nonsense value. So there is need to convert variable *temp* to type double. To do this, we use the *cast* operator, which consists of putting parentheses around the name of the data type as shown below:

(type) exp

where *exp* is either a constant, a variable, an array element or a function. For the above example, we can write

result = sqrt ((double) temp);

The expression *(double)* causes the value of variable *temp* to be converted from type *float* to type *double* before it is used.

An operator must have operands of the same type before it can carry out the operation. Because of this, C will perform some automatic conversion of data types.

These are the general rules for binary operators (* + / % etc):

If either operand is long double the other is converted to long double.

Otherwise, if either operand is double the other is converted to double

Otherwise, if either operand is float the other is converted to float

Otherwise, convert char and short to int

Then, if an operand is long convert the other to long.

Output format specifier :

Format Specifier	Used For
%d	signed decimal integer
%ld	signed long decimal integer
%u	unsigned decimal integer
%f	single precision floating real number
%lf	double precision floating real number
%e	floating point (exponential notation)
%x	unsigned hexadecimal integer
%o	unsigned octal integer
%c	single character
%s	string

Escape Sequence	Represents	Effect
\n	Newline	has the effect of both a carriage return and linefeed i.e. the subsequent output starts from new line.
\r	tab	move over to the next eight-space-wide field.
\b	backspace	moves the cursor one space left.
\r	carriage return	carriage return.
\f	formfeed	advances to the top of the next page on printer.
\a	beep	produces one audio tone of the speaker.
\’	single quote	insert character’ in the output.
\”	double quote	insert character” in the output.
\\	backslash	insert character\ in the output.

Logical Operator Example :

A company insures its drivers in the following cases:

- If the driver is married.
- If the driver is unmarried, male & above 30 years of age.
- If the driver is unmarried, female & above 25 years of age.

In all other cases the driver is not insured. If the marital status, sex and age of the driver are the inputs, write a program to determine whether the driver is to be insured or not.

We can write a program for the above problem in two ways:

(a) Without using && and || operators
(b) Using && and || operators

Method (a)

```
/* Insurance of driver-without using logical operators */
main( )
{
char sex, ms:
int age:

printf ( " Enter age, sex, marital status" ) ;
scant ( " %d %c %c", &age, &sex, &ms) ;

if ( ms == M )
printf ( " Driver is insured" ) ;
else
{
if  ( sex  == 'M')
{
if (age > 30 )
printf ( " Driver is insured " ) ;

else
printf ( " Driver is not insured " ) ;

}
else
{
if  ( age > 25 )
printf " Driver is insured" ) ;
else
printf ( " Driver is not insured " ) ;
}
}
}
```

Method (b)

As mentioned above, in this example we expect the answer to be either 'Driver is insured' or 'Driver is not insured'. If we list down all those cases in which the driver is insured, then they would be:

(a) Driver is married.
(b) Driver is an unmarried male above 30 years of age.
(c) Driver is an unmarried female above 25 years of age.

Since all these cases lead to the driver being insured, they can be combined together using && and ll as shown in the program below:

```
/* insurance of driver – using logical operators */
main ( )
{
char sex, ms :
int age:
printf ( " Enter age, sex, marital status " ) :
scanf ( " %d %c %c " &age, &sex, &ms ) :

if ( ( ms – 'M' ) ll (ms == 'U' && sex == 'M' && age > 30 ) ll
/ms == 'U' && sex == 'F' "&& age> 25 , ))
printf ( 'Driver is insured' ) ;
else
printf ( " Driver is not insured " ) ;
}
```

In this program it is important to note that :

➢ The driver will be insured only if one of the conditions enclosed in parentheses evaluates to true.

➢ For the second pair of parentheses to evaluate to true, each condition in the parentheses separated by && must evaluate to true.

➢ Even if one of the conditions in the second parentheses evaluates of false, then the whole of the parentheses evaluates to false.

➢ The last two of the above arguments apply to third pair of parentheses as well.

Thus, we can conclude that the && and || are useful in the following programming situations :

(a) When it is to be tested whether a value falls within a particular range or not.
(b) When after testing several conditions the outcome is only one of the two answers.

If & Switch

If statement

The syntax of the if statement is as follows:

if(expression)
statement);

The expression must be enclosed in parenthesis. The statement may be a compound statement.

for example

if (y>5)
x=0;

The statement will be executed only if the expression is true. The syntax of the if else statement is as follows:

if(expression)
statement-1;
else
statement-2;

if expression is true statement –1 is executed. If expression is false, statement –2 is executed. So depending on the truth value of expression, either statement-1 or statement 2 is executed,

Nested if statements :

The statement sequence of if or else may contain another statement i.e. the if else statement can be nested within one another as shown below:

Syntax of nested if statement :

```
if (expression-1)
{
    if(expression-2)
{
statement;
}
else
      if(expression-3)
      {
statement;
      }
      else
{
statement;
}
```

}
there may be one problem raised with nested if that is to decide "which if does the else match".

☞ Each else matches to its nearest unmatched preceding if.
For example

```
if(a<10)
{
if(b>5)
Sum=Sum + a + b;
else
Sum=Sum – a – b ;
```

Multiple if statement :

Syntax of multiple if statement :

```
if(expression-1)
statement –1;
else if (expression –2)
    statement –2;
else if(expression –3)
statement-3;
..
,.
else if(expression –n)
statement-n;
else
    default statement;
```

the expression are evaluated in order and if any condition is true then the statement associated with it is executed and this terminated the whole chain. The last else part is execute as default statement.

Example of If :

```
#include <stdio.h>

main()
{
  int i=1;        /* Define an integer variable.*/

        /*
         * i == 1 expression is evaluated. If TRUE the
         * first block is executed.
```

```
        * if i == 1 is FALSE the optional else block
        * is executed  */
  if (i == 1)
  {
    puts ("i is equal to 1\n");
  }
  else
  {
    puts("i is NOT equal to 1");
  }
}
```

The switch statement :

If you have a long series of conditions to check, a large block of if ; else statements can get tiresome and confusing to write (and read, later on). For this reason, C++ provides the switch statement. The general syntax is:

```
Switch (expression)
{
   case value1:
   statements
   [break;]
   case value 2:
   statements
   [break:]
   ....
         default:
    Statements
}
```

An expression is evaluated in the first line of a switch statement, and its value is used to determine the action or actions to take. The value of the expression is compared in turn with each value listed next to a case statement. If a match occurs, the statements following that case statement are executed. The break statement (shown in square brackets to indicate that it is optional; the square brackets are not actually part of the code), if present, causes the switch statement to be terminated after the statements in the current case block are executed., that is, control will pass to the statement immediately after the final brace ending the switch statement without any further case statements being tested, if the break statement is not present , the next case statement will be checked as well . In other words, a switch statement offers greater flexibility that an if.. Else statement in that it allows more than one block of statements to be executed.

Example of Switch :

```
main(int argc, char *argv[])
{
  switch (argc) /* Switch evaluates an expression
(argc)*/
   {
        /* If expression resolves to 1, jump here */
   case 1:
     puts("Only the command was entered.");
     break; /* break - cases the execution to jump
              out of the 'switch' block.*/

        /* If expression resolves to 2, jump here */
   case 2:
     puts("Command plus one parm entered");
     break;
        /* If expression resolves to 3, jump here */
   case 3:
     puts("Command plus two parm entered");
     break;
                /* Any other value jumps here.*/
   default:
     printf("Command plus %d parms entered\n", argc-1);
     break;
   }
}
```

Loop

The while Loop :

It is often the case in programming that you want to do something a fixed number of times. Perhaps you want to calculate gross salaries of then different persons, or you want to convert temperatures from centigrade to Fahrenheit for 15 different cities. The while loop is ideally suited for such cases. Let us look at a simple example which uses a while loop.

```
/* Calculation of simple interest for 3 sets of p, n and r*/
main( )
{
```

```
int p, n, count :
float r, sl ;

count = 1 :
while (count <= 3)
{
printf ("\Enter values of p, n, and r");
scanf ("%d %d %f, &p, &n, &r );
si = p * n * r / 100;
printf ( " Simple interest = Rs. %f, si );
count = count + 1 ;
}
}
```

And here are a few sample runs ....

Enter values of p, n and r 1000 5 13.5
Simple interest = Rs. 675,000000
Enter values of p, n and r 2000 5 13.5
Simple interest = Rs. 1350. 000000
Enter values of p, n and r 3500 5 3.5
Simple interest = Rs. 612.500000

Example of While :

```
#include <stdio.h>

main()
{
    int i=1;  /* Define an integer variable. */

     /*
      * i <= 10 expression is evaluated. If TRUE the
      * block is executed.
      */

    while (i <= 10)
    {
        printf ("i is %i\n", i);
        i++;
    }
}
```

The for Loop :

Perhaps one reason why few programmers use while is that they are too busy using the for, which is probably the most popular looping control. The for allows us to specify three things about a loop in a single line:

(a) Setting a loop counter to an initial value.

(b) Testing the loop counter to determine whether its value has reached the number of repetitions desired.

(c) Increasing the value of loop counter each time the program segment within the loop has been executed.

The general form of for statement is as under:

```
For ( initialize counter : test counter : increment counter)
{
do this ;
and this ;
and this ;
}
```

Let us write down the simple interest program using for. Compare this program with the one which we wrote using while.

```
/* Calculation of simple interest for 3 sets of p, n and r */
main ( )
{
int p, n, count ;
float r, si ;
for ( count = 1 ; count <= 3 ; count = count + 1)
{
printf ( "Enter values of p, n, and r ");
scanf( " %d %d %f , &p, &n, &r ");
si = p * n * r /100 ;
printf ( * Simple interest = Rs. %f\n", si );
}
}
```

Example of For :

```
#include <stdio.h>

main()
{
  int i;                    /* Define an integer */
                            /*
```

```
 * i=1 is executed the first time into the loop.
 * i<=10 is then tested, if true, the block is ex-
ecuted.
 * ++1 is the increment, before i<=10 is retested.
                              */
  for (i=1; i<=10; ++i)
  {
    printf ("loop counter = %i\n", i);
  }
}
```

Example of For (Advanced) :

```
#include <stdio.h>

main()
{
  int i,j;        /* Define integers */
 /* 'i' and 'j' get initalised on the 'for'.
 * Then they both are incremented and decremented
 * before 'i' is tested.
 */
  for (i=1, j=10; i<=10; ++i, --j)
  {
    printf ("   i = %02d  j = %02d\n", i, j);
  }
}
/
*****************************************************************
   O/P will look like this:

   i = 01  j = 10
   i = 02  j = 09
   i = 03  j = 08
   i = 04  j = 07
   i = 05  j = 06
   i = 06  j = 05
   i = 07  j = 04
   i = 08  j = 03
   i = 09  j = 02
   i = 10  j = 01
*****************************************************************/
```

The do-while Loop :

The do-while loop looks like this :

```
Do
{
this ;
and this ;
and this ;
and this ;
} while ( this condition is true ) ;
```

There is a minor difference between the working of while and do-while loops. This difference is the place where the condition is tested. The while teste the condition before executing any of the statements within the while loop. As against this, the do-while tests the condition after having executed the statements within the loop.

This means that do-while would execute its statements at least once, even if the condition fails for the first time itself. The while, on the other hand will not execute its statements if the condition fails for the first time. This difference is brought about more clearly by the following program.

```
main ()
{
while (4<1)
printf (“Hello there \n”) ;
}
```

Here, since the condition fails for the first time itself the printf () will not get executed at all. Let’s now write the same program using a do-while loop.

```
main()
{
do
{
printf (“Hello there \n”) ;
} while (4< 1) ;
}
```

In this program the printf ( ) would be executed once, since first the body of the loop is executed and then the condition is tested.

Functions

Why Use Functions :

Why write separate functions at all ? Why not squeeze the entire logic into one function, main ( ) ? Two reasons:

(a) Writing functions avoids rewriting the same code over and over. Suppose you have a section of code in your program that calculates area of a triangle. If, later in the program, you want to calculate the area of a different triangle, you won't like it if you are required to write the same instructions all over again. Instead, you would prefer to jump back to the place from where you left off. This section of code is nothing but a function.

(b) Using functions it becomes easier to write programs and keep track of what they are doing. If the operation of a program can be divided into separate activities, and each activity placed in a different function, then each be written and checked more or less independently. Separating the code into modular functions also makes the program easier to design and understand.

Passing Values between Functions :

Consider the following program. In this program, in main ( ) we receive the values of a, b and c through the keyboard and then output the sum of a, b and c. However, the calculation of sum is done in different function called calsum ( ). If sum is to be calculated in calsum ( ) and values of a,b and c are received in main( ), then we must pass on these values to calsum ( ), and once calsum ( ) calculates the sum we must return it from calsum( ) back to main( ).

```
/* Sending and receiving values between functions*/
main( )
{
int a, b, c, sum;
printf ("\nEnter any three numbers");
scanf ("%d %d %d, &a, &b, &c);
sum = calsum (a , b , c);
printf ("nSum = %d", sum );
}
calsum (x, y, z)
int x, y, z ;
{
int d ;
d = x + y + z ;
return (d) /; See what Happen if return (d) if not given.
}
```

And here is the output...

Enter any three numbers 10 20 30

Sum = 60

Exmple of Function :

```
int add( int, int);      /* Function declaration */

main()
{
  int i=1;
  printf("i starts out life as %d.", i);

  i = add(1, 1);         /* Function call*/

 printf(" And becomes %d after function is
executed.\n",i);
}

/
***********************************************************************/

int add( int a, int b)  /* Function definition*/
{
  int c;
  c = a + b;
  return c;
}
```

Example of Global and Local Variables :

```
int counter = 0;
/* global because we are outside all blocks.*/
int func(void);

main()
{
  counter++;
/* global because it has not been declared within this
block */
  printf("counter is %2d before the call to func\n",
counter);

  func();                  /* call a function.*/
  printf("counter is %2d after the call to func\n",
counter);
}
```

```
int func(void)
{
  int counter = 10;                /* local.
                                   */
  printf("counter is %2d within func\n", counter);
}
```

Example of Increment and Decrement :

```
main()
{

                /*
* ++i - i incremented before i is used.
* --i - i decremented before i is used.
* j++ - j is incremented AFTER j has been used.
* j-- - j is decremented AFTER j has been used.
                 */

  int i=1,j=1;

  puts("\tDemo 1");
  printf("\t%d %d\n",++i, j++);  /* O/P 2 1 */
  printf("\t%d %d\n",i, j);     /* O/P  2 2     */

  i=1;j=1;

  puts("\n\tDemo 2");
  printf("\t%d \n",i=j++);
/* O/P  1 */
  printf("\t%d \n",i=++j);
/* O/P  3 */

/
*************************************************************************
                         Comments
*************************************************************************/
           /* Consider this code */

  i = 0; j = 0;

  puts("\n\tDemo 3");
```

```
  if ( (i++ == 1) && (j++ == 1)) puts("Some text");

/* Will i and j get incremented? The answer is NO!
Because
* the expression in the left of '&&' resolves to false
the
* compiler does NOT execute the expression on the
right and
* so 'j' does not get executed!!!!! */

  printf("\t%d %d\n",i, j);
/* O/P 1 0 */

}
```

Example of Command Line :

```
#include <stdio.h>

main(int argc, char *argv[])
{
  int count;

/* Main takes two variables 'argc' is the number of
parms on * the
* command line and 'argv' is a pointer to each of the
* parameters.
* int argc    -- integer number called 'argc'
* char *argv[] -- Character pointer array!
*/

  printf("%i parameters entered on the command
line.\n", argc);

                /*
         * progname argc = 1
         * progname parm1 parm2 argc = 3
                 */
        /*
         * We take 1 from argc because
         * the argv array starts at zero
         * an ends at argc -1
```

```
        */

  for ( count = 0; count <= argc -1 ; count++)
  {
        /* printf expects a pointer
         * to the text
         */

    printf("parm %d is %s\n", count, argv[count]);
  }
}
```

Array Pointer and Arrays ::

(1) An array is a collection of variables of the same type that are referenced by a common name. Arrays are a way to group a numbers of terms into a larger unit.

Arrays are of different type.

(1) One dimensional arrays.

(2) Multi dimensional arrays.

C++ a class arrays of mare than two dimensions, the exact limit, if any is determined by the computes you use.

Single Dimensional Arrays.

The Simplest form of an array is a single dimensional array. The array is given a name and its elements are referred it by their subscripts or indices.

The general form of an array declaration is as shown below.

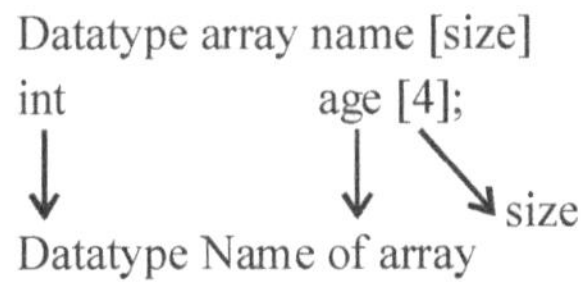

Syntax

Type array - name [size]:

The data type of array elements is known as the same as type of the array.

Accessing Array Elements

Scanf ("%d", $age[0]);

me insert the a value into the array with line.

Printf ("%d", age[0]);

it we read it out with the line.

(1) Initializing Array elements

```
# include <stdio.h>
void main ( )
int month, day, total day:
int days - per month [12] = {31, 28, 31, 30, 31, 30, 31, 31, 31, 30, 31, 30,
21};
```

Arrays can be created from any of the C data types int, float, char. I start with int and float as these are the easiest to understand. Then move onto int and float multi dimensional arrays and finally char arrays.

1) int or float arrays.
2) Two dimensional int or float arrays.
3) char arrays.
4) char multidimensional arrays.
5) int and float arrays

To define an integer or floating point variable you would say.

```
main()
{
 int   Count;              /* integer variable                */
 float Miles;              /* floating point variable         */
}
```

The syntax for an array is :

```
main()
{
 int   Count[5];           /* 5 element integer array         */
 float Miles[10];          /* 10 element floating point array */
}
```

Now, the important fact is that the elements start at 0 (ZERO), so, 'Count' above has elements 0, 1, 2, 3, 4.

To change the value of the 5th element we would code:

```
main()
{
 int Count[5];
 Count[4] = 20;            /* code 4 to update the 5th element */
}
```

If we want to initialise 'Count' at definition we can say:

```
main()
{
```

```
  int i;
  int Count[5]={10, 20, 30};
  for (i=0; i< 5; i++)
  {
    printf("%d ", Count[i]);
  }
  puts("");
}
```

The result will be:

10 20 30 0 0

We can see from the example above that the elements that have NOT been initialised have been set to zero.

One last thing to show you. If all the elements are being initialized when the variable is being defined, the compiler can work out the number of elements for you.

So this example will create an array with 3 elements.

```
main()
    { int i;
      int Count[]={10, 20, 30};
    }
```

Don't forget, all the stuff so far also applies to float.

Two dimensional int and float arrays

C does not actually support multidimensional arrays, but you can emulate them.

```
main()
{ int Count[5];
  int Matrix[10][4];
}
```

Count has been seen before, it defines an array of 5 elements.

Matrix is defined as 10 arrays, all with 4 elements.

To initialise Matrix at definition, you would code the following.

```
main()
{ int Matrix[4][2]={{1, 2},
                    {3, 4},
                    {5, 6},
                    {7, 8}};
}
```

Don't forget the last element will be Matrix[3][1]

char arrays

char arrays work in the same way as int and float

```
main()
{
  char Letter;
  char Letters[10];
}
```

'Letter' can only hold one character but 'the 'Letters' array could hold 10. It is important to think of 'char' as an array and NOT a string.

To initialise 'char' variables you can use the following syntax.

```
main()
{
  char Letter='x';
    char Letters[10]='f','a','x',' ','m','o','d','e','m','\0';
  char Text[10]="fax modem";
}
```

☞ Note that the double quotes mean 'text string' and so they will add the NULL automatically. This is the only time that text can be loaded into an array in this way. If you want to change the contents of the array you should use the function strcpy.

Two dimensional char arrays :

Two dimensional arrays are a different kettle of fish! We can follow the rules above to define the array like this.

```
main()
{
  char Colours[3][6]={"red","green","blue"};
  printf ("%c \n", Colours[0][0]);      /* O/P 'r' */
  printf ("%s \n", Colours[1]);         /* O/P 'green' */
}
```

Pointer

First Principles :

To understand pointers, it may be worth understanding how normal variables are stored. If you disagree, Click here to move on.

What does the following program really mean?

```
main()
{
   int Length;
}
```

In my mind, it means, reserve enough storage to hold an integer and assign the variable name 'Length' to it. The data held in this storage is undefined. Graphically it looks like:

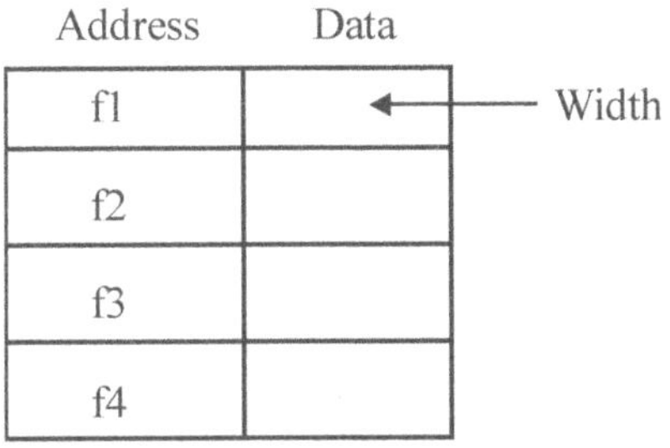

Address	Data
f1	← Width
f2	
f3	
f4	

To put a known value into 'Length' we code,

```
main()
{
int Length;
   Length = 20;
}
```

the decimal value 20 (Hex 14) is placed into the storage location.

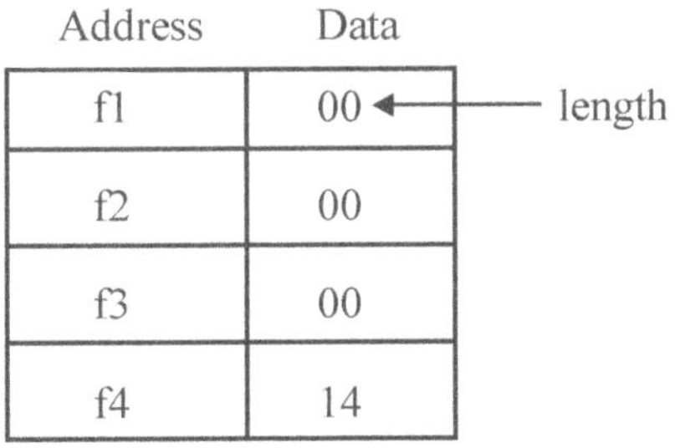

Address	Data
f1	00 ← length
f2	00
f3	00
f4	14

Finally, if the program is expanded to become

```
main()
{
   int Length;
   Length = 20;
printf("Length is %d\n", Length);
printf("Address of Length is %p\n", &Length);
```

```
}
```

The output would look something like this .....

```
Length is 20
Address of Length is 0xF1
```

☞ Please *note the '& Length' on the second printf statement. The &means address of Length. If you are happy with this, you should push onto the pointers below.*

Pointer definition :

A pointer is a variable which contains the address in memory of another variable. We can have a pointer to any variable type.

The ***unary*** or ***monadic*** operator **&** gives the "address of a variable".

The ***indirection*** or ***deference*** operator * gives the "contents of an object ***pointed to*** by a pointer"

☞ *When a pointer is declared it does not point anywhere. You must set it to point somewhere before you use it.*

A pointer to any variable type is an address in memory — which is an integer address. A pointer is definitely NOT an integer.

The reason we associate a pointer to a data type is so that it knows how many bytes the data is stored in. When we increment a pointer we increase the pointer by one "block" memory. So for a character pointer ++ch_ptr adds 1 byte to the address. For an integer or float ++ip or ++flp adds 4 bytes to the address.

An example of code defining a pointer could be...

```
main()
{
  int *Width;
}
```

A graphical representation could be...

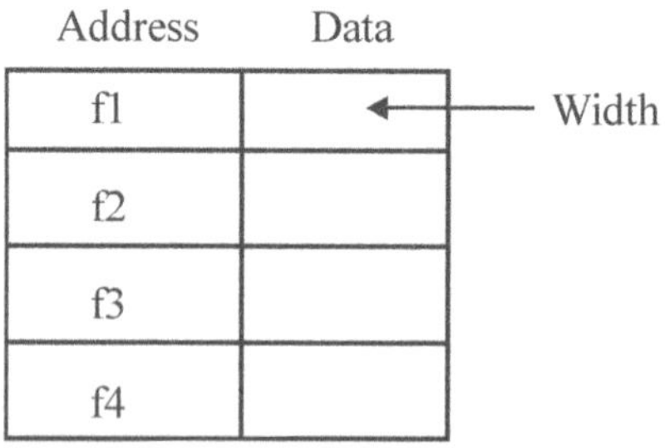

Address	Data
f1	← Width
f2	
f3	
f4	

So far, this variable looks the same as above, the value stored at 'Width' is unknown. To place a value in 'Width' you could code.

```
main()
{
  int *Width;                              /* 1 */
  Width = (int *)malloc(sizeof(int));      /* 2 */
  *Width = 34;                             /* 3 */
}
```

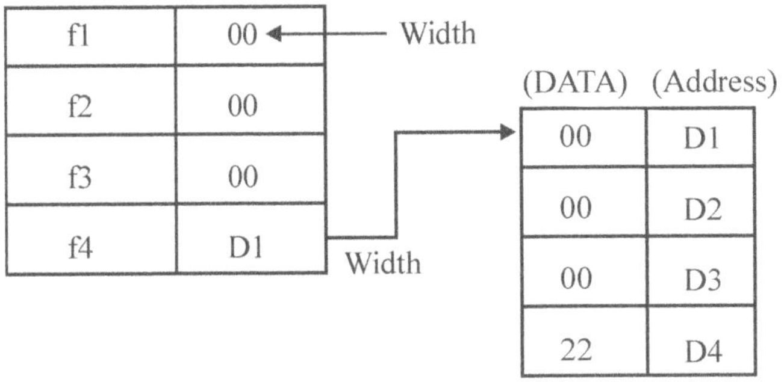

f1	00 ← Width
f2	00
f3	00
f4	D1 → Width

(DATA)	(Address)
00	D1
00	D2
00	D3
22	D4

Statements 2 and 3 are important here:
2) The malloc function reserves some storage and puts the address of the storage into Width.
3) *Width puts a value into the storage pointed to by Width.

Unlike the Length = 20 example above, the storage pointed to by 'Width' does NOT contain 34 (22 in Hex), it contains the address where the value 34 can be found. The final program is...

```
main()
 {
   int *Width;
   Width  = (int *)malloc(sizeof(int));
   *Width = 34;
   printf("  Data stored at *Width is %d\n", *Width);
   printf("       Address of Width is %p\n", &Width);
   printf("Address stored at Width is %p\n",  Width);
 }
```

The program output is something like.

```
  Data stored at *Width is 34
       Address of Width is 0xF1
Address stored at Width is 0xD1
```

A pointer can point to any data type, i.e. int, float, char. When defining a pointer you place an * (asterisk) character between the data type and the variable name, here are a few examples.

```
main()
{
  int   count;          /* an integer variable                 */
  int   *pcount;        /* a pointer to an integer variable    */
  float miles;          /* a floating point variable.          */
  float *m;             /* a pointer                           */
  char  ans;            /* character variable                  */
  char  *charpointer;   /* pointer to a character variable     */
}
```

Void Pointers :

There are times when you write a function but do not know the datatype of the returned value. When this is the case, you can use a void pointer.

```
int func(void *Ptr);
main()
{
    char *Str = "abc";
    func(Str);
}
int func(void *Ptr)
{
    printf("%s\n", Ptr);
}
```

Please note, you cant do pointer arithmetic on void pointers.

Advantages of Using Pointers :

Some of the advantages offered by the use of pointers are:

✓ to return more than one value from a function

✓ to pass arrays and strings more efficiently as arguments to a function

✓ to create complex data structures, such as *linked lists, binary trees* and *graphs*, where one data structure element must contain references to the other data structures of same type

✓ to communicate with operating system about memory. For example, the function *malloc()* returns the location of free memory block by using a pointer and the function *free()* returns the memory block pointed to by a pointer to the operating system.

✓ the pointer notation compiles into faster and more efficient code.

Q1. Differentiate between the following with an example $\left[2\frac{1}{2}\times 2=5\right]$

(i) Arrays vs Pointers Arrays

Arrays	Pointers
(1) Static memory i.e. number of calls remain same. E.g. int a [10] constant	Implement dynamic memory i.e. number of calls can decrease or increase. E.g. int *P; P = (int *) malloc (size of (int) * n);
(2) Overflow of bounds is there	Bounds overflow not there
(3) Array's base address is constant e.g. so you cannot write int a[10]; a = a+1;	Pointer address can be changed int * p = "Gph"; P = P+1;

Q2. Mention any three advantages of use of pointers over arrays. Also, write a program (using pointers) to insert and delete an element in an ordered list. [JUNE05, Q3(a)] [10]

The three advantages of pointers over arrays are:

1. There is no need to specify size in case of pointers whereas in case of arrays size must be specified prior to use.

2. There is no wastage of memory in case of pointers whereas memory is wasted in arrays if size of array is large as compared to required size.

3. Insertion and deletion from the middle of a list is easy and feasible in case of pointers whereas these operation requires more overhead in case of arrays implementation.

```
#include <stdio.h>
#include <conio.h>

void insert ( int *, int , int  ) ;
void del ( int *, int ,int) ;

void main( )
{
        int list[10] ;
        int n,element1,element2,i;
        clrscr( ) ;
        printf("Enter the size of list ");
        scanf("%d",&n);
        printf("\nEnter elements of list ");
        for(i=0;i<n;i++)
        scanf("%d",&list[i]);
        printf("\nEnter element to insert:-" );
```

```
        scanf("%d",&element1);
        insert ( list, n, element1 ) ;

        printf("\nEnter element to delete");
        scanf("%d",&element2);
        del ( list, element2 ,n) ;
        getch( ) ;
}

void insert ( int *list, int size, int num )
{
        int i ,j,n,swap;

        for ( i = 0 ; i < size ; i++ )
        {
        for(j=0;j<size;j++)
        {
        if(list[i] < list[j])
         {
         swap=list[i];
         list[i]=list[j];
         list[j]=swap;
         }
        }
        }

        list[size]=num;

        for ( i = 0 ; i < size+1 ; i++ )
        {
        for(j=0;j<size;j++)
        {
        if(list[i] < list[j])
         {
         swap=list[i];
         list[i]=list[j];
         list[j]=swap;
         }
        }
        }
```

```
        for(i=0;i<size+1;i++)
        printf(" %d",list[i]);
        getch();
}

void del ( int *list, int num,int size )
{
        int i,j ;
                for(i=0;i<size+1;i++)
                {
                if(list[i]==num)
                {
                j=i;
                }
                }

                for(i=j;i<size+1;i++)
                list[i]=list[i+1];

                for(i=0;i<size;i++)
                {
                printf("  %d",list[i]);
                }
}
```

Q3. List atleast 4 differences between Arrays and Pointers in 'C' language.

Array

1) array uses continues memory allocation.
2) array size is declared in advance.
3) array size cannot be increased and decreased at run time.
4) array stores the value.
5) declaration of array is
   int arr_name[size];
6) for example

```
    char arr[20]="dinesh "
    char brr[20]="verma"
    arr=brr;  // not valid
```

you cannot assign the value of one complete array to other array.
But you can do this by using pointer,
declare
char *c="dinesh"

char *d=”verma”;
c=d this is valid

Pointer

1) pointer is called dynamic memory allocation.
2) pointer size is not declared in advance
3) because its size is not declared in advance so there size is increased and decreased at runtime.
4) there is no space is allocated for pointer.
5) declaration of pointer is :
int *point;
6) pointer stores the address of variable.

Q4. Write a program EXPR in C language which evaluates a Reverse Polish expression from the command line, where each operator or operand is a separate argument. For example, EXPR 2 3 4 + * evaluates 2 × (3 + 4).

```
#include <stdio.h>
#include <ctype.h>
 int max=50;
main (int argc, char *argv [])
  {
   int stack[50],i;
   char *p;
  int j=0;
  if(argc<2)
  {printf("Insufficient number of arguments");
   getch();
  exit(0);
  }
  p=argv[1];
  for(i=0;i<strlen(argv[1]);i++)
  {
  if(*(p+i)>=48&&*(p+i)<=57)
  {
   stack[j]=*(p+i)-48;
  j++;
  }
  else
   if(*(p+i)=='+')
  {
```

```
 stack[j-2]=stack[j-1]+stack[j-2];
j=j-1;
}
else
 if(*(p+i)=='-')
{
 stack[j-2]=stack[j-1]-stack[j-2];
j=j-1;
}
else
 if(*(p+i)=='*')
{
 stack[j-2]=stack[j-1]*stack[j-2];
j=j-1;
}
else
 if(*(p+i)=='/')
{
 stack[j-2]=stack[j-1]+stack[j-2];
j=j-1;
}
}
j--;
printf("Final evaluation is %d",stack[j]);
 getch();
}
```

Structures & Union :

Just as the entity we call a 'book' is a collection of things such as title, author, isbn number, publisher, number of pages, date of publication etc. As you can see all this data is dissimilar, for example author is a string, whereas number of pages is an integer. For dealing with such collections, C provides a data type called 'structure'. A structure gathers together, different atoms of information that comprise a given entity.

Declaring A Structure

The following statement declares the structure type:

```
Struct book
{
char name;
```

```
float price;
int pages;
};
```

This statement defines a new data type called struct book. Each variable of this data type will consist of a character variable called name, a float variable called price and an integer variable called pages. The general form of a structure declaration statement is given below :

```
Struct <structure name>
{
structure element 1 ;
structure element 2 ;
structure element 3 ;
........
........
};
```

Once the new structure data type has been defined one or more variables can be declared to be of that type. For example the variables b1, b2, b3, can be declared to be of the type struct book, as,

```
Struct book b1, b2, b3;
```

How Structure Elements are Stored

```
Struct book
{
char name ;
float price;
int pages ;
};
struct book b1 = { 'B', 130.0, 500 };
```

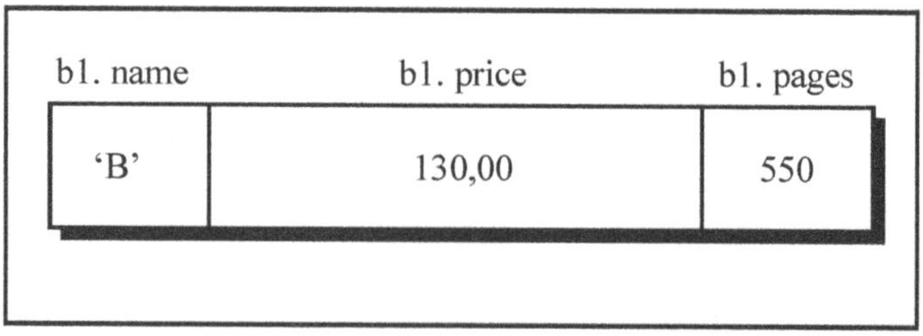

b1. name	b1. price	b1. pages
'B'	130,00	550

Unions ::

Both structures and unions are used to group a number of different variables together. But while a structure enables us to treat a number of different variables stored at different places in memory, a union enables us to treat the same space in memory as a number of different variables. That is, a union offers a way for a section of memory to be treated as a variable of one type on one occasion, and as a different variable of a different type on another occasion. You might wonder why it would be necessary to do such a thing, Let us take a look at a simple example :

```
/* Demo of union at work*/
main( )
{
union a
{
int I ;
char ch [2]
};
union a key ;
key, I = 512 ;
printf ("\nkey, I = %d" , key, I ) ;
printf ("\nkey, ch [0] = %d" , key. Ch [0] ) ;
printf ("\nkey, ch [1] = %d" , key. Ch [1] )
}
```

And here s the output ....

```
Key. I =512
Key,ch[0]=0
Key,ch[1]=2
```

```
struct a
int ;
char ch[2] ;
} ;
struct a key ;
```

This data type would occupy 4 bytes in memory, 2 for key. I and one each for key.ch[0] and key.ch[1], as shown below.

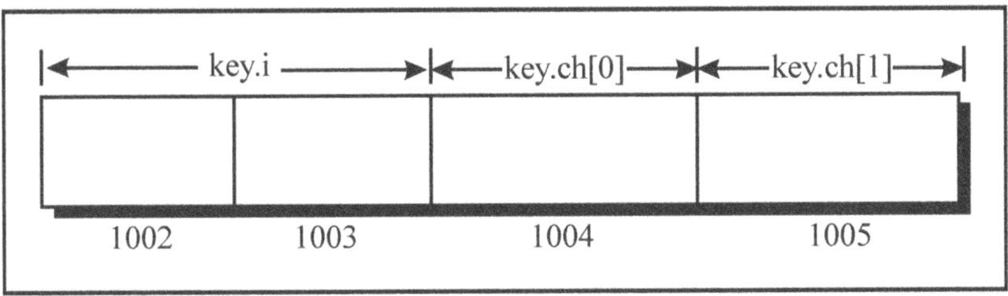

union a {

```
Int I ;
char ch [2] ;
} ;
union a key ;
```

Representation of this data type in memory is shown below .

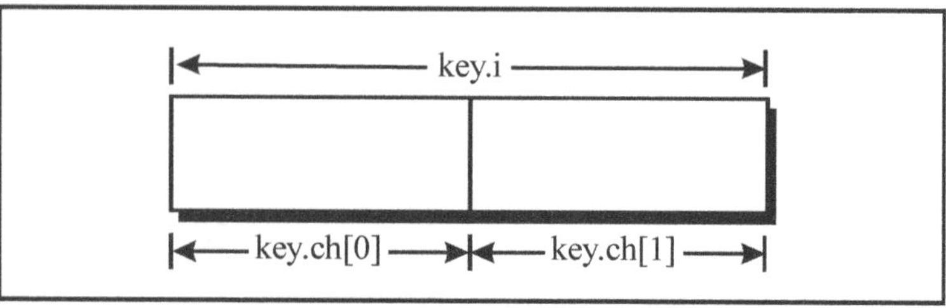

Q5. Write at least two differences between a Structure and a Union in 'C' language. Give an example each of a structure and Union.

The difference between structures and unions lies in the way their members are stored and initialized, as follows:

- Within a structure, the members have addresses that increase as the declarators are read left-to-right. That is, the members of a structure all begin at different offsets from the base of the structure. The offset of a particular member corresponds to the order of its declaration; the first member is at offset 0.

A pointer to a structure points to its first member, so no unnamed holes can reside at the beginning of a structure.

- In a union, every member begins at offset 0 from the address of the union. The size of the union in memory is the size of its largest member. The value of only one member can be stored in a union object at a time. When the storage space allocated to the union contains a smaller member, the extra space between the end of the smaller member and the end of the allocated memory remains unaltered. A pointer to a union member, converted to the proper type, points to the beginning of the union object.
- Several members of a structure can be initialized at once; only the first member of a union can be given an initialiser.

Example of structure :

```
structure book
{
        char name ;
```

```
        float price ;
        int pages ;
};
structure book b1 = {'B' 130,00, 550};
```

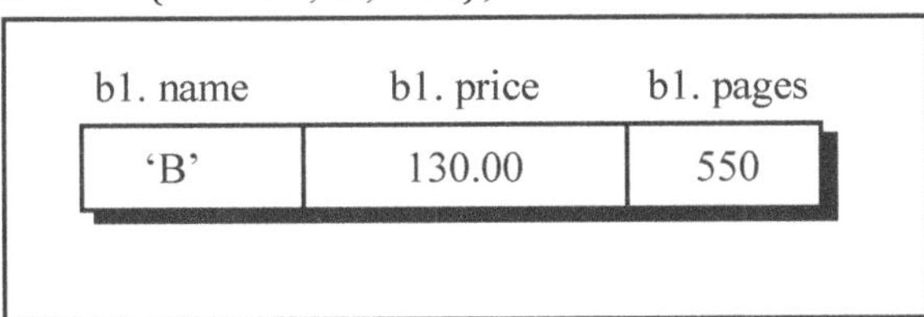

Example of union :

```
Union a
{
        int i ;
        char ch[2] ;
};
union a key ;
```

Representation of this data type in memory is shown below.

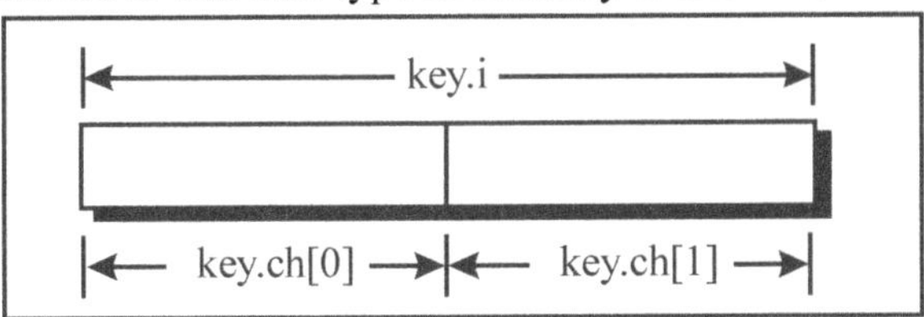

Q6. Write the syntax of any five file handling commands supported by 'C'.

(i) A call to fopen( ) to read the file **passbook.dat** looks like.

fopen (passbook.dat","r")

(ii) To connect your program to the file that fopen opens, your program must also declare a pointer of type FILE as :

FILE * file_ptr;

Now you can assign to fileptr the pointer that fopen returned: file_ptr = fopen ("passbook.dat", "r');

(iii) fscanf(file_ptr, "control string", list of pointers);

(iv) fwrite(numbers, sizeof(double), NUM_EL, f1)* ;

(v) fread(copy, sizeof(double), NUM_EL, f1);

Q7. Write a 'C' program to count the number of characters and lines in a text whose name is supplied command line.

```
#include<stdio.h>
main(int argc,char *argv[])
{
FILE *fs,*ft;
char ch;
int nol=0,noc=0;

if(argc!=2)
{
puts("Insufficient arguments");
getch();
exit(0);
}

fs=fopen(argv[1],"r");
if(fs==NULL)
{
puts("Cannot open file");
getch();
exit(0);
}
while(1)
{
ch=fgetc(fs);
if(ch==EOF)
break;
noc++;
if(ch=='\n')
nol++;
}
fclose(fs);
printf("Number of characters=%d",noc);
printf("\nNumber of lines=%d",nol);
getch();
}
```

Q8. What is a variable length argument ? Give an example of such an argument. How are variable length arguments passed to a function ?

It is frequently necessary to deal with situations where the number of arguments in a function's call may be arbitrary. Two common examples are printf () and scanf (). There are three macros available in the file "stdarg.h" called **va_start,**

va_arg and **va_list**

These macros provide a method for accessing the arguments of the functions when a function takes a fixed number of arguments followed by a variable number of arguments. The fixed number of arguments are accessed in the normal way, whereas the optimal arguments are accessed using the macros **va_start** and **va_arg**. Out of these macros **va_start** is used to initialize a pointer to the beginning of the list of optional arguments. On the other hand the macro **va_arg** is used to advance the pointer to the next argument. Let us put these concepts into action using a program. Suppose we wish to write a function **findmax( )** which would find out the maximum value from a set of values, irrespective of the number of values passed to it.

```
# include "stdarg.h"
        main( )
        {
   int max ;
   max = findmax (5, 23, 15, 1, 92, 50) ;
   printf ("\nmaximum = %d", max) ;
        }

        findmax (int tot_num)
        {
     int max, count_num ;
     va_list ptr ;
   va_start (ptr, tot_num) ;
   max = va_arg (ptr, int) ;

     for (count = 1 ; count < tot_nun ; count++)
        {
        nun = va_arg (ptr, int) ;
        if (num > max)
                max = num ;
             }
             return (max) ;
        }
```

Here, we are making two calls to findmax( ) first time to find maximum out 5 values and second time to find maximum out of 3 values. Note that for each call the first argument is the count of arguments that follow the first argument. The value of the first argument passed to **findmax( )** is collected in the values **tot_num. findmax( )** begins with a declaration of a pointer **ptr** of the type **va_list**. Observe the next statement carefully va_start (ptr) ;

This statement sets up **ptr** such that it points to the first variable argument in the list. If we are considering the first call to **findmax( ) ptr** would assign the integer being pointed to by **ptr** to **max**. Thus 23 would be assigned to **max,** and **ptr** would now start pointing to the next argument i.e., 15. The rest of the program is fairly straight forward. We just keep picking up successive numbers in the list and keep comparing them with the latest value in **max**, till all the arguments in the list have been scanned. The final value in **max** is then returned to **main**( ).

Files ::

Our program will read a file and count how many characters, spaces, tabs and newlines are present in the file. We will first list the program and show what it does, and then dissect it line by line. Here is the listing.

```
/* Count chars, spaces, tabs and newlines in a file */
#include "stdio.h"
main( )
{
FILE *fp;
char ch;
int not= 0, nos = 0, noc = 0;
fp = fopen ("PR1.C", "r");
While ( 1 )
{
ch = fgetc ( fp ) ;
if ( ch = = EOF )
break
noc ++ ;
if ( ch = = ' ' )
nob ++;
if ( ch = = '\n' )
nol ++ ;
if ( ch = = '\t' )
nol ++ ;
fclose ( fp ) ;
printf ( "\nNumber of  characters = %d" , noc ) ;
printf ( "\nNumber of  blanks  = %d" , noc ) ;
printf ( "\nNumber of  tabs  = %d" , noc ) ;
printf ( "\nNumber of  lines  = %d" , noc ) ;
}
```

And here is a sample run ……….

Number of character = 155
Number of blanks = 20
Number of tabs = 14
Number of tabs = 28
The above statistics are true for a file "PRI.C", which we had on our disk. You may give any other filename and obtain different results. More important than the actual statistics, is how the program calculates these. So let us now take a look at how it does it.

Opening A File

Before we can write information to a file on a disk or read it, we must open the file. Opening a file establishes a link between the program and the operating system, about, which file we are going to access and how. We provide the operating system with the name of the file and whether we plan to read or write to it. The link between our program and the operating system is a structure called FILE which has been defined in the header file "stdio.h" (standing for standard input/output header file). Therefore, it is necessary to always include this file when we are doing high level disk I/O. When we request the operating system to open a file, what we get back (if the request is indeed granted), is a pointer to the structure FILE. That is why, we make the following declaration before opening the file.
FILE *fp ;
Each file we open will have its own FILE structure. The FILE structure contains information about the file being used as its current size, its location in memory etc. More importantly it contains a character pointer which points to the character that is about to get read.
Now let us understand the following statements,
FILE *fp ;
fp = fopen ("PR1.C", "R") ;
fp is a pointer variable, which contains address of the structure FILE which has been defined in the header file stdio.h".
fopen () will open a file "PRI.C" in 'read mode, which tells the C compiler that we would be reading the contents of the file. Note that "r" is a string and not a character; hence the double quotes and not single quotes. In fact, fopen() Performs three important tasks when you open the file in "r" mode :

(a) Firstly it searches on the disk the file to be opened.
(b) If the file is present, it loads the file from the disk into memory. Of course if the file is very big, then it loads the file part by part.
If the file is absent, fopen( ) returns a NULL, NULL is a macro defined in "stdio.h" which indicates that you failed to open the file.

(c) It sets up a character pointer (which is part of the FILE structure) which points to the first character of the of if memory where the file has been loaded.

Reading from A File

Once the file has been opened for reading using fopen ( ), as we have seen be file's contents are brought into memory (partly or wholly) and a pointer points to the very first character. The read the file's contents from memory there exists a function called fgetc( ). This has been used in our sample program through,

ch = fgetc (fp) ;

fgetc ( ) reads the character from current pointer position, advances the pointer position so that it now points to the next character, and returns the character that is read, which collected in the variable ch. Note that once the file has been opened, we no longer refer to the file by its name, but through the file pointer fp.

We have used the function fgetc( ) within an indefinite while loop. There has to be a way to break out of this while. When shall we break out… the moment we reach the end of file. But what is end of file? End of file is signified by a special character, whose ASCII value is 26. This character is inserted beyond the last character in the file, when it is created. This character can also be generated from the keyboard by typing ctrl z.

While reading from the file, when fgetc( ) encounters this special character, instead of returning the character that it has read, it returns the macro EOF. The EOF macro has been defined in the file "stdio.h". In place of the function fgetc( ) we could have as well used the macro getc( ) with the same effect.

In our sample program, we go on reading each character from the file till end of file is met. As each character is being read we keep running totals of number of characters, number of blanks, number of tabs and number of lines read. Note that the end of the line is marked by a \n. Once out of the loop, we print these running totals.

Reading a File :

```
#include <stdio.h>

main()
{
 int c;                          /* Character read from the file.*/
 FILE *ptr;
          /* Pointer to the file. FILE is a structure  defined in <stdio.h> */
```

```
                              /* Open the file - no error checking done */
  ptr = fopen("/etc/hosts","r");
                              /* Read one character at a time, checking
                                 for the End of File. EOF is defined
                                 in <stdio.h> as -1 */
  while ((c = fgetc(ptr)) != EOF)
  {
    printf("%c",c);                  /* O/P the character to the screen
*/
  }
  fclose(ptr);                 /* Close the file. */
}
```

Using argc and argv

To execute program we are required to first type the program, compile it, and then execute it. This program can be improved in two ways:

(a) There should be no need to compile the program everytime to use the file-copy utility. It means the program must be executable at command prompt (A> or C> if you are using MS DOS, $ if you are using Unix).

(b) Instead of the program prompting us to enter the source and target filenames, we must be able to supply them at command prompt, in the form:

C>filecopy PR1.C PR2.C

Where, PR1.C is the source filename and PR2.C is the target filename.

The first improvement is simple. In MS-DOS, the executable file (the one which can be executed at DOS prompt and has an extension.EXE) can be created in Turbo C by using the key F9 to compile the program.

The second improvement is possible by passing the source filename and target filename to the function main( ). This is illustrated below:

```
#include "stdio.h"
main(int argc, char * argv[])
{
FILE *fs, *ft ;
char ch ;
If (argc ! = 3 )
{
puts("Insufficient arguments" ) ;
exit( ) ;
}
fs = fopen ( argv[1}, "1") ;
if (fs = = NULL)
{
```

```
puts ("Cannot open source file") ;
exit ( ) ;
}
ft = fopen(argv [2], "w") ;
if ( ft = = NULL )
puts ("Cannot open target file") ;
fclose(fs) ;
exit( ) ;
}
while ( 1 )
{
ch = fgetc ( fs ) ;
if (ch = = EOF )
break ;
else
fputc ( ch, ft ) ;
}
fclose ( fs ) ;
fclose ( ft ) ;
}
```

The arguments that we pass on to main ( ) at the command prompt are called command line arguments. The function main ( ) can have two arguments, traditionally named as argc and argv. Out of these, argv is an array of pointers to strings and argc is an int whose value is equal to the number of strings to which argv points. When the program is executed, the strings on the command line are passed to main ( ). More precisely, the strings at the command line are stored in memory and address of the first string is stored in argv [0], address of the second string is stored in argv [1] and so on. The argument argc is set to the number of strings given on the command line. For example, in our sample program, if at the command prompt we give,
argc would contain 3
argc [0] would contain base address of the string "filecopy"
argc [1] would contain base address of the string "PR1.C "
argc [2] would contain base address of the string "PR2.C "

Q9. Design an algorithm and draw corresponding flowchart to convert a decimal number to its hexadecimal equivalent. [DEC05, Q5(b)]

<u>ALGORITHM</u>

START:

```
const MAX = 16;
BASE = 16;
 i, j, remainder, number

Step1: Enter input number[1..MAX]

Step2: while (number > 0)
        remainder := number mod BASE
        number := number divide BASE

Step3: if (remainder < 10) then
        hexno[i] :=  remainder
        else
        hexno[i] := Char('A' + (remainder-10))
        i := i + 1;
        end;

Step4: Print in reverse order
        for j := (i-1) downto 1 do
        write(hexno[j]);

END
```

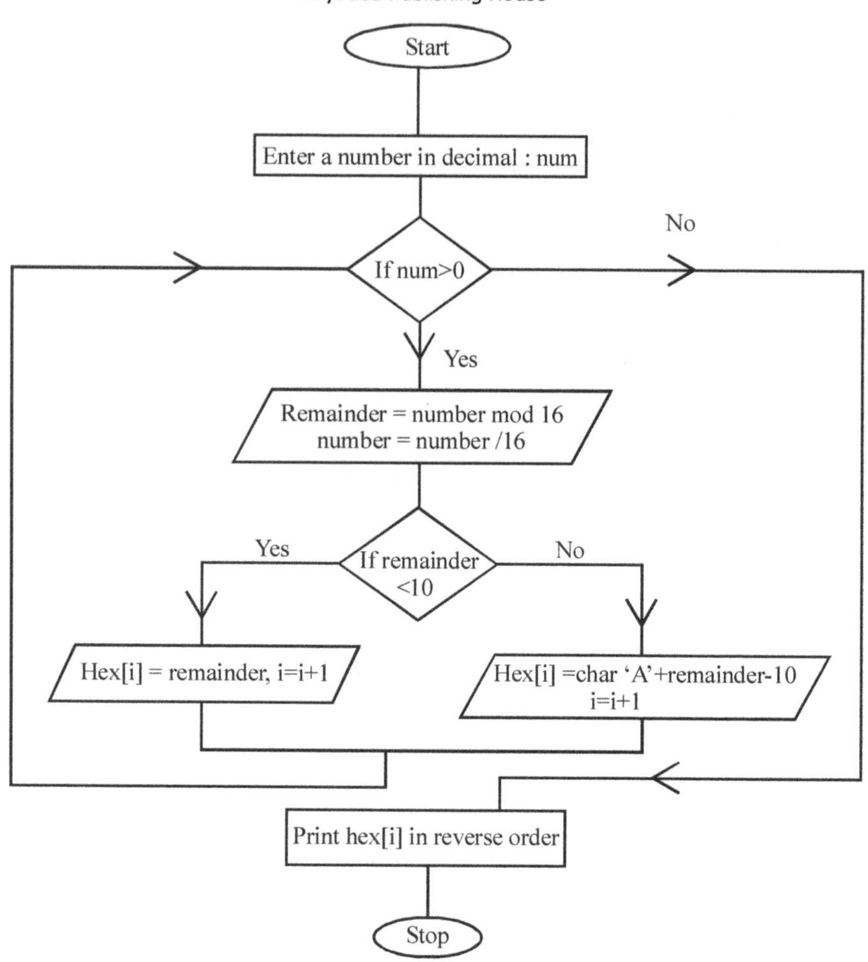
Start
Enter a number in decimal : num
If num>0
No
Yes
Remainder = number mod 16
number = number /16
If remainder
<10
Yes
No
Hex[i] = remainder, i=i+1
Hex[i] =char 'A'+remainder-10
i=i+1
Print hex[i] in reverse order
Stop

Chapter - 3

UNDERSTANDING A PROGRAM (MUST READ)

Example 1 : a program that counts the number of lines, words, and characters in its input. This program has examples of comments, `#includes`, constant and variable declarations, a `main()` function, and `if`, `while`, `printf()`, expression, and assignment statements.

SOLUTION :

Program Objectives

This program reports the number of lines, words, and characters in a file. The file is read from standard input.

A word is any sequence of non-blank characters that

- begins at the start of a line or immediately after a blank character, and
- ends at the end of a line or is followed by a blank character.

Algorithm Overview

Most of the processing in this program is done in a character processing loop. In this loop character, word, and line counts are updated to reflect the counts up to and including the current (most recently read) character. The character count is updated for each character. The word count is incremented each time a word is entered. This requires using a state variable to keep track of whether or not the current character is inside a word. The line count is updated at the end of each line.

Variables

- char ch - the current character from input.
- int wordState - the word state *before* reading the current character. This variable can have two possible values:

in - inside a word

notIn - not inside a word

- int numChars - the number of characters read so far
- int numWords - the number of words read so far
- int numLines - the number of lines read so far

Algorithm

initialize wordState and counts
- wordState = notIn
- numChars = numWords = numLines = 0

for each character ch in the input
    count characters
        - always increment numChars
    count lines
        - increment numLines if ch is a newline
    count words and adjust word state
        - increment numWords and set wordState to in when entering a new word (wordState is notIn and ch is not a space character)
        - set wordState to notIn when ch is a space character

print numChars, numWords, and numLines

Design Notes

• The algorithm has a minor flaw: it fails to count the last line of input if there is no trailing newline character. This could be corrected by adding a variable `lastCh` which is initialized to a newline character and set equal to `ch` at the end of each iteration of the character processing loop. If `lastCh` is not a newline character after the end of the character processing loop then `numLines` should be incremented. This program, however, is designed to mimic the UNIX wc program, which just counts newline characters.

```
/**                                                    // Comment 1.
 * Usage: understandC < fileName
 *
 * Reports the number of lines, words, and
 * characters in the file named by fileName.
 *
 * A word is any sequence of non-blank
 * characters that
 *    - begins at the start of a line or immediately
 *      after a blank character, and
 *    - ends at the end of a line or is followed
 *      by a blank character.
 */                                                    // Comment 1.

#include <stdio.h>                                     // Comment 2.
#include <ctype.h>                                     // Comment 2.
```

```
const int notIn = 0;  // not inside a word       // Comment 3.
const int in = 1;     // inside a word           // Comment 3.

int main(void) {                                 // Comment 4.
   char ch;           // current character       // Comment 5.
   int wordState;     // current word state:     // Comment 5.
                      //    notIn or in          // Comment 5.
   int numChars;      // characters so far       // Comment 5.
   int numWords;      // words so far            // Comment 5.
   int numLines;      // lines so far            // Comment 5.

   wordState = notIn;                            // Comment 6.
   numChars = 0;                                 // Comment 6.
   numWords = 0;                                 // Comment 6.
   numLines = 0;                                 // Comment 6.
   // for each character in the input            // Comment 1.
   ch = getchar();                               // Comment 7.
   while (ch != EOF) {                           // Comment 8.
    // count characters                          // Comment 1.
    numChars++;                                  // Comment 9.
    // count lines                               // Comment 1.
    if (ch == '\n') {                            // Comment 10.
       numLines++;                               // Comment 9.
    }                                            // Comment 10.
    // count words and adjust word state         // Comment 1.
    if (wordState == notIn) {                    // Comment 11.
       if (!isspace(ch)) {                       // Comment 12.
             numWords++;                         // Comment 9.
             wordState = in;                     // Comment 6.
       }                                         // Comment 12.
    } else {                                     // Comment 11.
       if (isspace(ch)) {                        // Comment 13.
             wordState = notIn;                  // Comment 6.
       }                                         // Comment 13.
    }                                            // Comment 11.
    ch = getchar();                              // Comment 7.
  }                                              // Comment 8.
  printf("%d %d %d\n", numLines, numWords,       // Comment 14.
       numChars);                                // Comment 14.
  return 0;                                      // Comment 15.
```

```
} // int main(void)
```

NOTES ABOUT COMMENT :

understandC.C - Step by Step Notes on comments mentioned in code line by line to throughly understand the code

Note on Comment 1 : Comments in C begin with `/*` and end with `*/`. If you are using a C++ compiler to compile a C program then you can also use `//` comments. These comments are terminated at the end of the line.
Comments are ignored by the compiler. They are intended to help people that need to read a program. Unless you have an exceptional memory, you will need to read your own program several times as you are debugging it in order to refresh your memory.

Note on Comment 2 : A line that begins with a # is a *compiler directive*. It directs the compiler to do something while the program is being compiled. Most of the other C code that you write in a program directs the computer do something while the compiled program is executing.
A `#include` directive tells the compiler to read a header file before processing the C code that follows. The angle brackets indicate header files for system library functions, which are located in a directory that is known to the compiler.
Almost all programs include `stdio.h`. This header file declares input and output library functions, including `getchar()` (Comment 7) and `printf()` (Comment 15). This header file also declares the constant `EOF` (Comment 8). The header file `ctype.h` declares functions for classifying characters, such as `isspace()` (Comment 12 and Comment 13).

Note on Comment 3 : These lines define constants `notIn` and `in` to be integers with values 0 and 1, respectively. A simple constant definition has the following form.
`const` *`type identifier`* `=` *`expression;`*
The type indicates the kind of value specified by the constant. The identifier specifies its name. Whenever that name is used in the code, the compiler replaces it by the value of the expression. This value cannot be changed.

Note on Comment 4 : The C code between the Comment 4 comments defines a function named `main()`. All C programs have a `main()` function. The portion `int main(void)` is the *prototype* for the function. The prototype determines the syntax for a function call by indicating the type of value that the function returns and the types of values that can be passed as function arguments or parameters. The rest of the function definition is a sequence of statements enclosed in braces. This construction forms a single statement called a *block statement*. The block statement is executed whenever the function is called.

The `int` at the beginning of the prototype indicates that `main()` returns an integer. Comment 15 describes the meaning of the returned value for the `main()` function. The `void` inside the parentheses of the prototype indicates that `main()` has no parameters.

Most functions are called by the programmer's C code, as in Comment 7, Comment 12, and Comment 13. The `main()` function is an exception. It is called by the operating system when the program is executed.

Note on Comment 5 : These lines are variable definition statements. Any number of variable definition statements can be placed at the beginning of a block statement.

A variable is a place in the computer where a data value can be stored. The value can be changed during program execution with an assignment statement, as in Comment 6, and some other kinds of statements, as in Comment 9.

A simple variable declaration has the following form.

`type identifier;`

The type specifies what kind of data is stored in the variable. `ch` is a `char` variable, which means it can hold a single character. `wordState` is an `int` variable, which means it can hold a single integer. The identifier specifies the name of the variable. This name is used in the program whenever you need to access the current value of the variable.

A variables that is declared inside a function is called a *local variable*: it is directly accessible only inside that function. A variables whose declaration is not inside a function is called a *global variable*: it is directly accessible by all functions.

Note on Comment 6 : These lines are assignment statements. A assignment statement has the following form.

`variable-expression = expression;`

The simplest (and most common) kind of variable expression is just the name of a variable. When an assignment statement is executed, the value of the expression is placed in the data storage location specified by the variable expression.

Note on Comment 7 : Here is another assignment statement. In this one, the expression on the right-hand side is a function call using the standard library function `getchar()`. It has the following prototype, declared in the stdio.h header file.

```
int getchar(void)
```

The `void` inside the parentheses indicates that `getchar()` should be called with no arguments. The `int` in front of the name `getchar` indicates that `getchar()` returns an integer. The returned value is the next character from `stdin`, converted to an integer. When there are no more characters, `getchar()` returns an integer constant `EOF`. This constant is defined in the stdio.h header file.

`stdin` is a standard input file that can be accessed in any C program. It is connected to the keyboard unless a command receives input from a file using redirection or from another program using pipes.

Note on Comment 8 : The lines of C code between the Note 8 comments form a while loop. A while loop is a type of statement. It has the following form.

`while (`*`conditional-expression`*`)` *`nested-statement`*

Usually the nested statement is a block statement (see Comment on Note 4), which allows the loop to contain multiple statements.

When the while loop is executed, its nested statement can be executed any number of times, depending on the value of its conditional expression. Each execution of the inner statement is called an *iteration* of the loop. The conditional expression is evaluated *before* each iteration of the while loop. If it is false the execution of the loop terminates.

In the conditional expression for this while statement, != is a C operator that compares two values for inequality, and `EOF` is a special character constant defined in the stdio.h header file. `getchar()` returns this value when there are no more characters in the input. The value of the expression `ch != EOF` is true when the most recent call to `getchar()` (Comment 7) found another character in the input.

Note on Comment 9 : ++ is a C operator that increments (adds 1 to) an integer variable.

Note on Comment 10 : The lines of C code between the Note 10 comments form an if statement. An if statement has the following form.

`if (`*`conditional-expression`*`)` *`then-clause`*

The then clause is a statement. It is usually a block statement (see Comment on Note 4), which allows the clause to contain multiple statements. When the if statement is executed its conditional expression is evaluated. If the value is true then the then clause is executed. If the conditional expression is false then the then clause is not executed.

In the conditional expression for this if statement, == is a C a C operator that compares two values for equality, and `'\n'` is a literal character constant representing the newline character. Thus `ch == '\n'` is true when `ch` is a newline character; otherwise it is false.

WARNING : If you use a single equals sign in the conditional expression, the code will often compile without error, but it will execute incorrectly. When you are having trouble figuring out why a program does not run correctly, check all = and == operators to make sure you have the right one.
The pair of braces in this if statement could be omitted since there is only one statement inside. However, it is a good practice to use them anyway. If you later need to add another statement there will be no possibility that it unintentionally falls outside the `if` statement.

Note on Comment 11 : The lines of C code between the first and third Note 11 comments form an if-else statement. It is distinguished from a simple if statement by the keyword `else` at the second Comment 11 comment.
An if-else statement has the following form.

```
if (conditional-expression) then-clause
else else-clause
```

The then and else clauses are statements. They are usually block statements (see Comment on Note 4), which allows the clauses to contain multiple statements. When the if-else statement is executed, the then clause is executed if the conditional expression is true. The else clause is executed if the conditional expression is false.

Note on Comment 12 : The conditional expression for this if-else statement contains the function `isspace(ch)`. The function `isspace()` is declared in the header file ctype.h. It has the following prototype.

```
int isspace(char c)
```

`isspace()` returns true if its argument (`ch` in this example) is a blank, tab, newline, formfeed, or certain other non-printing characters.
The C operator `!` means "not". It changes the meaning of a true expression to false and vice-versa.

Note on Comment 13 : The conditional expression for this if-else statement contains another call to the function `isspace(ch)`. See Comment 12.

Note on Comment 14 : The `printf()` function is used for program output. The double quotes in the first argument indicate that the argument is a string literal constant. This argument is the `printf()` *format* argument. Each `%d` is a *format specifier* that indicates that an integer should be printed in decimal form. The integers are passed as additional `printf()` parameters. The spaces in the format are printed as spaces in the output, and the `/n` is C notation for a newline character. So this statement prints the values of `numLines`, `numWords`, and `numChars` in decimal form separated by spaces and followed by a newline character.

WARNING : Compilers do not always check to see if there is a parameter for each of the `%d`'s. If a parameter is missing you will get a run-time error or garbage in the printout.

Note on Comment 15 : This program should be compiled with a C++ compiler since it uses `//` comments. C++ is an extension of the C language. It requires declaring the `main()` function to return an `int`. The value that is returned is an error code that is passed to the operating system. When you are not concerned with this, the `main()` function can return 0, which indicates that there were no errors.

Chapter - 4

Some More Examples

Example 1: a program that prints a conversion table for converting from degrees Fahrenheit to degrees Celsius. This program has examples of functions, for loops, and the use of floating point numbers.

Functions are an important aspect of program design. Good program design involves breaking up the computation into small functions that are easy to comprehend.

```
/**
 * Usage: ftoc
 *
 * Prints a table of conversions from degrees
 * Fahrenheit to degrees Celsius for Fahrenheit
 * temperatures from -40.0 to 100.0.
 *
 * This program demonstrates the use of for loops,
 * functions, and floating point numbers.
 */

#include <stdio.h>

const float fMin  = -40.0;          // min F temperature
const float fStep =   5.0;  // F temperature step
const float fMax  = 100.0;          // max F temperature

/**
 * fToC(fdeg) returns the Celsius equivalent of fdeg
 * degrees Fahrenheit.
 */
float fToC(float fdeg) {
   return (fdeg - 32.0)/1.8;
}  // int fToC(int)

int main(void) {
```

```
    float f;

    printf("Degrees F   Degrees C\n");
     printf("---------    ---------\n");
    for (f = fMin; f <= fMax; f += fStep) {
          printf("%7.1f%12.1f\n", f, fToC(f));
    }
    printf("\n");
    return 0;
} // int main(void)
```

Example 2 : a program that computes the factorial of a number. This program illustrates the behavior of C function parameters.

```
/**
 * Usage: fact
 *
 * Prints a number and its factorial.
 */
#include <stdio.h>
/**
 *  factorial(n) returns n*(n-1)*...*2*1 for
 * small values of n.
 */
int factorial(int n) {
    int fact;

    fact = 1;
    while (n > 1) {
          fact *= n;
          n--;
    }
    return fact;
} // int factorial(int)

int main(void) {
    int x; // an integer
    int f; // the factorial of x
    x = 5;
    f = factorial(x);
    printf("x = %d, f = %d.\n", x, f);
    return 0;
```

```
} // int main(void)
```

Example 3 : a program that echoes the arguments in its command line. This program illustrates the use of command-line parameters. It also illustrates the use of arrays.

```
/**
 * Usage: myecho arg ...
 *
 * Displays each of the command-line arguments,
 * separated by spaces.
 *
 * This program demonstrates the use of argc and
 * argv for handling command-line arguments.
 */

#include <stdio.h>

int main(int argc, char * argv[]) {
   int i;
   for (i = 1; i < argc - 1; i++) {
      printf("%s ", argv[i]);
   }
   if (argc > 1) {
         printf("%s\n", argv[argc - 1]);
   }
}
```

Example 4 : to read and verify a password.

```
   urpose: To read and verify a password.
 * Notes:  To read text from the keyboard on a UNIX system without
 *            it being echoed to the screen you can use noecho() and
 *            getch() from curses.h In DOS you can use getch() in conio.h
 * Author: Gullybaba.com, IgnouOnline.com, DegreeWala.com
 * Date:   12-Mar-06
```

```
#include <curses.h>
main()
{
 int i;
 char buffer[80];                     /* work buffer*/

 initscr();                                        /*initialize the screen*/

 printw("Please enter a password => ");      /*update screen image*/
 refresh();                           /*Update screen with screen image*/
 noecho();                            /*Suppress echo to the screen*/
                                      /*Read characters until C/R*/
 while((buffer[i] = getch()) != '\n') i++;

 printw("\nPassword is %s - press return to continue.",buffer);
 refresh();
 getch();
 endwin();                            /*Shut down curses*/
```

Chapter - 5

TOPIC WISE EXAMPLES

ARRAYS

Q1. Write a program for linear search using array.

```
#include<iostream.h>
#include<conio.h>
#include<string.h>
#include<stdio.h>
#include<stdlib.h>
main(void)
{
 clrscr() ;
 int n, x[10] ;
 int val;
 int flag=1 ;
 cout<<"\nhow many values:" ;
 cin>>n ;
 cout<<"enter values in the array :"<<endl ;
 for(int i=0;i<n;i++)
{
 cout<<"x"<<i+1<<":" ;
 cin>>x[i] ;
}
 cout<<"enter which value to be searched :" ;
 cin>>val ;
 for(int j=0;j<n;j++)
{
 if(x[j]==val)
   {
   flag=0 ;
   cout<<"search successful and value is find out at position "<<j<<" in the
array" ;
```

```
  }
}
 if(flag==1)
    cout<<"search unsuccessful" ;

 getch() ;
 return(0) ;
}
```

Q2. Write a program to find the product of two matrices.

```
#include<stdio.h>
#include<conio.h>

main()
{
 clrscr() ;
 int i, j, m, n, k ;
 int A[10][10], B[10][10], C[10][10] ;
 printf("enter m: ") ;
 scanf("%d", &m) ;
 printf("enter n: ") ;
 scanf("%d", &n) ;
 printf("\nenter the values for matrix A: ") ;
 printf("\n") ;
 for(i=0;i<m;i++)
{
printf("\nenter data for row no. %d\n", i+1) ;
 for(j=0;j<n;j++)
{
scanf("%d", &A[i][j] ) ;
}
}
printf("\nenter the values for matrix B: ") ;
printf("\n") ;
 for(i=0;i<n;i++)
{
printf("\nenter data for row no. %d\n", i+1) ;
 for(j=0;j<m;j++)
```

```
{
scanf("%d", &B[i][j] );
}
}
printf("\nthe entries for matrix C are : ");
printf("\n");
for(i=0;i<=m;i++)
{
for(j=0;j<=m;j++)
{
C[i][j]=0 ;
for(k=0;k<=m;k++)
{
C[i][j] = A[i][k] * B[k][j] + C[i][j] ;
}
}
}
for(i=0;i<m;i++)
{
for(j=0;j<m;j++)
{
printf("%d ", C[i][j] );
}
printf("\n");
}
getch() ;
return(0) ;
}
```

Q3. Write a program to sort a list of 10 numbers in ascending order.

```
#include<stdio.h>
#include<conio.h>
#include<process.h>
void main()
{
int i,j,temp,input[10];
    clrscr();
   printf("\nEnter elements of list :- ");
```

```
for(i=0;i<10;i++)
{
scanf("%d",&input[i]);
}

for(i=0;i<10;i++)
{
 for(j=0;j<10;j++)
 {
 if(input[j] >= input[i])
  {
   temp = input[j];
   input[j] = input[i];
   input[i]=temp;
  }
 }
}
for(i=0;i<10;i++)
 {
 printf("%d\n",input[i]);
 }
getch();
  }
```

FILES

Q4. Write a program to read the contents of one 'file 1' // and copy it into another file 'file 2' and count the number of character in that file.

```
#include<conio.h>
#include<stdio.h>
main()
{

FILE *fs,*ft;
int noc=0;
char ch,ch1;
clrscr();
fs=fopen("C:\\file1.c","r");
if(fs==NULL)
{
```

```
puts("Could not open source file");
exit();
}
ft= fopen("C:\\file2.c","ar");
if(ft==NULL)
{
puts("Cannot open target file");
fclose(fs);
exit();
}

while(1)
{
ch = fgetc(fs);
if(ch==EOF)
break;
else
fputc(ch,ft);
}


fclose(ft);

ft= fopen("C:\\file2.c","a+");
if(ft==NULL)
{
puts("Cannot open target file");
fclose(fs);
exit();
}


ch1=fgetc(ft);
while(ch1!=EOF)
{
noc++;
ch1=fgetc(ft);
}

printf("\n The number of character in the file is :- %d ",noc);
```

```
fclose(fs);
fclose(ft);
getch();
}
```

Q5. Write a program to open a file and read its content.

```
#include<stdio.h>
#include<conio.h>
main()
{
 clrscr() ;
 FILE *fpt ;
 char c ;
 fpt= fopen("f1.obj", "r") ;
 if(fpt==NULL)
  {
   puts("cannot open file") ;
  }
 else
   do
       putchar(c=fgetc(fpt));
   while(c!='\n') ;
 fclose(fpt) ;
 getch() ;
 return(0) ;
}
```

Q6. Write a program to read the contents of one 'file 1' and copy it into another file 'file 2'.

```
#include<conio.h>
#include<stdio.h>
main()
{
FILE *fs,*ft;
char ch;
fs=fopen("C:\\file1.c","r");
if(fs==NULL)
{
puts("Could not open source file");
exit();
}
```

```
ft= fopen("C:\\file2.c","w");
if(ft==NULL)
{
puts("Cannot open target file");
fclose(fs);
exit();
}
while(1)
{
ch = fgetc(fs);
if(ch==EOF)
break;
else
fputc(ch,ft);
}
fclose(fs);
fclose(ft);
getch();
}
```

FUNCTIONS

Q7. Write a program for matrix multipication using functions.

```
#include <stdio.h>
#include <conio.h>
#include <math.h>

#define MAX 3

void create ( int [3][3] ) ;
void display ( int [3][3] ) ;
void matmul(int[3][3],int[3][3],int[3][3]);
void main( )
{
        int mat [3][3] ;

        clrscr( ) ;

        printf ( "\nEnter elements for array: \n\n" ) ;
        create ( mat ) ;
```

```
        printf ( "\nThe Matrix: \n" ) ;
        display ( mat ) ;

        getch( ) ;
}


/* creates matrix mat */
void create ( int mat[3][3] )
{
        int n, i, j ;
        for ( i = 0 ; i < MAX ; i++ )
        {
                for ( j = 0 ; j < MAX ; j++ )
                {
                        printf ( "Enter the element: " ) ;
                        scanf ( "%d", &n ) ;
                        mat[i][j] = n ;
                }
        }
}

/* displays the contents of matrix */
void display ( int mat[3][3] )
{
        int i, j ;
        for ( i = 0 ; i < MAX ; i++ )
        {
                for ( j = 0 ; j < MAX ; j++ )
                        printf ( "%d\t", mat[i][j] ) ;
                printf ( "\n" ) ;
        }
}

/* multiplies two matrices */
void matmul ( int mat1[3][3], int mat2[3][3], int mat3[3][3] )
{
        int i, j, k ;
        for ( k = 0 ; k < MAX ; k++ )
        {
                for ( i = 0 ; i < MAX ; i++ )
```

```
                {
                        mat3[k][i] = 0 ;
                        for ( j = 0 ; j < MAX ; j++ )
                                mat3[k][i] += mat1[k][j] * mat2[j][i] ;
                }
        }
}
```

Q8. Write a program to perform create and display of a matrix using functions.

```
#include <stdio.h>
#include <conio.h>

#define MAX 3

void create ( int [3][3] ) ;
void display ( int [3][3] ) ;

void main( )
{
        int mat1[3][3], mat2[3][3];

        clrscr( ) ;

        printf ( "\nEnter elements for first array: \n\n" ) ;
        create ( mat1 ) ;

        printf ( "\nEnter elements for second array: \n\n" ) ;
        create ( mat2 ) ;

        printf ( "\nFirst Array: \n" ) ;
        display ( mat1 ) ;
        printf ( "\nSecond Array:\n" ) ;
        display ( mat2 ) ;

        getch( ) ;
}

/* creates matrix mat */
void create ( int mat[3][3] )
{
```

```
        int i, j ;

        for ( i = 0 ; i < MAX ; i++ )
        {
                for ( j = 0 ; j < MAX ; j++ )
                {
                        printf ( "Enter the element: " ) ;
                        scanf ( "%d", &mat[i][j] ) ;
                }
        }
}

/* displays the contents of matrix */
void display ( int mat[3][3] )
{
        int i, j ;

        for ( i = 0 ; i < MAX ; i++ )
        {
                for ( j = 0 ; j < MAX ; j++ )
                        printf ( "%d\t", mat[i][j] ) ;
                printf ( "\n" ) ;
        }
}
```

Q9. Write a program which performs any complex function on file.

```
#include<iostream.h>
#include<conio.h>
#include<string.h>
#include<stdio.h>
#include<stdlib.h>

void merge(int x[], int n)
{
int aux[10],i,j, k, l1, l2, u1, u2 , size ;
size=1 ;                          /* merge file of size 1 */
 while(size<n)
 {
  l1=0 ;                          /*initialize lower bound of file1 */
  k=0 ;                           /*index of auxilliary file */
```

```
while(l1+size<n)
{
 l2=l1+size ;                          /*lower bound of file 2 */
 u1=l2-1 ;                             /*upper bound of file1 */
 u2=(l2+size-1<n)? l2+size-1 : n-1 ;

  for(i=l1,j=l2;i<=u1 && j<=u2;k++)
        if(x[i]<=x[j])
           aux[k]=x[i++] ;
        else
           aux[k]=x[j++] ;

   for( ; i<=u1;k++)
         aux[k]=x[i++] ;
   for( ; j<=u2;k++)
         aux[k]=x[j++] ;

   l1=u2+1 ;
 }
for(i=l1;k<n;i++)
   aux[k++]=x[i] ;
for(i=0;i<n;i++)
   x[i]=aux[i] ;
size=size*2 ;
for(int a=0;a<n;a++)
{
cout<<aux[a]<<"  " ;
}
cout<<"\n" ;
}
}

main(void)
{
clrscr() ;
int list[10] , i, j, num ;
cout<<"how many numbers: " ;
cin>>num ;
for(i=0;i<num;i++)
{
cout<<"num"<<i<<" : " ;
```

```
cin>>list[i] ;
}
merge(list,num) ;
getch() ;
return(0) ;
}
```

Q10. Write a program to find transpose of a matrix.

```
#include <stdio.h>
#include <conio.h>

#define MAX 3

void create ( int [3][3] ) ;
void display ( int [3][3] ) ;
void transpose ( int [3][3] ) ;

void main( )
{
        int mat[3][3] ;
        clrscr( ) ;
        printf ( "\nEnter elements for matrix: \n\n" ) ;
        create ( mat ) ;
        printf ( "\nEntered Matrix is: \n" ) ;
        display ( mat ) ;
        transpose ( mat ) ;
        getch( ) ;
}

void create ( int mat[3][3] )
{
        int i, j ;
        for ( i = 0 ; i < MAX ; i++ )
        {
        for ( j = 0 ; j < MAX ; j++ )
                {
                        printf ( "Enter the element: " ) ;
                        scanf ( "%d", &mat[i][j] ) ;
                }
        }
```

```
}

void display ( int mat[3][3] )
{
        int i, j ;
        for ( i = 0 ; i < MAX ; i++ )
        {
                for ( j = 0 ; j < MAX ; j++ )
                        printf ( "%d\t", mat[i][j] ) ;
                printf ( "\n" ) ;
        }
}


void transpose ( int m1[3][3] )
{
        int i, j ;
        int m2[3][3];
        for ( i = 0 ; i < MAX ; i++ )
        {
                for ( j = 0 ; j < MAX ; j++ )
                        m2[i][j] = m1[j][i] ;
        }

    printf("\nThe Tronspose of entered matrox is :");
        for ( i = 0 ; i < MAX ; i++ )
        {
                printf("\n");
                for ( j = 0 ; j < MAX ; j++ )
                        printf("  %d", m2[i][j] );
        }
}
```

LOOP AND DECISION

Q11. Write a program to check whether the number is prime or composite.

```
#include<stdio.h>
#include<conio.h>
```

```
main( )
{
 clrscr() ;
 int min,max,n,i ;
 printf("Enter range");
 scanf("%d",&min);
 scanf("%d",&max);
 for(i=min;i<max;i++)
   {
     for(n=1;n<i/2;n++)
     {
      if(i% n == 0)
      printf("\n no. is prime");
    }
  }
 getch() ;
 return(0) ;
}
```

Q12. Write a program to draw reverse pyramid.

```
#include<stdio.h>
#include<conio.h>
main( )
{
 clrscr( ) ;
 int i, j, n ;
 printf ("enter number") ;
 scanf ("%d", &n) ;
 for (i=n;i>=1;--i) {
 for (j=1;j<=i;++j) {
 printf ("%d", j) ;}
 printf ("\n") ;
 }
 getch ( ) ;
 return (0) ;
 }
```

Q13. Write a program to print table.

```
#include<stdio.h>
void main()
{
```

```
int i,n;
printf("Enter a number ");
scanf("%d",&n);
for(i=1;i<=10;i++)
{
printf("%d * %d = %d\n",n,i,n*i);
}
}
```

Q14. Write a program related to pyramid.

```
#include<stdio.h>          /* header files */
#include<conio.h>
                            /* to print the half pyramid of alphabets */
main( )
{
 clrscr() ;
 int i, j, n ;                      /* variable declarations */
 char z='a' ;
 printf ("enter number: ") ;          /* output statement */
 scanf ("%d", &n) ;                   /* input statement */
 for (i=1;i<=n;++i)
{                              /* for loops */
 for (j=1;j<=i;++j)
{
 printf ("%c", z) ;
 printf("\t") ;
}
 z+=1 ;
 printf ("\n\n") ;
}
 getch() ;
 return (0) ;
}
```

POINTERS

Q15. Write a program to allocate memory dynamically for strings, and store their addresses in array of pointers to strings.

```
#include <stdio.h>
#include <conio.h>
```

```
#include <alloc.h>
#include <string.h>

void main( )
{
        char *name[5] ;
        char str[20] ;
        int i ;

        clrscr( ) ;

        for ( i = 0 ; i < 5 ; i++ )
        {
                printf ( "Enter a String: " ) ;
                gets ( str ) ;
                name[i] = ( char * ) malloc ( strlen ( str ) + 1 ) ;
                strcpy ( name[i], str ) ;
        }

        printf ( "\nThe strings are:" ) ;

        for ( i = 0 ; i < 5 ; i++ )
                printf ( "\n%s", name[i] ) ;

        for ( i = 0 ; i < 5 ; i++ )
                free ( name[i] ) ;

        getch( ) ;
}
```

Q16. Write a program to merge two 1-D arrays.

```
#include <stdio.h>
#include <conio.h>
#include <alloc.h>

#define MAX1 5
#define MAX2 7

int *arr ;

int* create ( int ) ;
```

```
void sort ( int *, int ) ;
void display ( int *, int ) ;
int* merge ( int *, int * ) ;
void main( )
{
        int *a, *b, *c ;

        clrscr( ) ;

        printf (  "\nEnter elements for first array: \n\n" ) ;
        a = create ( MAX1 ) ;

        printf ( "\nEnter elements for second array: \n\n" ) ;
        b = create ( MAX2 ) ;

        sort ( a, MAX1 ) ;
        sort ( b, MAX2 ) ;

        printf ( "\nFirst array: \n" ) ;
        display ( a, MAX1 ) ;
        printf ( "\n\nSecond array: \n" ) ;
        display ( b, MAX2 ) ;
        printf ( "\n\nAfter Merging: \n" ) ;

        c = merge ( a, b ) ;
        display ( c, MAX1 + MAX2 ) ;

        getch( ) ;
}

/* creates array of given size, dynamically */
int* create ( int size )
{
        int *arr, i ;
        arr = ( int * ) malloc ( sizeof ( int ) * size ) ;

        for ( i = 0 ; i < size ; i++ )
        {
                printf ( "Enter the element no. %d: ", i + 1 ) ;
                scanf ( "%d", &arr[i] ) ;
        }
```

```
        return arr ;
}

/* sorts array in ascending order */
void sort ( int *arr, int size )
{
        int i, temp, j ;
        for ( i = 0 ; i < size ; i++ )
        {
                for ( j = i + 1 ; j < size ; j++ )
                {
                        if ( arr[i] > arr[j] )
                        {
                                temp = arr[i] ;
                                arr[i] = arr[j] ;
                                arr[j] = temp ;
                        }
                }
        }
}

/* displays the contents of array */
void display ( int *arr, int size )
{
        int i ;
        for ( i = 0 ; i < size ; i++)
                printf (  "%d\t", arr[i] ) ;
}

/* merges two arrays of different size */
int* merge ( int *a, int *b )
{
        int *arr ;
        int i, k, j ;
        int size = MAX1 + MAX2 ;
        arr = ( int * ) malloc ( sizeof ( int ) * ( size ) ) ;

        for ( k = 0, j = 0, i = 0 ; i <= size ; i++ )
        {
                if ( a[k] < b[j] )
                {
```

```
                arr[i] = a[k] ;
                k++ ;
                if ( k >= MAX1 )
                {
                        for ( i++ ; j < MAX2 ; j++, i++ )
                                arr[i] = b[j] ;
                }
            }
            else
            {
                arr[i] = b[j] ;
                j++ ;
                if ( j >= MAX2 )
                {
                        for ( i++ ; k < MAX1 ; k++, i++ )
                                arr[i] = a[k] ;
                }
            }
        }

        return arr ;
}
```

Q17. Write a program to compare string using pointer.

```
#include <stdio.h>
#include <conio.h>
#include <string.h>

int xstrcmp ( char *, char * ) ;

void main( )
{
        char s1[ ] = "kicit" ;
        char s2[ ] = "Nagpur" ;

        clrscr( ) ;

        printf ( "\nString s1: %s", s1 ) ;
        printf ( "\nString s2: %s", s2 ) ;
```

```
        if ( xstrcmp ( s1, s2 ) == 0 )
                printf( "\nThe strings s1 and s2 are similar" ) ;
        else
                printf ( "\nThe strings s1 and s2 are not similar" ) ;

        getch( ) ;
}


/* compares two strings s and t for equality */
int xstrcmp ( char *s, char *t )
{
        while ( *s == *t )
        {
                if ( ! ( *s ) )
                        return 0 ;
                s++ ;
                t++ ;
        }
        return ( *s - *t ) ;
}
```

PREPROCESSOR

Q18. Write a macro program.

```
#include <iostream>

#define NUM_ITERATIONS 3
// Note: the "macro" on the following line should have parentheses.
//      It is given this way to point out the need for parentheses.
#define MAX(a, b)   a > b ? a : b
#define SHOW_PROBLEMS
static int getAnInteger()
{
   cout << "Enter an integer\n";
   int num;
   cin >> num;
   return num;
}
```

```
static void define_example()
{
   int biggies[NUM_ITERATIONS];
   for (int i = 0; i < NUM_ITERATIONS; i++)
   {
      cout << "Enter two integers\n";
      int num1, num2;
      cin >> num1 >> num2;

      biggies[i] = MAX(num1, num2);
#ifdef SHOW_PROBLEMS
      int num3 = MAX(num1, 42) + 3;
      cout << "num3 is " << num3 << endl;
#endif
   }

   cout << "Biggies:\n";
   for (int i = 0; i < NUM_ITERATIONS; i++)
   {
      cout << biggies[i] << " ";
   }
   cout << endl;
}

int main(void)
{
   define_example();
   return 0;
}
```

Q19. Wrie a macro program.

```
#include <stdio.h>

#define WORD1
/* you don't have to put an expression after the defined word */

int main() {
#ifdef WORD1
 printf("1: WORD1 is defined so this bit is compiled.\n");
#endif
```

```
#ifndef WORD2
 printf("2: WORD2 is not defined so this bit is compiled.\n");
#endif

#undef WORD1
#define WORD2

#ifdef WORD1
 printf("3: WORD1 is now undefined so this bit is not compiled.\n");
#endif

#ifndef WORD2
 printf("4: WORD2 is now defined so this bit is not compiled.\n");
#endif

 return 0;
}
```

Q20. Write a macro program for minimum and maximum.

```
#include <stdio.h>

#define MIN 0   /* #defines */
#define MAX 10
#define TRUE 1
#define FALSE 0

int main() {    /* beginning of program */
 int a;
 int okay = FALSE; /* the compiler sees this as int okay = 0; */

  while(!okay) {
  printf("Input an integer between %d and %d: ", MIN, MAX);
  scanf("%d", &a);

   if(a>MAX) {
     printf("\nToo large.\n");
   }
  else if(a<MIN) {
   printf("\nToo small.\n");
  }
```

```
    else {
      printf("\nThanks.\n");
      okay = TRUE;
    }
  }
  return 0;
}
```

Q21. Write another macro program.

```
#include <stdio.h>

#define MAX(a,b) (a>b ? a : b) /* a "function" */
#define DIFF1  4-7
#define DIFF2 (4-7)
#define NUMBER 10

int main() {
  int a=4, b=7;

  printf("Out of %d and %d, %d is the bigger number.\n",
        a, b, MAX(a,b));
  printf("DIFF1 =  4-7.  DIFF1 times 10 equals %d.\n", DIFF1*10);
  printf("DIFF2 = (4-7). DIFF2 times 10 equals %d.\n", DIFF2*10);

  printf("I live at number %d.\n", NUMBER);
  printf("I'm moving soon...");

#undef NUMBER
/* now undefine NUMBER so that we can give it a different value */
#define NUMBER 7

  printf(" now I live at number %d.\n", NUMBER);

  return 0;
}
```

STRINGS

Q22. Write a program to concatenate two strings

```
#include<stdio.h>
#include<conio.h>
```

```
char *strcat1() ;
void main()

{
 char *s1[30],*s3[60];
 char *s2[30];
 clrscr();
 printf("Enter two strings");
scanf("%s %s", &s1,&s2);
 *s3= strcat1(s1,s2);
printf("The concatenated string is :%s",*s3);
getch();
}
char *strcat1(char first,char second)
char *first,*second
{
static char result[70];
char *ptr=result;
while(*ptr++=*first++);
ptr--;
 while(*ptr++=*second++);
 return(result);
}
```

Q23. Write a Program to copy one string to another using pointers.

```
#include<stdio.h>
#include<conio.h>

main()
{
 clrscr() ;
 char st2[20] ;
char st1[20] ;
char strcopy(char*,char*) ;
gets(st2) ;
fflush(stdin) ;
strcopy(st1,st2) ;
printf("source string is %s", st1) ;
printf("\ntarget string is %s", st2) ;
getch() ;
```

```
 return(0) ;
}
char strcopy(char*st1,char*st2)
{
 while(*st2!='\0')
  { *st1=*st2 ;
    st2++ ;
    st1++ ;
          }
 *st1='\0' ;
}
```

Q24. Write a program to print 'n' right most caharacters from a string.

```
#include <stdio.h>
#include <conio.h>
#include <string.h>
#include <alloc.h>

char * rightsub ( char *, int n ) ;

void main( )
{
        char s1[20];
        char s2[20];
        char ch, *s ;
        int n ;

        clrscr( ) ;
        printf ( "\nEnter a String s1: ") ;
        gets(s1);

        printf("Enter the number of characters to extracts:-  ");
        scanf("%d",&n);
        s = rightsub ( s1, n ) ;
        printf ( "\nRight sub string: %s", s ) ;
        free ( s ) ;


        getch( ) ;
}
```

```
/* extracts rightmost n characters from the string */
char * rightsub ( char *str, int n )
{
        char *t = ( char * ) malloc ( n + 1 ) ;
        int l = strlen ( str ) ;
        char *s = str + ( l - n ) ;
        int i = 0 ;

        while ( i < n )
        {
                t[i] = *s ;
                s++ ;
                i++ ;
        }
        t[i] = '\0' ;

        return t ;
}
```

Q25. Write a program to find length of a string.

```
#include<stdio.h>
#include<conio.h>
main()
{
 char arr[]="ankur" ;
 int len ;
 int strlen(char*) ;
 len=strlen(arr) ;
 printf("\nstring=%s length=%d", arr, len) ;
 getch() ;
 return(0) ;
}
int strlen(char*s)
{
int length=0 ;
while(*s!='\0')
  { length++ ;
    s++ ;    }
return (length) ;
}
```

STRUCTURE

Q26. Write a program for assessment of external and internal marks of a student.

```
#include<stdio.h>
#include<conio.h>
struct student{
            char name[80] ;
            int int_cource[4];
            int ext_cource[4];
            int total_int ;
            int total_ext;
            } data ;
main()
{
 int max,total,i,int_max,ext_max;
 float average;
 clrscr();
 printf("\nEnter maximum marks of internal assessment : ") ;
 scanf("%d", &int_max) ;
 printf("\nEnter maximum marks of external assessment : ") ;
 scanf("%d", &ext_max) ;
 printf("\nname: ") ;
 scanf("%s", &data.name) ;

 printf("\n\nEnter marks of internal assessment:- ");
 for(i=0;i<4;i++)
 {
 printf(" \nmarks in cource[%d]: ",i+1) ;
 scanf("%d", &data.int_cource[i]) ;
 }

 for(i=0;i<4;i++)
 {
 if(data.int_cource[i] <= int_max * 0.39 )
 printf(" \nFailed in cource[%d]: ",i+1) ;
 }


 printf("\n\nEnter marks of external examination:- ");
```

```
for(i=0;i<4;i++)
{
printf(" \nmarks in cource[%d]: ",i+1) ;
scanf("%d", &data.ext_cource[i]) ;
}

for(i=0;i<4;i++)
{
if(data.ext_cource[i] <= ext_max * 0.39 )
printf(" \nFailed in cource[%d]: ",i+1) ;
}

for(i=0;i<4;i++)
{
data.total_int+=data.int_cource[i];
}

for(i=0;i<4;i++)
{
data.total_ext+=data.ext_cource[i];
}

total = data.total_int+ data.total_ext;
max= ( (int_max * 4) + (ext_max * 4) ) ;

average = ((float)total/(float)max)*100 ;
printf("\n %f ",average) ;

if(average>=60)
printf("\n \nfirst grade");
else if(average < 60 && average > 50)
printf("\n\nSecond Grade");
else if(average < 50)
printf("\n\n Third Grade");

getch() ;
return(0) ;
}
```

Q27. Write a Program to store student details using structures.

```
#include<stdio.h>
#include<conio.h>
struct dob {
            int month ;
            int dd ;
            int year ;
            } date ;
struct {
        char name[20] ;
        int roll_no ;
        struct dob date ;
    } student[2] ;
main()
{
 int i ;
 for(i=0;i<2;i++)
{
 printf("name: ") ;
 scanf("%s", student[i].name) ;
 printf("roll_no: ") ;
 scanf("%d",&student[i].roll_no) ;
 printf("date of birth: ") ;
 scanf("%d %d %d",  &student[i].date.month, &student[i].date.dd,
&student[i].date.year) ;
}
 getch() ;
 return(0) ;
}
```

Q28. Write a Program to create student marksheet using structure.

```
#include<stdio.h>
#include<conio.h>
struct student{
            char name[80] ;
            int sub1, sub2, sub3, sub4 ;
              int total ;
            } data ;
main()
{
 int max=50 ;
```

```
printf("maximum marks: ") ;
scanf("%d", &max) ;
printf("name: ") ;
scanf("%s", &data.name) ;
printf(" marks in sub1: ") ;
scanf("%d", &data.sub1) ;
printf(" marks in sub2: ") ;
scanf("%d", &data.sub2) ;
printf(" marks in sub3: ") ;
scanf("%d", &data.sub3) ;
printf(" marks in sub4: ") ;
scanf("%d", &data.sub4) ;
printf(" total marks in all sub: ") ;
data.total=data.sub1 + data.sub2 + data.sub3 + data.sub4 ;
printf("%d", data.total) ;
getch() ;
return(0) ;
}
```

SOLVED PAPERS
MCS-11

MCS-011 : PROBLEM SOLVING AND PROGRAMMING
JUNE-2005

Note : *Question no. 1 is* ***compulsory.*** *Answer any three from the rest.*

Q1(a). Write an algorithm and draw a corresponding flowchart to find the greatest number and its position among the 6 given numbers. [10]

<u>ALGORITHM</u>

```
START
Max=0,pos=1,i=6
Step1: while( i>0)
         Max=Input[i]
         Pos = 1
If(max<input[i])
          Max=input[i]
          Pos = i
          End if
       End while
Step 2: print "maximum number is max"
Step 3: Print "location is pos"
End
```

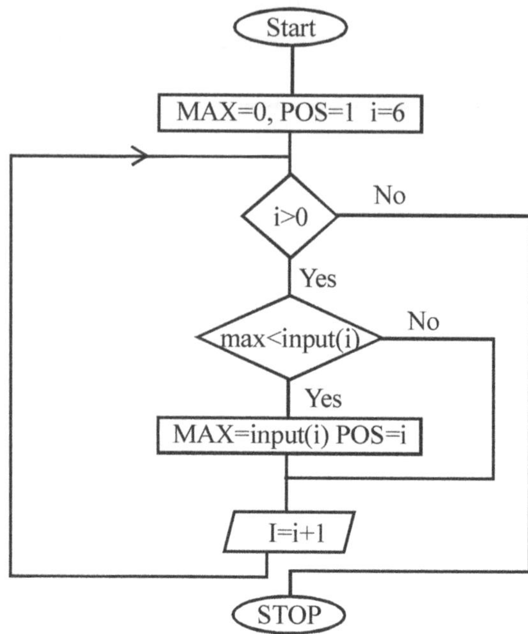

(b) Write a program in C language to add, subtract, multiply and divide two complex numbers (Use a Switch statement to select the operation). **[10]**

```
#include<stdio.h>
#include<conio.h>
#include<process.h>
void main()
{
float real1,real2,real,img1,img2,img;
int ch;
clrscr();
printf("\nEnter real part of first complex number:-  ");
scanf("%f",&real1);
printf("\nEnter complex part of first complex number:-  ");
scanf("%f",&img1);
printf("\nEnter real part of second complex number:-  ");
scanf("%f",&real2);
printf("\nEnter complex part of second complex number:-  ");
scanf("%f",&img2);
printf("\nThe first Complex number is : -  %f +  i (%f)",real1,img1);
```

```
printf("\nThe second Complex number is : -  %f +  i (%f)",real2,img2);
getch();
clrscr();
printf("\nENTER YOUR CHOICE :-");
printf("\n1.Add complex numbers");
printf("\n2.Subtract complex number");
printf("\n3.Multiply complex number");
printf("\n4.Divide complex number");
printf("\n5.Exit");
scanf("%d",&ch);
switch(ch)
{
case 1: printf("The result after addition is %f + i
(%f)",(real1+real2),(img1+img2));
        break;
case 2: printf("The result after subtraction is %f + i (%f)",(real1-real2),(img1-
img2));
        break;
case 3: printf("The result after multiplication is %f + i (%f)",((real1*real2)-
(img1*img2)),((real1*img2)+(real2*img1)));
        break;
case 4: printf("The result after division is %f + i
(%f)",(((real1*real2)+(img1*img2))/((real2 * real2)+(img2*img2))),((-1) *
((real1*img2)+(real2*img1))/((real2*real2)+(img2*img2))));
        break;
case 5: exit(0);
        break;
default: printf("Wrong choice....");
}

getch();
}
```

(c) Design an algorithm, draw a corresponding flowchart and write a program in C to reverse a given string and find whether it is a palindrome or not. [10]

ALGORITHM

START

Step 1: Enter a string : str , j=0 ,temp

Step 2: Find its length
Length = stringlength(str)

Step3 : while(length>0)
temp[j]= str[length]
j = j+1
length = length – 1
End while loop

Step 4: Print reverse String : temp

Step 5: If(temp = str)
String is palindrome
Else
String is not palindrome

STOP

**************************C Language Program*****************

```
#include<stdio.h>
#include<conio.h>
#include<string.h>

void main()
{
 char line[80],temp[80];
 int i,j,k=0,check;
 clrscr() ;
 printf("Enter a string \n");
 gets(line);
 i=strlen(line);
 for(j=i-1;j>=0;j--)
  {
   temp[k]=line[j];
   k++;
  }
  temp[k]='\0';
 printf("\n\nReversed line is :\n");
  puts(temp);

 check = strcmp(temp,line);
```

```
if(strcmp(temp,line))
printf("Not Palindrome");
else
printf("Palindrome");
getch();
}
```

Flowchart :

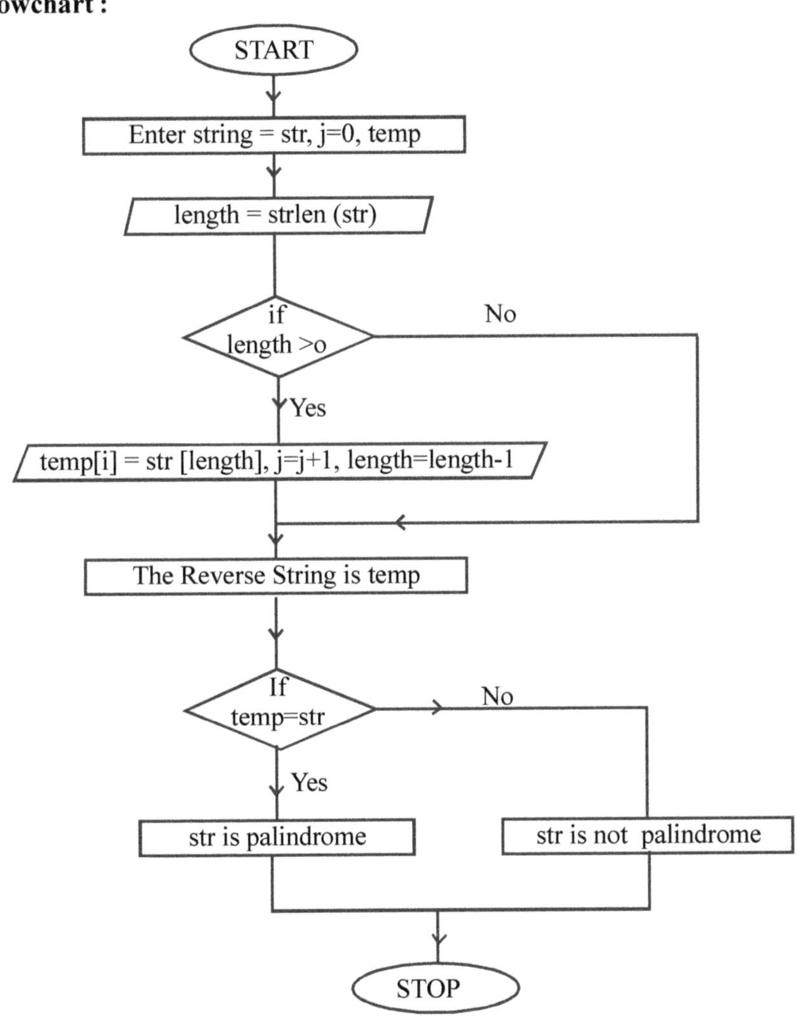

(d) Write a program in C, to multiply two matrices. **[10]**

```
#include<stdio.h>
#include<conio.h>
#include<process.h>
void main()
{
int s,k,i,j,r1,r2,c1,c2,m1[10][10],m2[10][10],m3[10][10];
    clrscr();
   printf("\nEnter rows & column of first matrix :- ");
    scanf("%d%d",&r1,&c1);
   printf("\nEnter rows & column of second matrix :- ");
    scanf("%d%d",&r2,&c2);
   if(c1!=r2)
   {
   printf("\n\n\tMATRIX MULTIPLICATION IS NOT POSSIBLE");
   getch();
   exit(0);
   }
   printf("\nEnter elements of first matrix");
     for(i=0;i<r1;i++)
      {
      for(j=0;j<c1;j++)
           {
             scanf("%d",&m1[i][j]);
           }
      }

   printf("\nEnter elements of second matrix");
    for(i=0;i<r2;i++)
     {
     for(j=0;j<c2;j++)
      {
          scanf("%d",&m2[i][j]);
      }
     }

   clrscr();
  printf("\t\nThe first matrix entered by you is ");
   for(i=0;i<r1;i++)
  {
  printf("\n");
```

```
    for(j=0;j<c1;j++)
     {
      printf("\t%d",m1[i][j]);
     }
  }

  printf("\t\n\nThe second matrix entered by you is ");
   for(i=0;i<r2;i++)
   {
   printf("\n");
    for(j=0;j<c2;j++)
    {
   printf("\t%d",m2[i][j]);
    }
   }

printf("\nThe Result is : - \n");
for(i=0;i<r1;i++)
{
printf("\n");
for(j=0;j<c2;j++)
{
s=0;
printf("\t");
for(k=0;k<c1;k++)
{
s+=m1[i][k]*m2[k][j];
}
m3[i][j]=s;
printf("%d",m3[i][j]);
}
}
getch();
}
```

Q2(a). Write the steps involved in the top-down design process with the help of a diagram. [10]

The steps involved in top–down design process are:

Top-down design

➢ The design activity must begin with the analysis of the requirements definition and should not consider implementation details at first.

➢ A project is decomposed into subprojects, and this procedure is repeated until the subtasks have become so simple that an algorithm can be formulated as a solution.

➢ Top-down design is a successive concretization of abstractly described ideas for a solution.

➢ Abstraction proves to be the best medium to render complex systems comprehensible; the designer is involved only with those aspects of the system that are necessary for understanding before the next step or during the search for a solution.

Features:

· often used with data-flow notations (DFDs, flowcharts)
· state is typically shared: all parts of the program operate on the same data

Example:

· top level design for a compiler

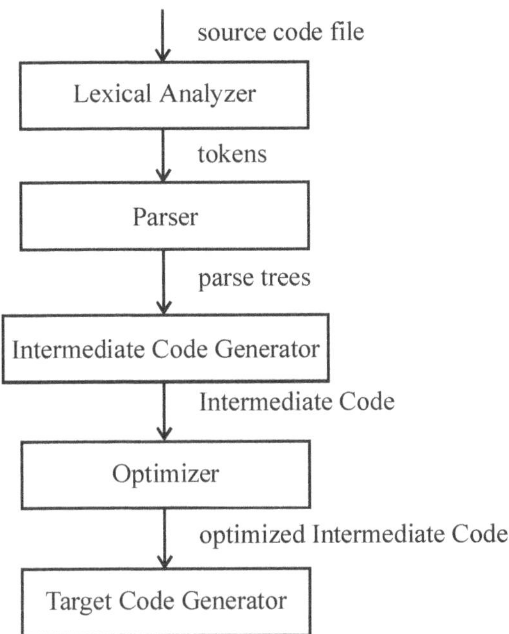

* each box represents a top-level function
* the lexical analysis box could be refined as follows:

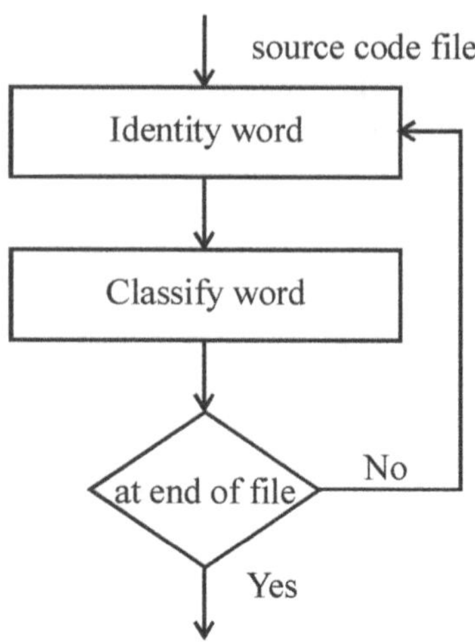

(b) Write a program in C (using files) to open the "file1", read the contents and copy the same into "file 2". [10]

```
#include<conio.h>
#include<stdio.h>
main()
{
FILE *fs,*ft;
char ch;
fs=fopen("C:\\file1.c","r");
if(fs==NULL)
{
puts("Could not open source file");
exit();
}
ft= fopen("C:\\file2.c","w");
if(ft==NULL)
{
puts("Cannot open target file");
fclose(fs);
exit();
}
while(1)
{
```

```
ch = fgetc(fs);
if(ch==EOF)
break;
else
fputc(ch,ft);
}
fclose(fs);
fclose(ft);
getch();
}
```

Q3(a). Mention any three advantages of use of pointers over arrays. Also, write a program (using pointers) to insert and delete an element in an ordered list. [10]

Refer to Chapter-2, Q-2, Page no.-43

(b) Write a program to do the following without the use of any string functions like strcat and strlen :

(i) Concatenate two strings

```
#include<stdio.h>
#include<conio.h>
#include<string.h>

 void main()
 {
  char str1[20],str2[20],str[40];
 int i,j,length1,length2,length;
  clrscr();
  printf("Enter a first string \n");
  gets(str1);
  printf("Enter a second string \n");
  gets(str2);
  length1=string_length(str1);
  length2=string_length(str2);
  length = length1 + length2;
  for(i=0;i<length1;i++)
  {
  str[i]=str1[i];
  }

  for(j=0;j<length2;j++)
```

```
  {
  str[i++]=str2[j];
   }
   for(i=0;i<length;i++)
  {
   printf("%c",str[i]);
   }
    getch();
}

string_length(char *s)
{
int length = 0;
while(*s!=NULL)
{
length++;
s++;
}
return(length);
}
```

(ii) To find the length of any given string **[10]**

```
#include<stdio.h>
#include<conio.h>
#include<string.h>

 void main()
 {
  char str[20];
  clrscr();
  printf("Enter a string \n");
  gets(str);
  string_length(str);
  getch();
}

string_length(char *s)
{
int length = 0;
while(*s!=NULL)
{
```

```
length++;
s++;
}
printf("The length of string is :- %d ",length);
}
```

Q4(a). What is a preprocessor directive ? Write the syntax for the following preprocessor conditional statments : [10]
(i) # if def
(ii) # if n def
(iii) # else
(iv) # pragma

C preprocessor is a special program in C language that allows us to define and associate symbolic names with constants. The C preprocessor uses the terminology macro names and macro body to refer to the symbolic names and the constants. The C preprocessor runs before the compiler. During preprocessing, the operation to replace a macro name with its associated macro body is called macro substitution or macro expansion. All preprocessor directives begin with # as the very first non-space character. This is important - the first non-space character must be #. Preprocessor directives do not end with a semicolon like C commands. A preprocessor directive ends with the end-of-line character, and can be continued on more than one line by hiding the carriage return with the \ character.

<u>(i) Syntax for #ifdef Directives</u>

The #ifdef and #endif directives control whether a given group of statements is to be included as part of your program.

The general form to use the #ifdef and #endif directives is

```
#ifdef macro_name
  statement1
  statement2
  . . .
  statementN
#endif
```

Here macro_name is any character string that can be defined by a #define directive. statement1, statement2, and statementN are statements that are included in the program if macro_name has been defined. If macro_name has not been defined, statement1, statement2, and statementN are skipped.

(ii) Syntax for #ifndef Directives

The #ifndef directive enables you to define code that is to be executed when a particular macro name is not defined.

The general format to use #ifndef is the same as for #ifdef:

```
#ifndef macro_name
  statement1
  statement2
  . . .
  statementN
#endif
```

Here macro_name, statement1, statement2, and statementN have the same meanings as those in the form of #ifdef. Again, the #endif directive is needed to mark the end of the #ifndef block.

(iii)Syntax for #else Directives

The #else directive provides an alternative to choose. It cannot be used without #if. It is used to just provide an alternative option. The following general form uses the #else directive to put statement_1, statement_2, and statement_N into the program if expression is zero:

```
#if expression
  statement1
  statement2
  . . .
  statementN
#else
  statement_1
  statement_2
  . . .
  statement_N
#endif
```

the #endif directive is used to mark the end of the #if block.

(iv) Syntax for #pragma Directives

The ICC11/ICC12 preprocessor recognizes pragma directives that is used to develop interrupt software. Interrupt_handler pragma are used to specify a function as an interrupt handler. The compiler will then use the rti instruction rather than the rts instruction to return from ExtHan.

```
#pragma interrupt_handler ExtHan()
void ExtHan(void){
  KWIFJ=0x80; // clear flag
  PutFifo(PORTJ&0x7F);}
```

(b) Design an algorithm and draw corresponding flowchart to convert a decimal number to its binary equivalent. [10]

Algorithm

```
START
Step 1.let num be an array of integer

Step2.input no.

Step3.let rem=0,ctr=0

Step4.while(rem!=1)
       begin
       q=no/2
       rem=no mod 2
       num[ctr]=rem
       ctr++
       no=q

       end

Step5.while(ctr>=0)
       begin
       print num[ctr]
       ctr=ctr-1
      end

       END
```

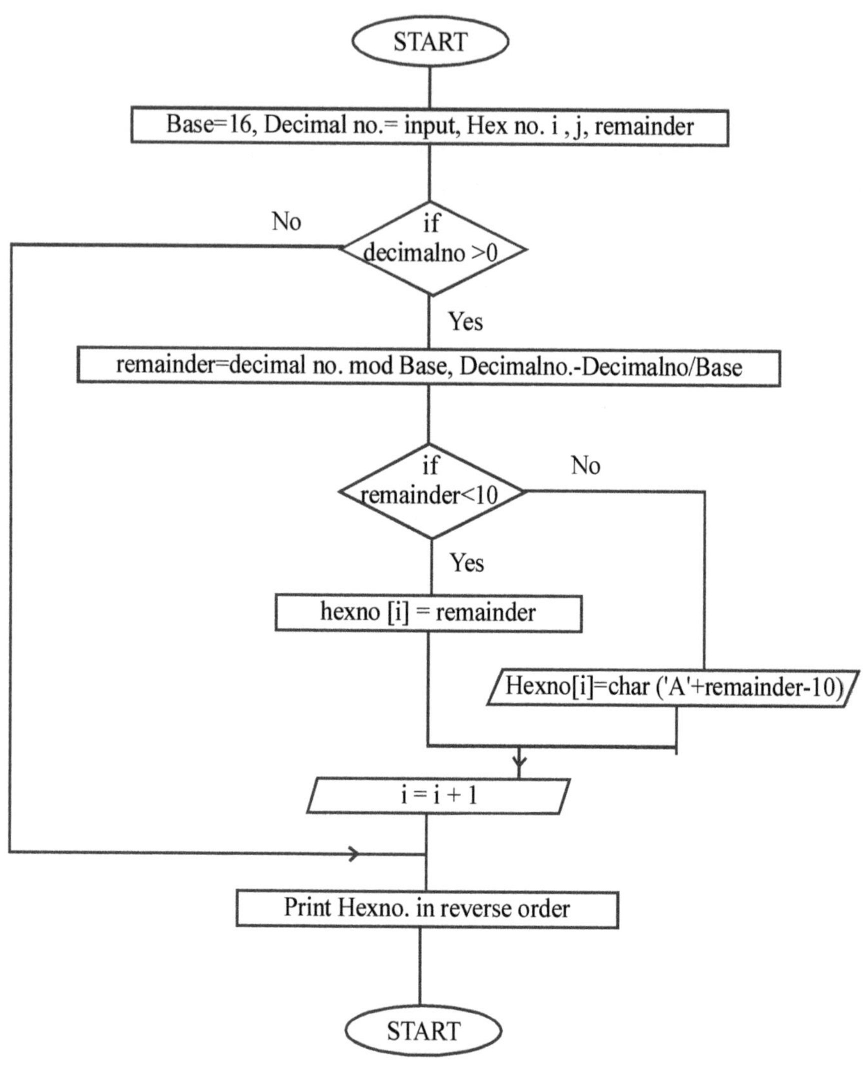

Q5(a). Mention the rules for using the Big-O Notation. **[5]**

<u>Defination of Big 'O'</u>

f(x) is O(g(x)) if there are constants C and k such that

$|f(x)| <= C\ |g(x)|$ whenever $x>k$

This is read as f(x) is big-oh of g(x).

In English, this means that the function f(x) grows no faster than g(x) as x gets larger. A function that is $O(x^3)$ grows faster than one that is $O(x^2)$. What we would like is to develop algorithms that have the smallest O values.

Rules for Big-Oh Notation:

The eight rules for using big-oh notation.

Let *f(n)*, *g(n)*, *h(n)*, and *p(n)* be functions from the set of non-negative integers to the set of non-negative real numbers.

1. Coefficient Rule: If f(n) is O(g(n)), then kf(n) is O(g(n)), for any constant $k > 0$.
2. Sum Rule: If f(n) is O(h(n)) and g(n) is O(p(n)), then f(n)+g(n) is O(h(n)+p(n)).
3. Product Rule: If f(n) is O(h(n)) and g(n) is O(p(n)), then f(n)g(n) is O(h(n)p(n)).
4. Transitive Rule: If f(n) is O(g(n)) and g(n) is O(h(n)), then f(n) is O(h(n)).
5. Polynomial Rule: If f(n) is a polynomial of degree k, then f(n) is $O(n^k)$.
6. Log of a Power Rule: $\log(n^k)$ is $O(\log(n))$ for any constant $k > 0$.
7. Comparison Rule 1: n^k is $O(a^n)$ for any constants $k > 0$ and $a > 1$.
8. Comparison Rule 2: $(\log(n))^k$ is $O(n^m)$ for any constants $k > 0$ and $m > 0$.

(b) What is a variable ? What are the rules to be followed to name a variable in "C" ? Write the syntax to declare the variables. Also metion the initialise a character variable with the help of an example. [6]

VARIABLE:- Variables represent named storage locations, whose values can be manipulated during program run. A Variable can also be considered as a name given to the location in memory where any constant value is stored.

The rules to be followed to name a variable in "C"

- Variable names must start with a letter or underscore. By convention a lowercase letter. The use of a leading underscore is NOT recommended.
- Then letters, numbers and the underscore_can be used.
- Spaces are NOT allowed.
- Do NOT use any of the C reserved keywords.
- Case is significant, num is a different variable to Num
- Only the first 31 characters are significant.

Syntax to Declare a Variable:

datatype variable_name;

ex:

int i;

char ch;

flaot s;

Syntax to initialize a char variable:

Char variable_name = 'character'
Ex: char = ' A';

(c) Write a program to sort the given list of 10 numbers in ascending order. **[9]**

```
#include<stdio.h>
#include<conio.h>
#include<process.h>
void main()
{
int i,j,temp,input[10];
    clrscr();
   printf("\nEnter elements of list :- ");

for(i=0;i<10;i++)
{
scanf("%d",&input[i]);
}
```

```
for(i=0;i<10;i++)
{
 for(j=0;j<10;j++)
 {
  if(input[j] >= input[i])
  {
    temp = input[j];
    input[j] = input[i];
    input[i]=temp;
  }
 }
}
for(i=0;i<10;i++)
 {
 printf("%d\n",input[i]);
 }
getch();
   }
```

Note : *Question no. 1 is* ***compulsory.*** *Answer any three from the rest.*

Q1(a). Write an algorithm and draw a corresponding flowchart to search a number in the given list of numbers and also display its position.[10]

ALGORITHM

```
START
num,pos=1,size
 while(i>size)
  If(num=list[i])
             Pos = i
         Print " Search Successful"
             Print "Position is pos"
 Else
              Print "Search Unsuccessful"
 End if
        i=i+1
 End while
END
```

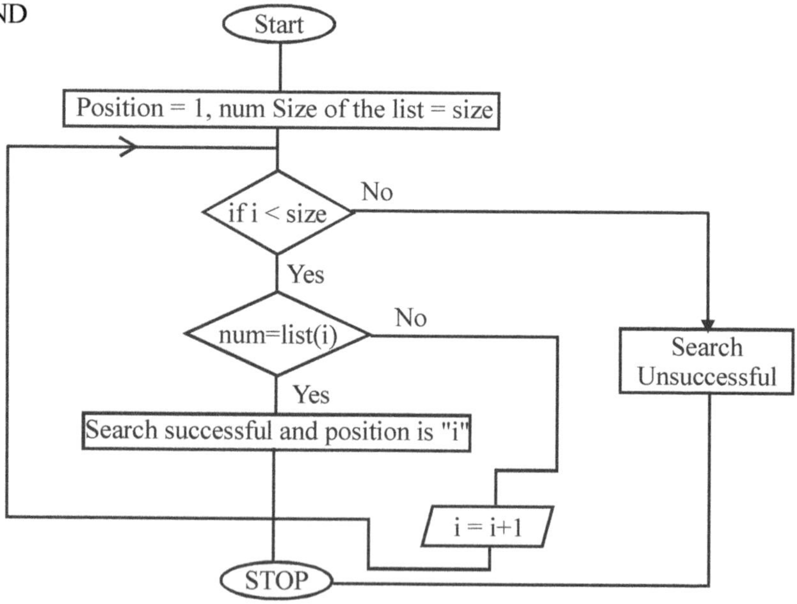

Start

Position = 1, num Size of the list = size

if i < size

No

Yes

num=list(i)

No

Search Unsuccessful

Yes

Search successful and position is "i"

i = i+1

STOP

(b) Write a Menu driven program in C to add, subtract and multiply two distances which are given in feet and inches. [e.g. 3 ft 9 inches + 2 ft 5 inches = 6 ft 2 inches] [10]

```
#include<stdio.h>
#include<conio.h>
#include<process.h>
void main()
{
int feet1,feet2,feet,inch1,inch2;
int ch,inch,toti;
clrscr();
printf("\nEnter feet of first distance:-  ");
scanf("%d",&feet1);
printf("\nEnter inches of first distance:-  ");
scanf("%d",&inch1);
printf("\nEnter feet of second distance:-  ");
scanf("%d",&feet2);
printf("\nEnter inches of second distance:-  ");
scanf("%d",&inch2);

printf("\nThe first distance is : -  %d '   (%d)"",feet1,inch1);
printf("\nThe second distance is : -  %d'   (%d)"",feet2,inch2);
getch();
clrscr();
printf("\nENTER YOUR CHOICE :-");
printf("\n1.Add Distances");
printf("\n2.Subtract  Distances");
printf("\n3.Multiply Distances");
printf("\n4.Exit");
scanf("%d",&ch);
switch(ch)
{
case 1: toti=inch1+inch2+(feet1*12)+(feet2*12);
      feet=toti/12;
      inch=(toti-(feet*12));
      printf("The result after addition is %d '  (%d)"",feet,inch);
      break;

case 2:
      toti=(inch1+(feet1*12))-(inch2+(feet2*12));
```

```
      feet=toti/12;
      inch=(toti-(feet*12));
      printf("The result after subtraction is %d '  (%d)"",feet,inch);
      break;
case 3: toti=(inch1*inch2);
      if(toti<12)
      {
      inch=toti;
      feet=feet1*feet2;
      }
      else
      {
      inch=(toti-(toti/12));
      feet=(feet*feet2)+(toti/12);
      }
      printf("The result after multiplication is %d'  %d"",feet,inch);
      break;
case 4: exit(0);
      break;
default: printf("Wrong choice....");
}

getch();
}
```

(c) Write a recursive program in 'C' to find whether a given five digit number is a palindrome or not. [10]

```
#include<stdio.h>
#include<string.h>
#include<conio.h>
#include<stdlib.h>
/* TO SEARCH FOR A PALINDROME */

void reverse(char num[],int a,int b)
{
if(a<b)
{
if(num[a++]==num[b--])
reverse(num,a,b);
else{
printf("not a palindrom");
```

```
getch();
exit(0);
}
}
else
{
printf("\n palindrom");
getch();
exit(0);
}
}

void main()
{
int len;
char num[6];
 printf("\nEnter the number: ") ;
 scanf("%s", num) ;
 len=strlen(num);
 len--;
 reverse(num,0,len);
 getch();
 }
```

(d) Write a program in 'C' to print automorphic numbers. The automorphic number is a number in which the square of the number contains the number in the end.

Examle : (a) 5; 25 (b) 6; 36 **[10]**

```
#include<stdio.h>
#include<conio.h>
main()
{
int i,k,square;
clrscr();
printf("Enter a Number:- ");
scanf("%d",&i);
square=i*i;
k=square%10;
if(i==k)
printf("\nThe Given Number is Automorphic ");
else
```

```
printf("\nThe Given Number is Not Automorphic");
getch();
}
```

Q2(a). Design an algorithm and draw corresponding flowchart to find all the prime numbers between two given numbers 'm' and 'n', where m, n > 0. [10]

ALGORITHM

```
START

Start=m,stop=n,flag=set,i=2

Step1:while(m<n)

Step:2while(i<m/2)
        If(m%i=0)
        Reset Flag
        i=i+1
        End step 2 while

Step3:  if(flag Is Set)
          Print i is prime
           m=m+1;

Step4: End step1 while
```

STOP

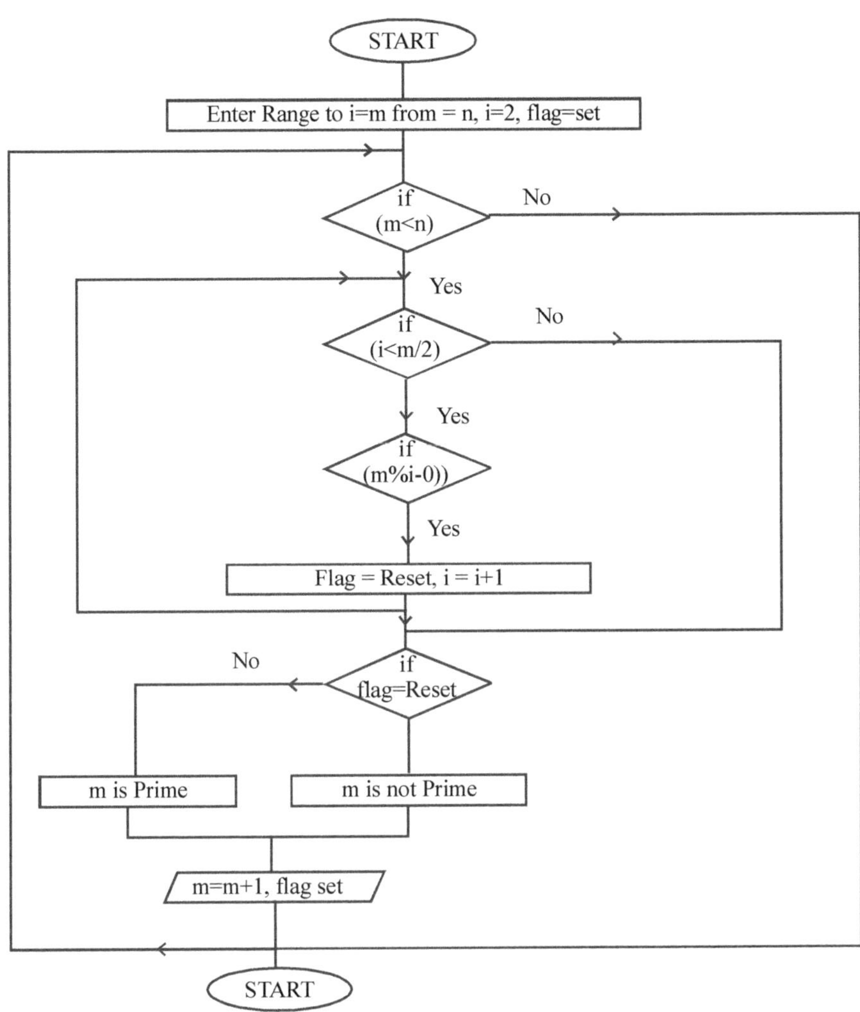

(b) Design an algorithm and write a program using 'C' to compute transpose of a matrix. [10]

ALGORITHM:

START

mat[][],trans[][],rows=I,column=j.

Step1: Enter the matrix mat[][].

Step2: while (I > row)

Step3: while(j > column)

Step4: trans[i][j]=matrix[j][i]

Step5:i=i+1
j=j+1
end while
end while

Step6: print trans .

End

*********************Program in C Language**********************

```
#include <stdio.h>
#include <conio.h>

#define MAX 3

void create ( int [3][3] ) ;
void display ( int [3][3] ) ;
void transpose ( int [3][3] ) ;

void main( )
{
    int mat[3][3] ;
    clrscr( ) ;
    printf ( "\nEnter elements for  matrix: \n\n" ) ;
    create ( mat ) ;
    printf ( "\nEntered Matrix is: \n" ) ;
    display ( mat ) ;
    transpose ( mat ) ;
    getch( ) ;
}

void create ( int mat[3][3] )
{
    int i, j ;
    for ( i = 0 ; i < MAX ; i++ )
    {
```

```
        for ( j = 0 ; j < MAX ; j++ )
            {
                    printf ( "Enter the element: " ) ;
                    scanf ( "%d", &mat[i][j] ) ;
            }
        }
}

void display ( int mat[3][3] )
{
        int i, j ;
        for ( i = 0 ; i < MAX ; i++ )
        {
            for ( j = 0 ; j < MAX ; j++ )
                    printf ( "%d\t", mat[i][j] ) ;
            printf ( "\n" ) ;
        }
}

void transpose ( int m1[3][3] )
{
        int i, j ;
        int m2[3][3];
        for ( i = 0 ; i < MAX ; i++ )
        {
            for ( j = 0 ; j < MAX ; j++ )
                    m2[i][j] = m1[j][i] ;
        }

        printf("\nThe Tronspose of entered matrox is :");
         for ( i = 0 ; i < MAX ; i++ )
        {
            printf("\n");
            for ( j = 0 ; j < MAX ; j++ )
                    printf("    %d", m2[i][j] );
        }
```

Q3(a). Write a program to process the marks for 4 courses in a semester. Each course contains 2 components namely internal assessment and external examination. Students need to pass in both the components individually by acquiring at least 40% in order to declare successful

completion in a course. Computer the total marks average and also display the Grade accordingly.

Note : You should use "Structures" concept. [10]

```
#include<stdio.h>
#include<conio.h>
struct student{
                char name[80] ;
                int int_cource[4];
                int ext_cource[4];
               int total_int ;
               int total_ext;
               } data ;
main()
{
 int max,total,i,int_max,ext_max;
 float average;
 clrscr();
 printf("\nEnter maximum marks of internal assessment : ") ;
 scanf("%d", &int_max) ;
 printf("\nEnter maximum marks of external assessment : ") ;
 scanf("%d", &ext_max) ;
 printf("\nname: ") ;
 scanf("%s", &data.name) ;

 printf("\n\nEnter marks of internal assessment:- ");
 for(i=0;i<4;i++)
 {
 printf(" \nmarks in cource[%d]:  ",i+1) ;
 scanf("%d", &data.int_cource[i]) ;
 }

 for(i=0;i<4;i++)
 {
 if(data.int_cource[i] <= int_max * 0.39 )
 printf(" \nFailed in  cource[%d]:  ",i+1) ;
 }

 printf("\n\nEnter marks of external examination:- ");
 for(i=0;i<4;i++)
 {
 printf(" \nmarks in cource[%d]:  ",i+1) ;
```

```
 scanf("%d", &data.ext_cource[i]) ;
 }

 for(i=0;i<4;i++)
 {
 if(data.ext_cource[i] <= ext_max * 0.39 )
 printf(" \nFailed in  cource[%d]:  ",i+1) ;
 }

 for(i=0;i<4;i++)
 {
 data.total_int+=data.int_cource[i];
 }

 for(i=0;i<4;i++)
 {
 data.total_ext+=data.ext_cource[i];
 }

total = data.total_int+ data.total_ext;
max= (  (int_max * 4) + (ext_max * 4) ) ;

average = ((float)total/(float)max)*100 ;
printf("\n %f ",average) ;

 if(average>=60)
 printf("\n \nfirst grade");
 else if(average < 60 && average > 50)
 printf("\n\nSecond Grade");
 else if(average < 50)
 printf("\n\n Third Grade");

 getch() ;
 return(0) ;
}
```

(b) Write the functions to perform the following : [10]

(i) To accept a string and print the rightmost "n" characters.

```
#include <stdio.h>
#include <conio.h>
#include <string.h>
```

```
#include <alloc.h>

char * rightsub ( char *, int n ) ;

void main( )
{
      char s1[20];
      char s2[20];
      char ch, *s ;
      int n ;

      clrscr( ) ;
      printf ( "\nEnter a String s1: ") ;
      gets(s1);

      printf("Enter the number of characters to extract:-  ");
      scanf("%d",&n);
      s = rightsub ( s1, n ) ;
      printf ( "\nRight sub string: %s", s ) ;
      free ( s ) ;


      getch( ) ;
}

/* extracts rightmost n characters from the string */
char * rightsub ( char *str, int n )
{
      char *t = ( char * ) malloc ( n + 1 ) ;
      int l = strlen ( str ) ;
      char *s = str + ( l - n ) ;
      int i = 0 ;

      while ( i < n )
      {
            t[i] = *s ;
            s++ ;
            i++ ;
      }
      t[i] = '\0' ;
      return t ;
```

```
}
```

(ii) To accept any two strings and check whether the first string is a substring of the second string.

```
#include <stdio.h>
#include <conio.h>
#include <string.h>

int xstrsearch ( char *, char * );

void main( )
{
    char s1[20];
    char s2[10];
    int pos;

    clrscr( );

    printf ( "Enter first String :-");
    gets(s1);
    printf ( "\nEnter String to be Searched :-" );
    gets(s2);
    /* search if s2 is present in s1 */
    pos = xstrsearch ( s1, s2 );
    if(pos==1)
    printf ( "\nThe string is found" );
    else
    printf( "\nThe string is not found");
    getch( );
}

/* searches for the given pattern s2 into the string s1 */
int xstrsearch ( char * s1, char * s2 )
{
    int i, j=0, k ;
    int l1 = strlen ( s1 );
    int l2 = strlen ( s2 );

    for ( i = 0 ; i <= l1 ; i++ )
    {
     k=0;
```

```
        j=0;
        if(s1[i]==s2[j])
        {
        while(s1[i]==s2[j])
        {
        j++;
        k++;
        i++;
        }
        }
        if(k==l2)
         return 1;
      }
      return -1;
}
```

Q4(a). Write a program in 'C' to find the length of a given string including blank spaces, tabs and other special symbols (new line character should be taken as a string terminating character).
Note : You should use "pointers" concept. **[10]**

```
#include <stdio.h>
#include <conio.h>
#include <string.h>
int xstrlen ( char * ) ;
void main( )
{
        char s1[20];
        int len ;
        clrscr( ) ;
        printf ( "\nEnter the String:- ") ;
        gets(s1);
        len = xstrlen ( s1 ) ;
        printf ( "\nlength of the string s1: %d", len ) ;
```

```
        getch( ) ;
}

/* finds the length of the string */

int xstrlen ( char *s )

{

        int l = 0 ;

        while ( *s )

        {

                l++ ;

                s++ ;

        }

        return l ;

}
```

(b) Write macros for the following :

(i) To find the value of
P (1+i)^n
P, i, n are arguments of a macro and n is an integer. [5]

(i) #define power(i , n) (pow((1+i) , n))

(ii) To find the maximum of two numbers A, B where A and B are arguments of a macro. [5]

```
(ii) #if(A > B)
printf("A is greater");
#else
printf("B is greater");
#endif
```

Q5(a). Write a program in 'C' to append some characters in an already existing file and also find the number of characters in the resultant file after appending. [10]

Refer to Chapter-1, Q-5, Page no.-13

(b) Design an algorithm and draw corresponding flowchart to convert a decimal number to its hexadecimal equivalent. [10]

ALGORITHM

```
START:
const MAX = 16;
BASE = 16;
 i, j, remainder, number

Step1: Enter input number[1..MAX]

Step2: while (number > 0)
        remainder := number mod BASE
        number := number divide BASE

Step3: if (remainder < 10) then
        hexno[i] :=  remainder
        else
        hexno[i] := Char('A' + (remainder-10))
        i := i + 1;
        end;

Step4: Print in reverse order
        for j := (i-1) downto 1 do
        write(hexno[j]);

END
```

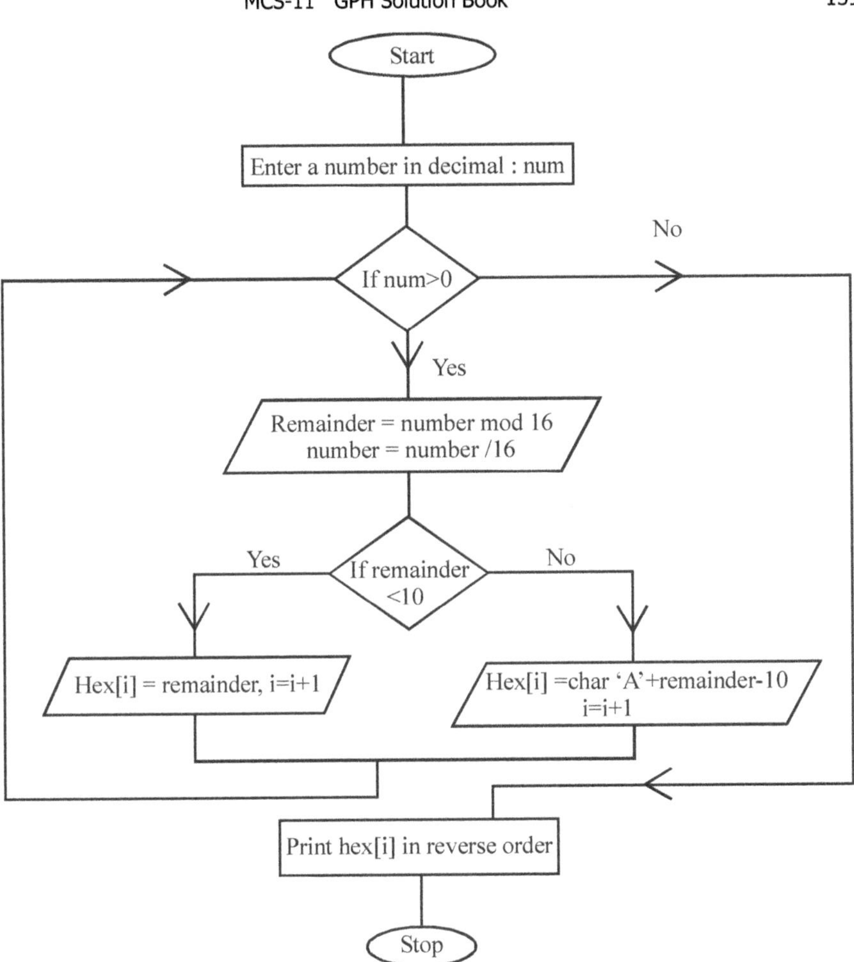
Start
Enter a number in decimal : num
No
If num>0
Yes
Remainder = number mod 16
number = number /16
Yes
If remainder
<10
No
Hex[i] = remainder, i=i+1
Hex[i] =char 'A'+remainder-10
i=i+1
Print hex[i] in reverse order
Stop

;

MCS-011 : PROBLEM SOLVING AND PROGRAMMING
JUNE-2006

Note : *Question number 1 is* ***compulsory.*** *Attempt any* ***three*** *questions from the rest.*

Q1(a). Design an algorithm, draw a corresponding flow chart and write a program in C, to print the Fibonacci series.

Ans. Algorithm

Step 1: Start

Step 2: Assign first $\leftarrow$ 0 and second $\leftarrow$ 1

Step 3: Print first, second

Step 4: Counter $\leftarrow$ 2;

Step 5: While (counter < N)
    third $\leftarrow$ first + second
    Print third
    Counter $\leftarrow$ counter + 1;
    First $\leftarrow$ second;
    Second $\leftarrow$ third;
    End while

Step 6: Exit

Flowchart

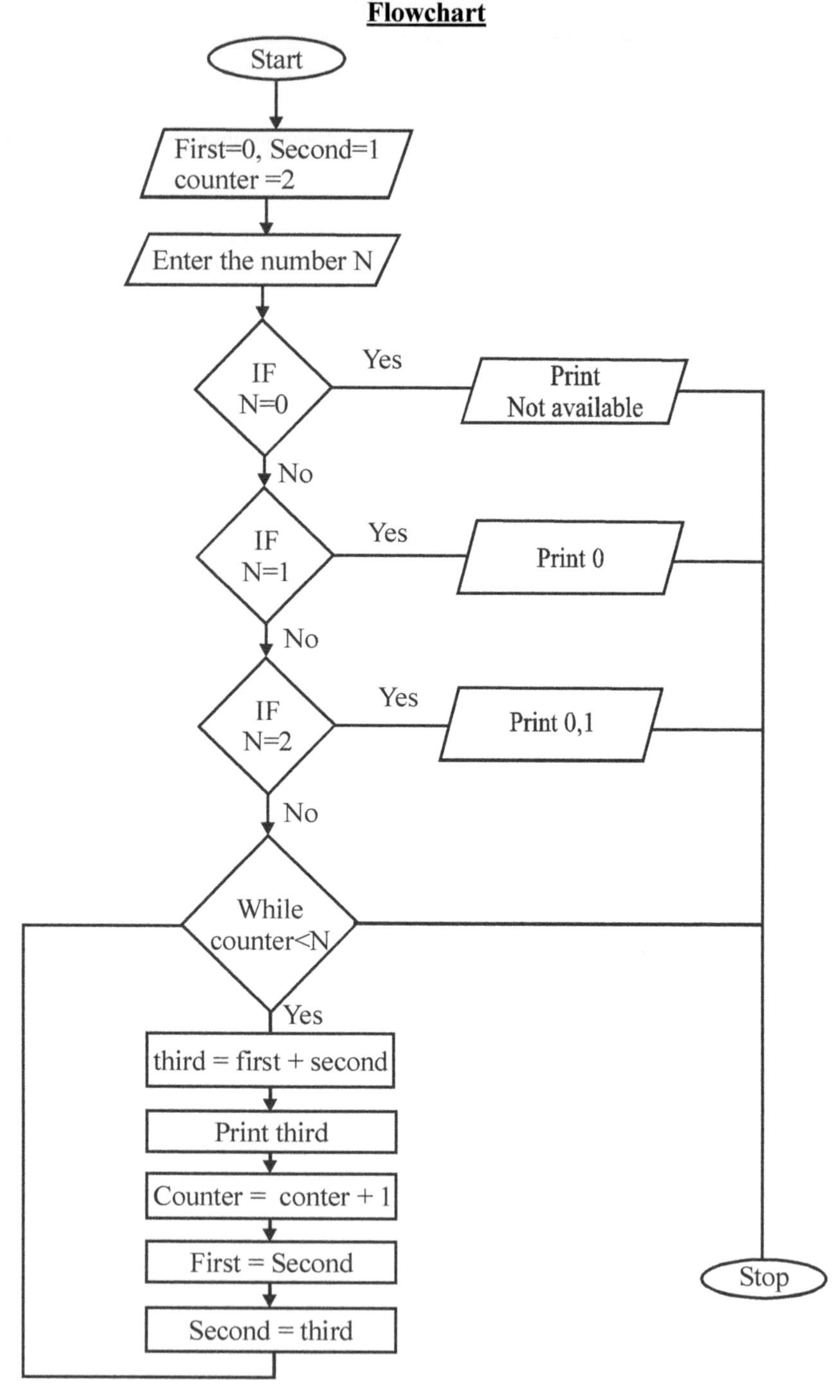
Start
First=0, Second=1
counter =2
Enter the number N
IF
N=0
Yes
Print
Not available
No
IF
N=1
Yes
Print 0
No
IF
N=2
Yes
Print 0,1
No
While
counter<N
Yes
third = first + second
Print third
Counter = conter + 1
First = Second
Second = third
Stop

```
void main ( )
{
int first, second, third, n, counter;
clrscr( );
counter = 2;
first = 0;
second = 1;
printf ("How many numbers you want to generate Fibonacci series \n");
scanf (" %d", &n);
if (n = = 0)
printf("Not available");
elseif (n = = 1)
printf (" %d", first);
elseif (n = = 2)
printf (" %d \t %d", first, second);
else
{
printf (" %d \t %d", first, second);
while (counter < N)
{
third = first + second;
printf (" %d", third);
counter = counter + 1;
first = second;
second = third;
}
}
getch( );
}
```

Or Refer to

(b) Write a program that does not use the inbuilt string functions to perform the following :

Ans.

(i) To compare two strings

Refer to Page No. 91, Q17.

(ii) To copy a string

Refer to Page No. 96, Q23.

(c) Design an algorithm, and write a program to find the factorial of a

number using recursion.

Ans. Algorithm

Step 1: Start
Step 2: Enter the number n
Step 3: if (n < 0) then
        Print "No factorial"
Step 4: if (n = = 0) then
        Print "Factorial is 1"
Step 5: For i = n to 2, > –1
        Fact = fact * i;
Step 6: Print the Factorial
Step 7: Stop

```
// Program to find factorial of a number
#include <stdio.h>
/**
 *  factorial(n) returns n*(n-1)*...*2*1 for
 *  small values of n.
 */
int factorial(int n) {
   int fact;

   fact = 1;
   while (n > 1) {
         fact *= n;
         n--;
   }
   return fact;
} // int factorial(int)

int main(void) {
   int x; // an integer
   int f; // the factorial of x
   x = 5;
   f = factorial(x);
   printf("x = %d, f = %d.\n", x, f);
   return 0;
} // int main(void)
```

(d) A C program contains the following declarations :
int i, j:

long iX,
short S;
float X;
double dX;
char C;
Determine the resultant data type of each of the following expressions:
(i) i + C
Ans. integer

(ii) X + C
Ans. float

(iii) dX + X
Ans. double

(iv) {(int) dX} + iX
Ans: double

(v) i + X
Ans. float

(vi) S + j
Ans. int

(vii) iX + j
Ans. long

(viii) S + C
Ans. short

(ix) iX + C
Ans. long

(x) i + j
Ans. int

Q2(a). Summarize the purpose of the format strings (like %s, %d, %c) that are commonly used within the printf function, with an example for each.
Ans. The purpose of format string to print the value of address. The commonly used format strings are:

(i) %s → To print string
(ii) %c → character
(iii) %d → integer

```
void main ( )
{
char name [10] = "GullyBaba Ki Jai";
printf ("%s", name);                //prints a string
getch( );
}

void main ( )
{
char x = 'a';
printf ("%c", x);                   //prints a single character value
getch( );
}

void main ( )
{
int a = 25;
printf ("%d", a);                   //prints integer value in a
getch( );
}
```

(b) When can two matrices of order a x b and c x d be subtracted ? Also write a program in C to find the difference of two such matrices.

Ans. Two metrics of order a x b and c x d be subtracted when a = c and b = d. It means when number of rows and number of column are same.

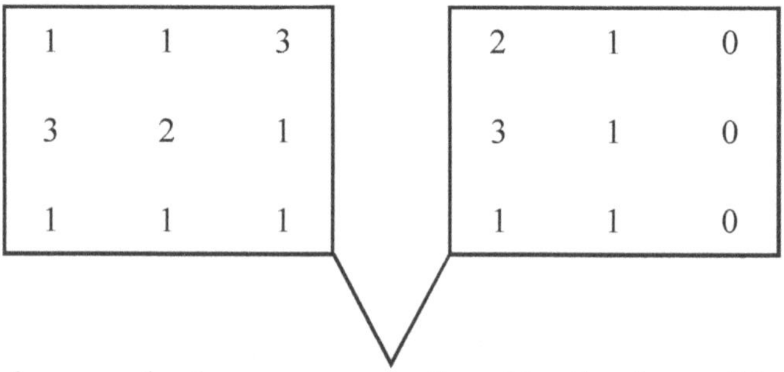

1	1	3
3	2	1
1	1	1

2	1	0
3	1	0
1	1	0

Number of rows and columns are same. So subtraction is possible.

/* subtract Two Matrices */

```
# include<stdio.h>
# include<stdlib.h>
# define row 10
# define col 10

int i, j;
int row1, col1;
int row2, col2;
float mat1[row][col];
float mat2[row][col];
float mat_res[row][col];

void mat_add(float mat1[row][col], int, int,
float mat2[row][col], int, int,
float mat_res[row][col]);

void display(float mat[row][col], int, int);
void input(float mat[row][col], int , int);

/* Function mat_add */

void mat_sub(float mat1[row][col], int row1, int col1,
float mat2[row][col], int row2, int col2,
float mat_res[row][col])
{
        int i, j;
        if((row1 == row2) && (col1 == col2))
        {
                printf("\n Subtraction is possible and Result is as follows\n");
                for(i = 0; i<row1; i++)
                        for(j = 0; j<col1; j++)
                                mat_res[i][j] = mat1[i][j]-mat2[i][j];
                display(mat_res,row1,col1);
        }
        else
                printf("\n Subtraction is not possible");
        exit(0);
}

/* Output function */
void display(float mat[row][col], int r, int c )
```

```
{
        for(i = 0; i < r; i++)
        {
                for(j = 0; j < c; j++)
                {
                        printf("  %f", mat[i][j]);
                }
                printf("\n");
        }
}

/* Input function */
void input(float mat[row][col], int r, int c)
{
        for( i = 0 ; i < r; i++)
        {
                for(j = 0 ; j < c; j++)
                {
                        printf("Input Value for : %d: %d: ", i+1, j+1);
                        scanf("%f", &mat[i][j]);
                }
        }
}

/* main function */
void main()
{
        int row1, col1;
        int row2, col2;
        float mat1[row][col];
        float mat2[row][col];
        float mat_res[row][col];
        clrscr();

        printf("\n Input the row  of the matrix->1:");
        scanf("%d", &row1);
        printf(" Input the col  of the matrix->1:");
        scanf("%d", &col1);
        printf("\n Input data for matrix-> 1\n");
        input(mat1, row1, col1);
        printf("\n Input the row  of the matrix ->2:");
```

```
        scanf("%d", &row2);
        printf("\n Input the col  of the matrix->2:");
        scanf("%d", &col2);

        printf("\n Input data for matrix-> 2\n");
        input(mat2, row2, col2);

        printf("\n Entered Matrix First is as follows:\n");
        display(mat1,row1,col1);

        printf("\n Entered Matrix Two is as follows:\n");
        display(mat2,row2,col2);
        mat_sub(mat1, row1, col1, mat2, row2, col2, mat_res);
}
```

Q3(a). Design an algorithm, draw a corresponding flow chart and write a C program to check whether a given string is a palindrome or note.

Ans. Refer to Page No. 107, Q1(c).

(b) Explain the meaning of each of the following function prototypes and mention the return data type of each of them :

(i) double f (double a, int b);

Ans. double f (double a, int b);

function name is f which contain two argument a and b. a is double data type and b is integer type. It can return the double value.

(ii) void f (long a, short b, unsigned c)

Ans. void f (long a, short b, unsigned c)

function name is f which contain three arguments a, b, and c. a is long type, b is short type and c is unsigned type. It can not return any value.

(iii) unsigned f (unsigned a, unsigned b);

Ans. unsigned f (unsigned a, unsigned b);

function name is f, which contain two arguments a and b. a is unsigned type and b is unsigned type. It can return unsigned value means only positive value

(iv) int(*f) (char*, int);

Ans: int (* f) (char *, int);

It means that f is a pointer to a function and it has two arguments. First denote the char pointer and other is integer argument. It returns integer type.

(v) int * f(char*, int);

Ans: int * f (char *, int)

It is a function f which have two arguments. First denote the pointer of character and second is integer value.
It is a function returning a pointer to an array of pointers to function returning an integer.

Q4(a). What is the difference between a function and a macro ? Find the largest number among two numbers using a function definition as well as a macro. Which is more efficient in terms of execution time and code size?

Ans. MACRO:
e.g.:# define ref-name 99
The code is substituted by the MACRO ref-name. So no overhead.
Execution is faster.
FUNCTION:
There will be a overhead due to function arguments. (Arguments are stored in the stack)

Where MACROs can not be used?
if the macro definition go like kind of x++ and y++. It's better to use functions and avoid macros. Use typedef instead of macros (while pointer declarations).

Where FUNCTIONs can be used?
Anywhere. But RELATIVELY there will be a overhead and takes more CPU cycles to execute the same. If it's a macro, just simple substitution.

Functions that assembles into 3-4 lines of assembly code or less can in some cases be handled more efficiently as macros. When using macros the macro name will be replaced by the actual code inside the macro at compile time. For very small functions the compiler generates less code and gives higher speed to use macros that to call a function.
Passing arguments to a function and getting back the returned value does take time and would therefore slow down the program. This gets avoided with macros since they have already been expanded and placed in the source code before compilation.
Like in our examples also the above explanation is true.
Function to find the largest number among two numbers :

```
int largest(int n1, int n2)
{ if (n1>n2)
return n1;
else
```

```
return n2;
}
```

Macro to find the largest number among two numbers :

```
#define largest(n1,n2) (n1>n2?n1:n2)
```

Now when we see the code size and execution time for macros and functions, we come to know that Code Size and Execution Time in case of Function is more than Macro. ***This implies, that macro is more efficient than function in terms of Execution Time and Code Size.***

Moral of story is: if the macro is simple and sweet like in our examples, it makes a nice shorthand and avoids the overhead associated with function calls. On the other hand, if we have a fairly large macro and it is fairly often, perhaps we ought to replace it with a function. Because if we use a macro hundred times in a program, the macro expansion goes into our source code at hundred different places, thus increasing the program size. On the other hand, if a function is used, then even if it is called from hundred different places in the program, it would take the same amount of space in the program.

(b). Write a program to sort a list of strings in alphabetical order, using an array of pointers.

Ans. // program to sort a list of string in alphabetical order.

```
void sort_s (char *array[ ], int);
void display (char *list[ ], int);
void sort_s (char *array[ ], int size)
{
char *temp;
int i, j;
for (i = 0; i < size; i++)
for (j = 0; j < size; j++)
if (strcmp(array[i], array[j]>0)
{
temp = (char*) malloc (size of (array[i]));
temp = array[i];
array[i] = array[j];
array[j] = temp;
}
void display (char *list[ ], int n)
{
int j;
for (i = 0; i < n; i++)
{
```

```
printf ("\n %s", list[i]);
}
}
void main (void)
{
char list[100] = {"Monday", "Tues", "Wed", "Thur", "Fri", "Sat", "Sun",};
Printf ("\n Input list as follows:");
display(list,7);
sort_s(list, 7);
printf("\n sorted list is as follows: \n");
display(list,7);
}
```

Q5(a). Write a program, using 'structures', to calculate the gross salary and net salary, if the details of an employee along with the basic pay, attendance and deductions are given as input.

Ans. struct emp

```
{
char name [20];
char address [20];
int bs;
int atten;
int dedu;
};
main ( )
{
int da, hra, pf, netsal, grosssal, x, sal;
struct emp e;
clrscr ( );
printf ("enter the name of employee\n");
scanf ("%s", e. name);
printf ("enter the address of employee\n");
scanf ("%s", e. address);
printf ("enter the basic salary of employee\n");
scanf ("%d", &e. bs);
printf ("enter the attendance of employee\n");
scanf ("%d", &e. atten);
printf ("enter the deduction of employee\n");
scanf ("%d", & e.dedu);
x=e.bs/e.atten;
```

```
sal = *e. atten;
da=sal *.1;
hra=sal *.9;
grosssal=sal+da+hra;
netsal=grosssal–e.dedu;
printf (“the net salary is %d\n”, netsal);
printf (“the gross salary is %d”, grosssal);
getch ( );
}
```

(b) Write a program to count the number of characters, number of words and number of lines in a given file.

Ans. // count character, word, number of lines in a given file;

```
void main( )
{
FILE *fopen( ), *fp;
int c, nc, nw, n lines;
char filename[40];
nlines = 0
nc = 0
nw = 0
printf (“Enter file name”);
gets(file name);
fp = fopen(filename, “r”);
if (fp = = NULL)
{
printf (“Cann’t open %s for reading \n”, filename);
exit(1);
}
c = gets (fp);
while (c != EOF)
{
 if (c = = ‘\n’)
 nlines++;
 if (ch = =  ‘ ’)
 nw++
 c = getc(fp);
}

fclose (fp);
if (nc != 0)
```

```
{
printf ("There are %d characters", nc);
printf ("There are %d words", nw);
printf ("There are %d lines", nlines);
}
else
printf("File is Empty");
 }
```

MCS-011 : PROBLEM SOLVING AND PROGRAMMING
DEC-2006

Note : *Question number 1 is* ***compulsory.*** *Attempt any* ***three*** *questions from the rest.*

Q1(a). Write an algorithm and draw a corresponding flow chart to print the sum of all integers starting from 2 to the given positive integer x where $x \geq 2$. **[10]**

Ans.

Algorithm

Step 1: Start

Step 2: Enter a number

Step 3: if number < 2 then

Print "Invalid number"

End if

Step 4: While (C < = N)

Sum = Sum + C

C = C + 1

End loop

Step 5: Print Sum

Step 6: Exit

Flow chart

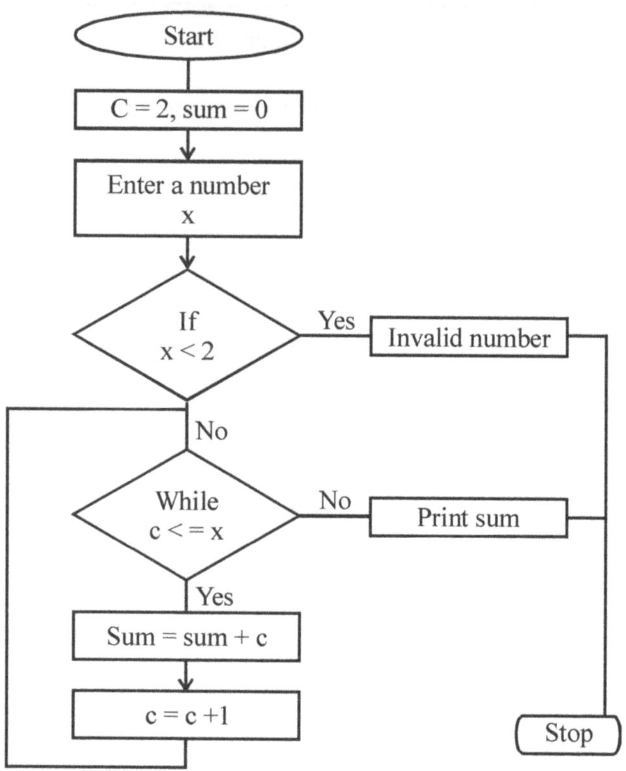

(b) Write a recursive program in 'C' to find the L.C.M. (Least Common Multiple) of two given numbers. **[10]**

Ans.

```
# include<stdio.h>
int n=1;
int l_C_Mul(int , int);

int l_C_Mul( int x, int y)
{
        if((n % x==0) && ((n % y) == 0))
                return(n);
        else
                l_C_Mul(x,y);
}

/* main function */
void main()
{
```

```
        int x, y;
        int result;
        clrscr();
        printf("\n Input the first integer number: ");
        scanf("%d", &x);
        printf("\n Input the second integer number: ");
        scanf("%d", &y);
        result = l_C_Mul(x, y);
    printf("\n Least Common Multiple of : %d and %d is = %d", x, y, result);
        getch();
}
```

(c) Write a program in 'C' to print the following format: [10]

```
        C
      C C C
    C C C C C
  C C C C C C C
C C C C C C C C C
```

Ans.

```
void main()
{
int i,j;
clrscr();
for(i=0;i<=4;i++)
{
 for(j=1;j<=(2*i+1);j++)
 {
  printf("C");
  }
  printf("\n");
}
getch();
}
```

(d) Write a non-recursive procedure in 'C' for calculating power of a number 'm' raised by another number 'n' i.e. m^n . [10]

Ans.

```
void main()
{
  int m,n,pow=1,x,i;
```

```
 clrscr();
 printf("enter the mantissa\n");
 scanf("%d",&m);
 printf("enter the exponent\n");
 scanf("%d",&n);
 x=m;
 for(i=1;i<=n;i++)
 {
   pow=pow*x;
 }
 printf("the  power of %d^%d is %d ",m,n,pow);
 getch();
}
```

Q2(a). Design an algorithm and draw corresponding flow chart to print the value of the number in words when the number entered is in the range of 1 to 299. [10]

Ans:

Algorithm

Step 1: Start

Step 2: Enter a number N

Step 3: if (N < 1 or N > 299)

Print "Invalid number"

endif

Step 4: a = n/100

if a < 1 then

go to step 5

end if

Print a in its particular hundred's

Step 5: n = n % 100

b = n/10

if b < 1 then

go to step 6

end if

Print b in its particular ten's

Step 6: c = n % 10

Print particular c digit in word.

Step 7: Exit.

Flow chart

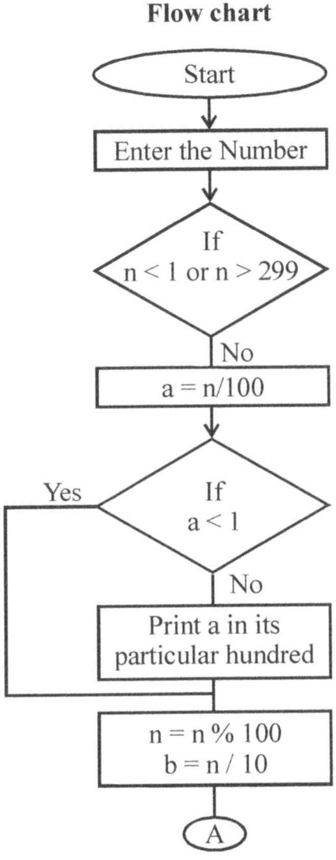

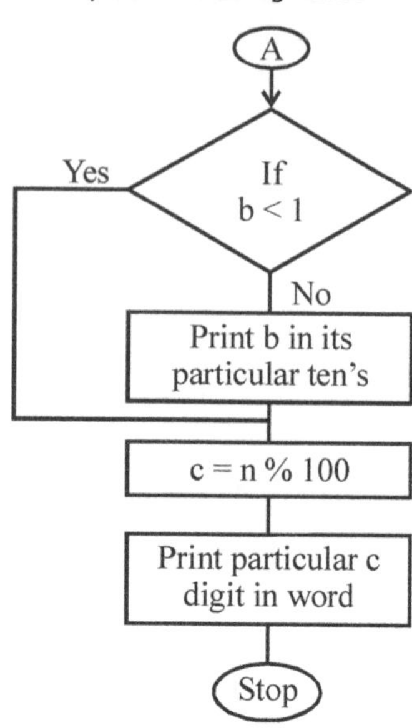

(b) Using pointers, write a program in 'C' to count the occurrence of each character in a given string. **[10]**

Ans.

```
void main()
{
char *str, *comp;
int n, a, j, count;
clrscr();
printf ("Enter the string: ");
scanf(" %s", str);
n=strlen(str);
for (a=0; a<n; a++)
{
 comp= str[a];
 if (comp!=' ')
{
 count =0;
 for (j=0; j<n; j++)
{
if (comp = = str[j])
{
count = count+1;
str[j]= ' ';
```

```
        }
      }
    }
printf (" %c occurs %d times \n", comp, count);
}
getch();
}
```

Q3(a). Write a program in 'C' that accept 10 words of varying length and arranges the words in the descending order of word length. Use arrays. [10]

Ans.

```
#define items 10
#define maxchar 20
main()
{
char string[items][maxchar],dummy[maxchar];
int i=0,j=0;
clrscr();
printf("enter the name of %d words\n",items);
while(i<=items)
scanf("%s",string[i++]);

for(i=1;i<items;i++)
{
 for(j=1;j<=items-i;j++)
 {
   if(strlen(string[j-1])>strlen(string[j]))
   {
    strcpy(dummy,string[j-1]);
    strcpy(string[j-1],string[j]);
    strcpy(string[j],dummy);
   }
 }
}
printf("\n alphabhet list\n\n");
for(i=0;i<items;i++)
printf("%s\n",string[i]);
getch();
}
```

(b) Write a program in 'C' for the multiplication of two matrices.[10]

Ans:

Using the program : mmultiply is the exe file of the code.

C:\>mmultiply input.txt input.txt

"input.txt" is an example of text files describing connectivity matrices. The first line includes the number of rows and columns of the matrix and the following lines include the elements of the matrix. The output will be displayed on the screen. To make further processing, please redirect the output into a file as follows.

Contents of File input.txt

```
6
0	1	0	0	0	0
1	0	1	0	0	0
0	1	0	1	1	0
0	0	1	0	0	0
0	0	1	0	0	1
0	0	0	0	1	0
```

C:\>mmultiply input.txt input.txt > input2.txt

You can multiply the matrix three times or more by processing the output as follows.

C:\>mmultiply input2.txt input.txt > input3.txt

```
#include <iostream.h>
#include <fstream.h>

main(int argc, char *argv[]) {
	//definition of the variables.
	int mtx1[20][20], mtx2[20][20], mtx3[20][20];
	int n, i, j, k;

	//exit if the number of arguments is not 2.
	if(argc != 3) {
		cerr << "Usage: mm <filename1> <filename2>\n";
		return 1;
	}
```

```
//open the input file 1. exit if an error occurs.
ifstream fin1(argv[1]);
if(!fin1) {
        cerr << "Can't open file1!\n";
        return 1;
}

//read the input file 1.
fin1 >> n;                  //read the number of rows and columns.
for(j=1; j<=n; j++) {
        for(i=1; i<=n; i++) {
                fin1 >> mtx1[i][j]; //read the elements of the matrix.
        }
}
fin1.close();                       //close the file 1.

//open the input file 2. exit if an error occurs.
ifstream fin2(argv[2]);
if(!fin2) {
        cerr << "Can't open file2!\n";
        return 1;
}

fin2 >> n;                  //read the number of rows and columns.
for(j=1; j<=n; j++) {
        for(i=1; i<=n; i++) {
                fin2 >> mtx2[i][j]; //read the elements of the matrix.
        }
}
fin2.close();                       //close the file 2.

//fill the matrix 3 for the result with zero.
for(j=1; j<=n; j++) {
        for(i=1; i<=n; i++) {
                mtx3[i][j] = 0;
        }
}

//multiply the matrices.
for(j=1; j<=n; j++) {
        for(i=1; i<=n; i++) {
```

```
                        for(k=1; k<=n; k++) {
                                mtx3[i][j] += mtx2[i][k] * mtx1[k][j];
                        }
                }
        }

        //output the result.
        cout << n << "\n";
        for(j=1; j<=n; j++) {
                for(i=1; i<=n; i++) {
                        cout << mtx3[i][j];
                        if(i < n) {
                                cout << "\t";
                        }
                }
        cout << "\n";
        }

        return 0;
}                                               //end of the program.
```

Q4(a). Write a program in 'C' to check whether a given string is palindrome. Use pointers. **[10]**

Ans.

```
# include <stdio.h>
# include<conio.h>
# include <stdlib.h>
main()
{
char *palin, c;
int i, count;
short int palindrome(char, int);
palin = (char*) malloc(no *sizeof(char));
printf ("\n Enter a word:");
do
{
c=getChar ();
palin[i] = c;
i++;
} while (c!='\n');
i=i-1;
```

```
palin[i] ='\0'
count=i;
if (palindrome (palin, count) = = 1)
        printf("\n Entered word is not a palindrome");
         else
        print ("\n Entered word is a palindrome");
 }
short int palindrome(char *palin, int len)
{
 short int i=0, j=0;
for (i=0; j=len-1; i<len/2; i++, j--)
{
if palin[i] = = palin[j]
continue;
else
return (1);
}
return (0);
}
```

(b) Write a program in 'C' for the addition of two polynomials. Use arrays and structures. **[10]**

Ans. struct poly

```
{
int coeff;
int expo;
};

void main()
{
int poly1[2][2], poly2[2][2], poly3[20][20], i, j, m, n, x;
struct poly e;
clrscr();
printf("how many terms u want to add in the poly1\n");
scanf("%d"&m,);
printf("enter exponent in ascending order");
for(i=0; j<2; j++)
{
for(j = =0)
{
printf("enter the coeff");
```

```
scanf ("%d", &e.coeff);
ploy1[i][j] =e. coeff;
}
if (j = =1)
{
printf ("enter the expo");
scanf ("%d", &e.expo);
ploy1[i][j] =e.expo;
}
}
}
printf ("how many terms u want to add in the poly2\n");
scanf ("%d, &n);
printf ("enter exponent in ascending order");
for (i=0; i< n; i++)
{
for (j =0; j<2; j++)
{
if (j = = 0)
{
printf ("enter the coeff");
scanf ("%d", &e.coeff);
ploy2[i][j]=e.coeff;
}
if (j = = 1)
{
printf ("enter the expo");
scanf ("%d", &e.expo);
ploy1[i][j]=e.expo;
}
}
}
x=0;
for (i= 0; i< n; i++)
{
if (poly[i][1] = = poly2[i][1])
{
poly3[x][1] = poly1[i][1];
poly3[x][0] = poly1[i][0] + poly2[i][0];
x=x+1;
}
```

```
if (poly1[i][1] < poly2[i][1])
{
poly3[x][1] = poly1[i][1];
poly3[x][0] = poly1[i][1];
x=x+1;
poly3[x][1] = poly2[i][1];
poly3[x][0] = poly2[i][0];
x=x+1;
}
if (poly1[i][1] > poly2[i][1]);
{
poly3[x][1] = poly2[i][1];
poly3[x][0] = poly2[i][0];
x=x+1;
poly3[x][1] = poly1[i][1];
poly3[x][0] = poly1[i][0];
x=x+1;
}
}
for (i=0; i< n; i++)
{
for (j=0; j<2; j++)
{
printf ("%d", poly1[i][j]);
}
printf( "\n");
}
printf ("\n");

for (i=0; i< n; i++)
{
for (j=0; j<2; j++)
{
printf ("%d", poly2 [i] [j]);
}
printf( "\n");
}
printf ("\n");

for (i=0; i< x; i++)
{
```

```
for (j=0; j<2; j++)
{
printf ("%d", poly3 [i] [j]);
}
printf("\n");
}
getch();
}
```

Q5(a). Write a program in 'C' that accept two files as input and creates a new file whose contents include the contents of two input files. [10]

Ans.

```
# include <stdio.h>
void main()
{
FILE *fp1, *fp2, *fp3, *fopen();
int c;
char fname1[40], fname2[90], fname3[90];
printf ("Enter the two input file name");
gets(fname1);
gets(fname2);
printf("Enter the destination file name");
gets(fname3);
fp1= fopen (frame1, "r");
fp2= fopen (frame2, "r");
fp3= fopen (frame3, "w");
if(fp1= = NULL)
{
printf ("Cannot open %s for reading", fname1);
exit(1);
}
elseif (fp2 = = NULL)
{
printf ("Cannot open %s for reading", fname2);
exit(1);
}
elseif(fp3 = = NULL)
{
printf ("Can't open %s for writing \n", frame3);
exit(1);
}
else
```

```
{
c=getc(fp1);
while(c!=EOF)
{
putc(c, fp3);
c = getc(fp1);
}
n=ftell(f3);
fseek (fp3, OL, 2);
c=getc(fp2)
while (c!= EOF)
{
putc(c, fp3)
c=getc(fp2)
}
fclose (fp1);
fclose (fp2);
fclose (fp3);
printf ("Files successfully copied. \n");
}
}
```

(b) Consider a data file containing some records of type STUDENT : **[10]**

```
Struct STUDENT
{
        char Name [20];
        int Roll_No;
        float marks;
};
```

(i) Write a function, which takes file name as an argument and returns the number of records in that file.

Ans.

```
void show_record()
{
    do
     {
       flag=0;
       cleardevice();
        settextstyle(SANS_SERIF_FONT,HORIZ_DIR,3);
       outtextxy(150,212,"ENTER FILE NAME :-");
```

```
        gotoxy(60,15);
        scanf("%s",&fname);

       rewind(fp);
        while(fread(&st,recsize,1,fp)==1)
       {
          if(record==st.recsize)
       {
       cleardevice();
      outtextxy(25,86,"ROLL NUMBER:-");
       gotoxy(30,7);
       printf("%d",st.roll);
      outtextxy(120,118,"STUDENT NAME:-");
                        gotoxy(42,9);
                        puts(st.name);
       outtextxy(120,150,"marks:-");
           gotoxy(42,11);
                        puts(st.marks);
   flag=1;
    break;
    }
}
    if(flag==0)
   {
       outtextxy(170,300,"RECORD DOES NOT EXIST");
       printf("\a\a");
    }
   outtextxy(40,390,"DO U WANT TO SHOW NEXT RECORD(Y/N)");
    fflush(stdin);
    ch=getche();
  }while(ch=='Y' || ch=='y');
}
```

(ii) Write a function, which takes two arguments: filename and Roll No(s) and deletes the corresponding records with these Roll_ No (s) from that file.

Ans:

```
void delete_ record ()
{
do
{
```

```
flag=0;
cleardevice ();
settextstyle (SANS_SERIF_FONT, HORIZ_DIR, 3);
outtextxy (150, 212, "ENTER FILE NAME : -");
gotoxy (60,15);
scanf ("%s",& fname);
settextstyle (SANS_SERIF"_FONT, HORIZ_DIR, 3);
outtextxy (150, 212," ENTER ROLL NUMBER : -");
gotoxy (60,15);
scanf ("%d", &roll);
rewind (fp);
while (fread (&st, recsize), 1, fp) = =1)
{
if (record !=st.recsize);
{
outtextxy (150,300, "RECORD DOES NOT EXIST");
flag=1;
}
}
if (flag = =1)
printf ("\a\a");
ft=fopen ("tpm1.txt", "wb");
rewind (fp);
while (fread (&st, recsize, 1, fp)= =1)
{
if (record!=st.recsize, 1, ft);
}
}
fclose (fp);
fclose (ft);
remove ("xyzl.txt");
rename ("tpml.txt", "xyzl.txt");
outtextxy (40, 390, "DO U WANT TO DELETE NEXT RECORD (Y/N)");
fflush (stdin);
ch=getche ();

}while (ch = = 'Y' | | ch = ='Y');
}
```

MCS-011 : PROBLEM SOLVING AND PROGRAMMING
June, 2007

Note : Question number 1 is **compulsory.** Attempt any **three** questions from the rest.

1. (a) Design an algorithm, draw a corresponding flow chart and write a program in C, to swap the values using pass by value and pass by reference methods. *10*

Ans. Algorithm : SWAP [NUM1, NUM2]

Step 1: START

Step 2: INPUT NUM1, NUM2, TEMP $\leftarrow$ 0

Step 3: TEMP := NUM1

Step 4: NUM1 := NUM2

Step 5: NUM2 := TEMP

Step 6: PRINT NUM1, NUM2

Step 7: EXIT

Flow Chart

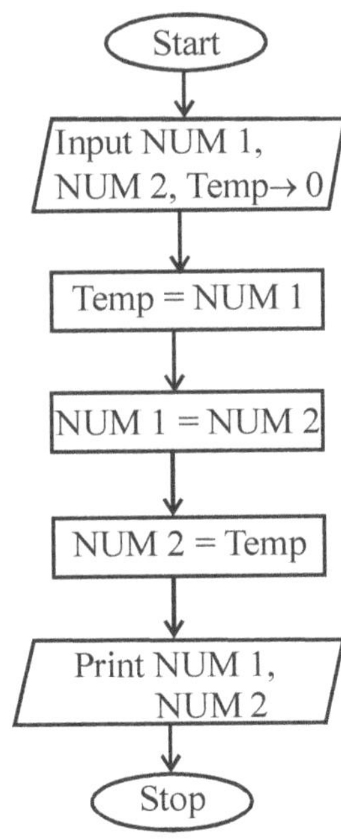

C program to swap the **values using pass by value method**

void swap (int a, int b);

```
{
int num1, num2;
printf("Enter two numbers::\n");
scanf("%d%d", &num1, &num2);
printf("The swapped values of num1 and num2 are:\n");
swap(num1, num2);
getch();
}
void swap (int a, int b)
{
int t;
t = a;
a = b;
b = t;
printf("Value of num1 = %d\n", a);
printf("Value of num2 = %d\n" b);
}
```

C program to swap the values using pass by reference method

```
void swap (int *a, int *b);
main()
{
int num1, num2;
printf("Enter two numbers::\n");
scanf("%d%d", &num1, &num2);
printf("The swapped values are:\n");
swap1(&num1, &num2);
getch();
}
void swap (int *a, int *b)
{
int t;
t = *a;
*a = *b;
*b = t;
printf("New value of num1 = %d\n", *a);
printf("New value of num2 = %d\n", *b);
}
```

(b) Write an algorithm and program in C to print Fibonacci series. ***10***

Ans. Algorithm: Fibonacci

Step 1: START

Step 2: Input First ← 0, Second ← 1, Sum ← 0, Final_sum

Step 3: Repeat Steps 4 to 7 until sum > Final_sum

Step 4: Sum := First + Second

Step 5: Print Sum

Step 6: First := Second

Step 7: Second := Sum
Step 8: Exit

Program in C for Fibonacci series

```
#include <stdio.h>
main()
{
long first, second, sum, final_sum;
int i, n;
first = 0;
second = 1;
printf("Enter the value of final sum for fibonacci series::");
scanf("%ld", &final_sum);
sum = first + second;
while (sum < = final_sum)
{
sum = first + second;
printf(:%ld", sum);
first = second;
second = sum;
printf("\n");
}
getch();
}
```

(c) Write a program to generate the pattern ***10***

1
1 2
1 2 3
1 2 3 4
1 2 3 4 5

Ans.

```
#include <stdio.h>
main()
{
int i, j, n;
printf("Enter n:");          //n is number of lines
scanf("%d", &n);
for(i = 1; i < = n; i++)     //loop for number of lines
{
for(j = 1; j < = i; j++)     //loop for number of digits
printf("%d", j);
printf("\n");
}
getch();
```

```
}
```

(d) When can 2 matrices of order a×b and c×d be multiplied? Also write a program in C to find the product of 2 such matrices. ***10***

Ans. Two matrices of order a×b and c×d can be multiplies when number of columns in first matrix are equal to the number or rows in second matrix i.e. if b = c in this case then we can multiply these two matrices of order a×b and c×d.

Program for Matrices Multiplication

Refer to June-2005, Q.No.-1(d), Page No.-110

2. (a) Explain the concept of a function returning a pointer with an example. ***6***

Ans. Function Returning Pointer : We can define a function that returns a pointer with the following syntax:

```
type *function(type 1, type2, .....);
example: float *fun1(int, char); //This function returns a pointer to float
int *fun2(int, int); //Fun2 function returns a pointer to int.
```

When a function returns a pointer, the memory address returned by the pointer will exist even after the termination of a function.

Program to show the use of a function that returns pointer

```
#include <stdio.h>
int *fun(int *p, int n);
main()
{
int arr[10] = {1, 2, 3, 4, 5, 6, 7, 8, 9, 10};
int n, *ptr;
n = 5;
ptr = fun(arr, n);
printf("Value of arr = %u, value of *ptr = %d\n", arr, ptr, *ptr);
}
int *fun(int *p, int n)
{
p = p + n;
return p;
}
```

(b) Write a macro to find the sum of n numbers. ***7***

Ans.

```
#include <stdio.h> /*The concept of macros with variable number of
            arguments is used here */
#include <stdarg.h>
int sum(int,.....);                //macro
main( )
{
printf("Total = %d\n", sum(2, 99, 56));    //running macro
printf("Total = %d\n", sum(3, 4, 11, 59)); //running macro
```

```
printf("Total = %d\n", sum(5, 23, 55, 17, 9, 78)); //running macro
}
int sum(int num,.....)      //macro definition
{
int i;
va_list ap;
int arg, total = 0;
va_start (ap, num);
for(i = 0; i < num; i++)
{
arg = va_arg(ap, int);
printf("%d", arg);
total + = arg;
}
va_end(ap);
return total;
}
```

(c) Write a program in C, to copy file 1 to another file 2 in the same directory. *7*

Ans.

```
#include <stdio.h>
main(int arg c, char *arg v[])
{
FILE *File1, *File2, *fopen();
int c;
if(arg c! = 3)
{
printf("Wrong number of arguments\n");
exit(1);
}
if((file 1 = fopen(argv[1], "r")) = = NULL)
{
printf("Cannot open File1\n");
exit(1);
}
if((file 2 = fopen(argv[2], "w")) = = NULL)
{
printf("Cannot open File2\n");
exit(1);
}
while((ch = fgetc(file1))! = EOF)
fputc(file2, c);
fclose(file1);
```

```
fclose(file2);
}
```

3. (a) Draw a flow chart and write a program in C to sort a given list of numbers. *7*

Ans.

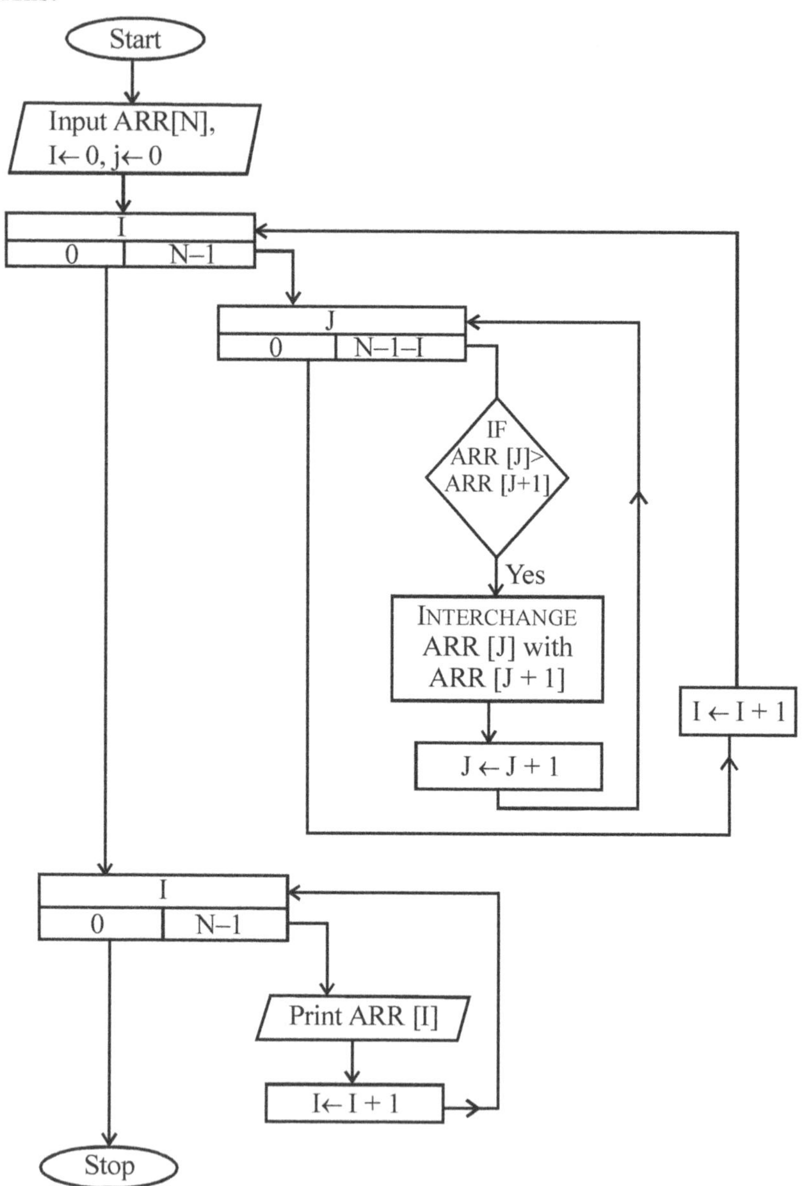

```
//Program to sort a list of elements using Bubble sort
#include <stdio.h>          /*Suppose number of elements in list are n*/
# define MAX 50
main( )
{
int arr[MAX];
int temp, i, j;
printf("Enter number of array elements:\n");
scanf("%d", &n);
for(i = 0; i < n; i++)
scanf("%d", &arr[i]);
for(i = 0; i < n – 1; i++)
{
for j = 0; j < n – 1 – i; j++)
{
if(arr[j] > arr[j + 1])
{
temp = arr[j];
arr[j] = arr[j + 1];
arr[j + 1] = temp;
}
}
}
printf("Sorted Array is:\n");
for(i = 0; i < n; i++)
printf("%d", arr[i]);
printf("\n");
getch();
}
```

(b) Write a program in C to compare two strings without using String Compare function. ***5***

Ans.

```
#include <stdio.h>
main( )
{
int i = 0, flag = 0;
static char str1[10], str2[10];
printf("Enter the first string");
scanf("%s", str1);
printf("Enter the second string");
scanf("%s", str2);
while(str1[i]! = '\0' && str2[i]! = '\0' && str1[i] = = str2[i])
```

```
i++;
if(str1[i] = = str2[i])
flag = 0;
else
flag = 1;
if(flag = = 0)
printf("Strings are equal");
else
printf("Strings are unequal");
getch();
}
```

(c) Explain various types of storage classes in C with examples for each. ***8***

Ans. 1) auto - storage class

auto is the default storage class for local variables.

```
{
   int Count;
   auto int Month;
}
```

The example above defines two variables with the same storage class. Auto can only be used within functions, i.e. local variables.

2) register - Storage Class

register is used to define local variables that should be stored in a register instead of RAM. This means that the variable has a maximum size equal to the register size (usually one word) and cant have the unary '&' operator applied to it (as it does not have a memory location).

```
{
  register int  Miles;
}
```

Register should only be used for variables that require quick access - such as counters. It should also be noted that defining 'register' goes not mean that the variable will be stored in a register. It means that it MIGHT be stored in a register - depending on hardware and implementation restrictions.

3) static - Storage Class

static is the default storage class for global variables. The two variables below (count and road) both have a static storage class.

```
static int Count;
int Road;

main()
{
  printf("%d\n", Count);
```

```
  printf("%d\n", Road);
}
```

'Static' can also be defined within a function. If this is done, the variable is initialised at compilation time and retains its value between calls. Because it is initialized at compilation time, the initialisation value must be a constant. This is serious stuff - tread with care.

```
void Func(void)
{
  static Count=1;
}
```

Here is an example

There is one very important use for 'static'. Consider this bit of code.

```
char *Func(void);
main()
{
  char *Text1;
  Text1 = Func();
}
char *Func(void)
{
  char Text2[10]="martin";
  return(Text2);
}
```

'Func' returns a pointer to the memory location where 'Text2' starts BUT Text2 has a storage class of auto and will disappear when we exit the function and could be overwritten by something else. The answer is to specify:

```
static char Text[10]="martin";
```

The storage assigned to 'Text2' will remain reserved for the duration if the program.

4) Extern - storage Class

extern defines a global variable that is visible to ALL object modules. When you use 'extern' the variable cannot be initialized as all it does is point the variable name at a storage location that has been previously defined.

Source 1	**Source 2**
extern int count;	int count=5;
write( )	main( )
{	{
printf("count is %d\n", count);	write( );
}	}

Count in 'source 1' will have a value of 5. If source 1 changes the value of count - source 2 will see the new value.

4. (a) Explain use of comma operator in C with the help of an example. 5

Ans. The comma operator (,) is used to link the related expressions together. Comma is used to permit different expressions to appear in situations where one expression would be used. The comma separated expressions are evaluated from left to right.

Example: a = 8, b = 7, c = 9, a + b + c   // It is a single expression separated by comma

Comma operator is not only used in expressions but we can use it in statements also like :

sum = (a = 8, b = 7, c = 9, a + b + c);

Here sum will be equal to 24.

By using comma operator we have made the program more compact as four statements are embedded in single statement using comma operator.

a = 4;
b = 7;
c = 9;
sum = a + b + c;

These four statements are reduced to single statement using comma operator.

(b) What is the difference between & and &&? Explain with an example. 5

Ans. & - It is an address operator in C when used with pointer.

& - It is a Bitwise AND operator. This binary operator takes operands of integer type and performs Bitwise AND operation on that operands.

Example: We assume that the size of integer is 8 bits.

int a = 5;   Binary: [00000 101]
int b = 9;   Binary: [0000 1001]

Expression :

a & b will give outputs as Binary AND: [0000 0001]

Therefore & is a Bitwise Logical AND operator used for manipulating the data at Bit Level.

Bitwise Logical AND operator is applicable to integer datatype only.

& & - It is a Logical AND operator used to combine two or more than two relational expression in C language.

&& is a binary operator and applicable to all datatypes of C language.

Example:

```
#include <stdlib.h>
main()
{
int num1 = 25, num2 = 10, num3 = 15;
```

```
if(num1 > = num2 && num1 > = num3)
printf("%d" is largest of three numbers", num1);
getch();
}
```

(c) Write a program in C using structures to stimulate salary calculation for employees of a company. Assumptions can be made wherever necessary. ***10***

Refer to June-2006, Q.No.-5(a), Page No.-151

5. (a) Write a program to count the number of characters and words in a given file. ***10***

Ans. Refer to June-2006, Q.No.-5(b), Page No.-152

(b) Write a program to display the string "EARTH" in the following format: ***10***

E
E A
E A R
E A R T
E A R T H
E A R T
E A R
E A
E

Ans.

```
# include <stdio.h>
#include <conio.h>
void main()
{
int i, j, k = 4;
char arr[6] = {'E', 'A', 'R', 'T', 'H', '\O'}'
for(i = 1; i < = 5; i++)
{
for (j = 0; j < = i – 1; j++)
printf("%s", arr[j]);
printf("\n");
}
for(i = 1; i < = 4; i++)
{
for(j = 0; j < = 4 – i; j++)
printf("%s", arr[j]);
printf("\n");
}
getch();
}        //main ends
```

MCS-011 : PROBLEM SOLVING AND PROGRAMMING
December, 2007

Note : (i) Question number 1 is **compulsory.**
(ii) Attempt any **three** questions from the rest.

---

1. (a) Design an algorithm, draw a corresponding flow chart and write a 'C' program for Binary Search, to search a given number among the list of numbers. *10*

Ans. Algorithm: Binary Search (A, n, item, loc)
Step 1: START
Step 2: INPUT THE ITEM TO BE SEARCHED
Step 3: SET beg := 0, end := n – 1 and mid := (beg + end)/2
Step 4: REPEAT Step 5 to 6 WHILE ((beg < = end) AND (A[mid] ≠ item)
Step 5: IF(item < A[mid]) THEN
SET end := mid – 1
ELSE
SET beg := mid + 1
ENDIF
Step 6: SET mid := (beg + end)/2
Step 7: IF(beg > end) THEN
SET loc : = –1
ELSE
SET loc : = mid
ENDIF
Step 8: END

Flowchart of Binary Search

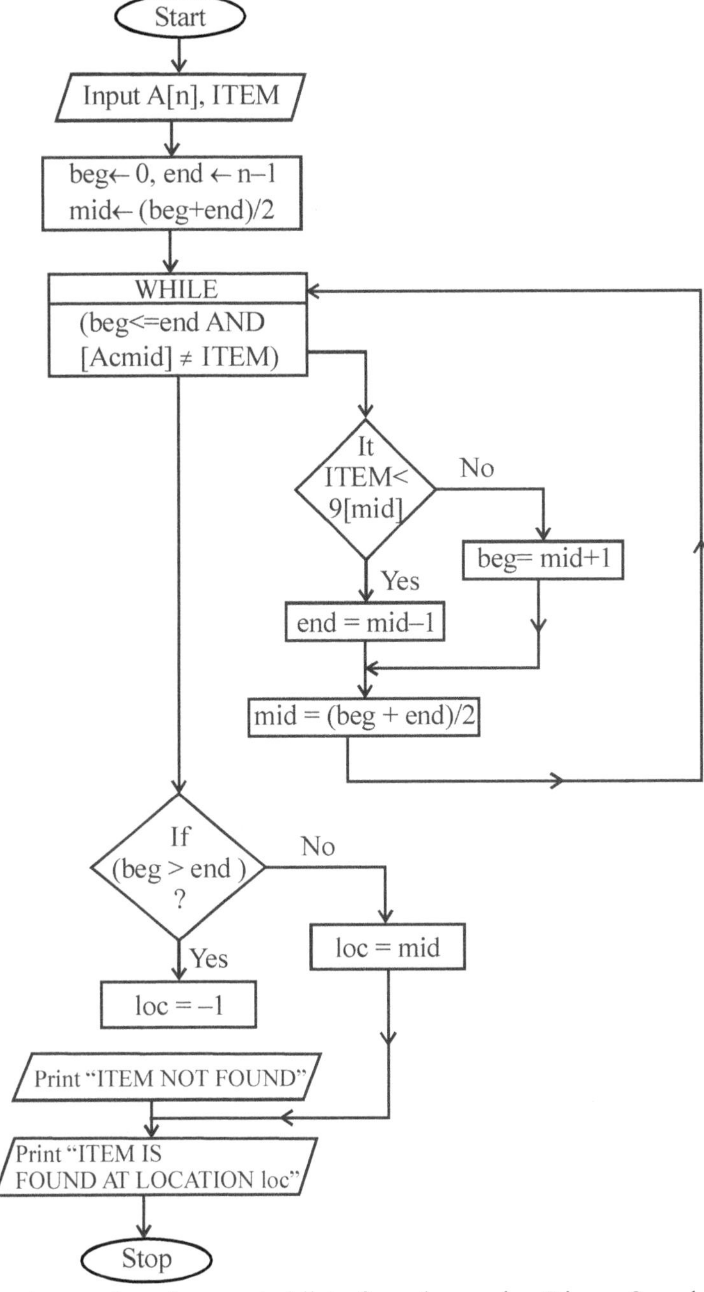

Program to search a given sorted list of numbers using Binary Search

```
#define MAX 50
int binarysearch (int a[ ], int beg, int end, int item)
void main()
{
int a[MAX], i, n, item, loc;
printf("Enter size of array:");
scanf("%d", &n);
printf("Enter %d element of array in ascending order", n);
for(i = 0; i < n; i++)
scanf("%d", &a[i]);
if(n > MAX)
{
printf("\n Input size greater than Max \n");
exit(1);
}
printf("Enter the element to search:");
scanf("%d", &item);
loc = binarysearch (a, 0, n – 1, item);
if(loc = = –1)
printf("Element not found::\n");
else
printf("Element found at location %d\n", loc);
getch();
}
int binarysearch(int a[ ], int beg, int end, int item)
{
int mid;
if(beg > end)
return = -1;
else
{
mid = (beg + end)/2;
if(item = = a[mid])
return mid;
else if(item < a[mid])
return binarysearch(a, beg, mid – 1, item);
else
return binarysearch(a, mid + 1, end, item);
}
}
```

(b) Write the syntax for the declaration of a function. Also discuss the parameter passing methods with an example program. *10*

Ans. Syntax and Definition of a Function : The general form of function definition is

```
Returntype Function Name (List of Arguments)
{
Local declarations;
----------------
Executable body?
----------------
----------------
}
```

→ The first statement of function must be the function defining statement specifying the return-type, name and formal arguments.

→ If the type of function is omitted, then it is assumed of type integer (int).

→ The formal arguments should neither be constants nor expressions.

→ The return statement need not be at the end of function. It may be used anywhere in the function.

Passing Arguments to a Function : Arguments to a function can be passed in two ways:

(1) Call by value

(2) Call by address or Call by reference

(1) Call by Value Approach : Here the names of the actual arguments are used in the function call. In this way the values of actual arguments are passed to the function. When control is transferred to the called function, the values of actual arguments are substituted to the corresponding formal arguments and the body of the function is executed.

(2) Call by Address or Call by Reference : Here the address of actual arguments are used in the function call. In this way the addresses of the actual arguments are passed to the function. When the control is transferred to the called function, the address of the actual arguments are substituted to corresponding formal arguments and the body of the function is executed.

For example of each type : Refer to June-07, Q,No-1.(a) Swap Function.

(c) Write a recursive function in 'C' that computes the factorial of a given integer. *10*

Ans. The factorial function can be recursively defined as:

$$n! = \begin{cases} 1 & \text{if } n = 0 \\ n(n-1) & \text{if } n > 0 \end{cases}$$

```
int factorial(int n)        //'C' Recursive Function for factorial
{
(if n = = 0)
return 1;
else
return(n * factorial (n – 1));
```

(d) List and explain the precedence of Arithmetic, Logical and Relational operators in 'C'. *10*

Ans. The Precedence Table in 'C' for Arithmetic, Logical and Relational Operators is shown below :

Description of Operator	Operator	Precedence Level	Associativity
Logical NOT	!	I	Light to Left
Multiplication	*	II	Left to Right
Division	/	II	Left to Right
Modulus (Remainder)	%	II	Left to Right
Addition	+	III	Left to Right
Subtraction	-	III	Left to Right
Less than	<	IV	Left to Right
Less than equal to	<=	IV	Left to Right
Greater than	>	IV	Left to Right
Greater than equal to	>=	IV	Left to Right
Equal to	= =	V	Left to Right
Not Equal to	!=	V	Left to Right

2.(a) Write an algorithm and draw flowchart to find whether a given string SI is substring of another string S2. *10*

Ans.

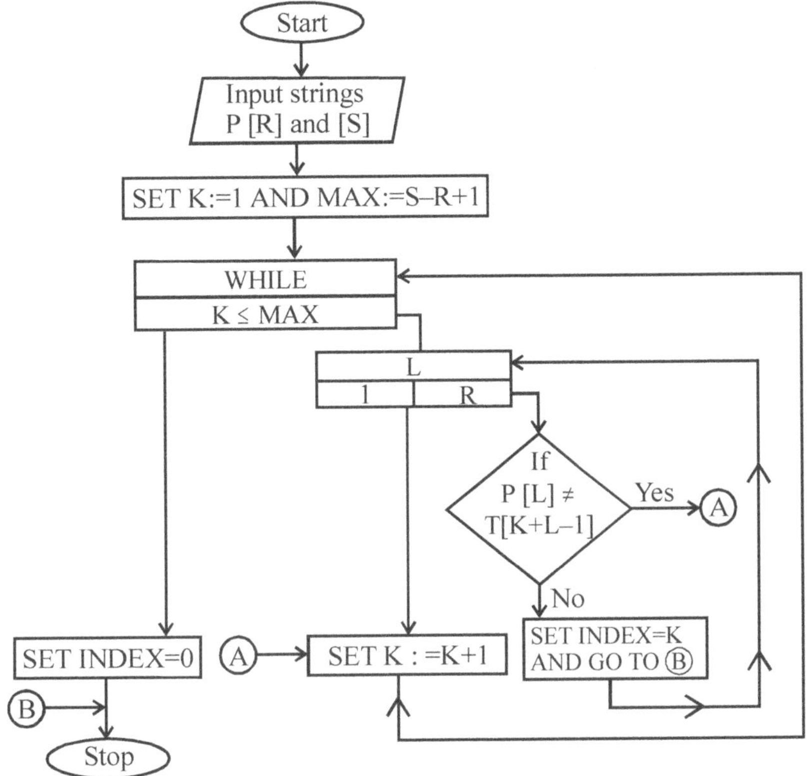

Note: We have taken string S1 in char array P and string S2 in char array T.

Algorithm Substring (P[R], T[S], K, MAX, INDEX)

Step 1: START

Step 2: [INITIAL 12E] SET K:=1 and MAX:= S – R + 1

Step 3: REPEAT Steps 4 to 6 while K < = MAX

Step 4: REPEAT FOR L = 1 to R [Test for each character of P]

IF P[L] $\neq$ T[K + L – 1], then Go to Step 6

Step 5: [Success] Set INDEX = K and EXIT

Step 6: SET K:= K + 1

Step 7: [Failure] SET INDEX:=0

Step 8: EXIT

(b) Write a program in 'C' language which accepts the enrollment number of a students as input and prints the name of that student. The program should initially store information about the (name, enrollment number) pairs of students in the from of a matrix. ***10***

Ans. #define MAX 50

```
#include <stdio.h>
struct student          //Arrays with in structure are used
{
char name[20];
int enrollment no;
};
void main()
{
int i, j, n;
clrscr( );
printf("Enter how many records for student are required");
scanf("%d", &n);
struct student stuarr[n];
for(i = 0; i < n; i++)
{
printf("Enter data for student %d\n", i + 1);
printf("Enter student name:");
scanf("%s", stuarr[i].name);
printf("Enter student's Enrollment number:");
scanf(:%d", &stuarr[i].enrollment no);
}
for(i = 0; i < n; i++)
{
printf("Data of student %d\n", i + 1);
printf("Name: %s, Enrollment No: %d", stuarr[i].name, stuarr[i].enrollment
no);
printf("\n");
}
getch();
}
```

3.(a) Write a program in 'C' language to display the names and seat numbers of all passengers of a bus in the form of a singly linked list. Use pointers. ***10***

Ans.

```
#include <stdio.h>
#include <string.h>
#include <alloc.h>
#include <conio.h>
typedef struct passenger
{
char name[25];
```

```
int seatno;
struct passenger *next;
} node;
node *start, *last_ptr;
void input(void);
void display(void);
void delete(void);
main()
{
int option;
start = last_ptr = (node*) NULL;
while(1)
{
printf("Select One of the following option");
printf("\n------------------------------------");
printf("\n 1. Enter New Passenger");
printf("\n 2. Display List of Passenger");
printf("\n 3. Exit from program");
printf("\n Enter your option (1 – 3):");
scanf(:%d", &option);
switch(option)
{
case 1: input();
break;
case 2: display();
break;
case 3: delete();
exit(1);
}
}
}
void input(void)
{
node *this_ptr;
char pname[25];
int pseatno;
printf("Enter passenger name");
scanf("%s", pname);
printf("Enter seat number");
scanf("%d", &pseatno);
this_ptr = (node *) malloc(size of (node));
```

```
this_ptr→seatno = pseatno;
strcpy(this_ptr→name, pname);
this_ptr→next = (node *) NULL;
if(start = =(node *) NULL)
start = last_ptr = this_ptr;
else
{
last_ptr→next = this_ptr;
last_ptr = this_ptr;
}
}
void display(void)
{
int i = 1;
node *this_ptr;
if(start = =(node *) NULL)
{
printf("\n" List is empty");
getch();
return;
}
printf("List of Passengers\n");
for(this_ptr = start; this_ptr!=(node *) NULL; this_ptr = this_ptr→next)
{
printf("Passenger Name:%s", this_ptr→name);
printf("Passenger Seat No:%d", this_ptr→seatno);
getch();
}
}
void delete(void)
{
node * this_ptr;
while(start!=(node *) NULL)
{
this_ptr = start;
start = startnext;
free(this_ptr);
}
}
```

(b) Explain any five functions of <stdlib.h> library. ***10***

Ans. The various data conversion functions are declared in header file <stdlib.h>. Some of these functions are:

atof( ), atoi( ), atol( ), strtod( ), strtol( ), strtoul( ), free( ), malloc( ), calloc() and realloc ( ) etc. are the various functions included in stdlib.h header file.

(1) atof( ): It is a data conversion function to convert character data into float type.

(2) atoi( ): It is a data conversion function to convert character data into integer type.

(3) malloc( )

Declaration: void *malloc(size_t, size);

It is a function used to allocate memory dynamically. The argument size specifies the number of bytes to be allocated. The type size_t is defined in stdlib.h as unsigned int.

(4) calloc( )

Declaration: void *calloc(size_t n, size_t size);

This function is used to allocate multiple blocks of memory. It takes 2 arguments. The first argument specifies the number of blocks and second one specifies the size of each block.

(5) realloc( )

Declaration: void *realloc(void *ptr, size_t newsize)

If we want to increase or decrease the memory allocated by malloc() or calloc() function then realloc( ) function is used to change the size of that memory block. It changes the size of memory block without losing the old data.

4. (a) Write a program in 'C' that accepts a sentence 's' and a word 'w' as input. Now, the program should print the starting position or right-most occurrence of 'w' in 's'. ***10***

Ans.
```
#include <string.h>
#include <stdio.h>
main()
{
char s[100], w[25]
int i, j, flag = 0;
printf("Enter the sentence:");
scanf("%s", s);
printf("Enter the word:");
scanf("%s", w);
for(i = 0; i < strlen(s); i++)
{
flag = 0;
```

```
for(j = 0; j < strlen(w); j++)
{
if(s)
{
flag = 1;
break;
}
}
if(flag!= 1)
printf("The word w is not present in string s");
else
printf("The starting position of w in s is %d", i + 1);
getch();
}        //main ends
```

(b) Write a program in 'C' language that accepts the name of a file as input and prints those lines of the file which have the word 'this'. *10*

Ans.

```
#include <string.h>
#include <stdio.h>
#include <stdlib.h>
int display(char line[], char wordtext[]);
main()
{
char line[81], char name[30];
int total = 0;
FILE *fptr;
printf("Enter the input file name:");
scanf("%s", name);
if(fptr = fopen(name, "r")) = = NULL)
{
printf("File does not exist\n");
exit(1);
}
while(fgets(line, 81, fptr))!= NULL)
total = total + display(line, "this");
printf("Number of times the given word occurs in the file is %d\n", total);
fclose(fptr);
}        //main ends
int display(char line[], char wordtext[])
{
int i, j, k, len;
char str[80];
int count = 0;
```

```
len = strlen(word_text);
for(i = 0; line[i]!='\0'; i++)
{
k = 0;
if(is_end(line[i – 1] && is_end(line[i + len]))
{
for(k = 0; j = i; k < len; j++, k++)
str[k] = line[j];
str[k] = '\0';
if(strcmp(str, wordtext) = = 0)
count ++;
}
}
if(count > 0)
{
printf("%s", line);
printf("count = %d\n", count)
}
return count;
}        //end of function display
is_end(int ch)
{
switch(ch)
{
case '\n':
case '\t':
case ' ':
case ',':
case '.':
case ':':
case ';':
case '-';
return 1;
}
return ( );
}        //end of is_end function
```

5. (a) Write a program in 'C' language to convert a decimal number into binary number. *10*

Ans. long int binary(long int num);

```
main()
{
long int num;
printf("Enter the decimal number:");
```

```
scanf("%ld", &num);
printf("Decimal = %ld, Binary = %ld\n", num, binary(num));
}
long binary(long int num)
{
long rem, a = 1, bin = 0;
while(num > 0)
{
rem = num%2;
bin = bin + rem * a;
num/=2;
a * = 10;
}
return bin;
}
```

(b) Write a program in 'C' language to add two matrices. *10*

Ans.

```
#define R 3
#define C 4
#include <stdio.h>
main( )
{
int i, j;
int mat1[R][C], mat2[R][C], mat3[R][C];
printf("Enter matrix mat1 Row-wise\n");
for(i = 0; i < R; i++)
for(j = 0; j < C; j++)
scanf("%d", &mat1[i][j]);
printf("Enter matrix mat2 Row-wise\n");
for(i = 0; i < R; i++)
for(j = 0; j < C; j++)
scanf("%d", &mat2[i][j]);
/*Addition of matrix mat1 and mat2*/
for(i = 0; i < R; i++)
for(j = 0; j < C; j++)
mat3[i][j] = mat1[i][j] + mat2[i][j];
printf("The Resultant Matrix Mat3 is::\n");
for(i = 0; i < R; i++)
{
for(j = 0; j < C; j++)
printf("%5d", mat3[i][j]);
printf("\n");
}
getch( );
}
```

MCS-011 : Problem Solving and Programming
June, 2008

Note : (i) Question number 1 is **compulsory.**
(ii) Attempt any three questions from the rest.

Q1. (a) Design an algorithm, draw a corresponding flowchart and then write a program in C to convert a given string to lower case.

Ans. Algorithm:

Step 1: Initialize i = 1
Step 2: Accept a string into S.
Step 3: Repeat Step 4 through Step 6 until end of string
Step 4: if s[i] is a capital letter then
Step 5: Replace capital letter with lower case letter
Step 6: Increment i with 1
Step 7: Print S
Step 8: End

Flowchart:

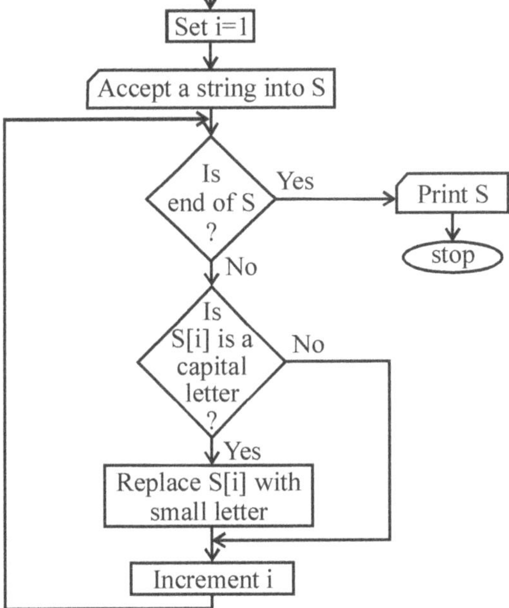

Program:

```
#include <stdio.h>
#include <conio.h>
void main( )
{
char s[100];
int i;
```

```
printf("\n Enter a String:");
scanf("%s", s);
for(i = 0; s[i] != NULL; i++)
if(s[i] >= 65 && s[i] <= 90)
s[i] = s[i] + 32;
printf("\n The converted string is: %s", s);
}
```

(b) Write an algorithm and program in C to generate Fibonacci series. Use recursion.

Ans. Algorithm :

Step 1: Set F1 = 0, F2 = 1, F3 = 0, i = 3

Step 2: Accept "Number of terms" into N

Step 3: Print F1

Step 4: Print F2

Step 5: Repeat Step 6 through Step 8 until i > N

Step 6: F3 = F1 + F2

Step 7: Print F3

Step 8: increment i

Step 9: End

Program:

```
#include <stdio.h>
#include <conio.h>
long fib(long);
void main( )
{ printf("\n%d term of the Fibonacci Series is: %d", 10, fib(10));
}
long fib(long n)
{ if(n <= 1)
return 0;
else if(n = = 2)
return 1;
else
return(fib(n – 1) + fib(n – 2));
}
```

(c) Draw a flowchart and write a program in C to calculate the number of vowels in a given string.

Ans. Program:

```
#include <stdio.h>
#include <conio.h>
```

```
void main( )
{
char s[100];
int i, cnt = 0;
printf("\n Enter a string:");
scanf("%s", s);
for(i= 0; s[i] != NULL; i++)
{
if(s[i] = = 'a' || s[i] = = 'e' || s[i] = = 'i' || s[i] = = 'o' || s[i] = = 'u' ||
s[i] = = 'A' || s[i] = = 'E' || s[i] = = 'I' || s[i] = = 'O' || s[i] = = 'U')
cnt++;
} printf("\n The total number of vowels in %s is %d", s, cnt);
}
```

Flowchart:

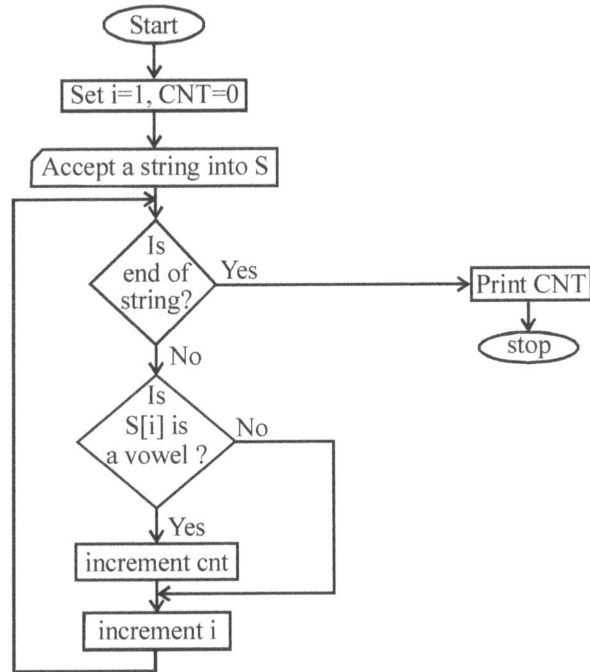

(d) What do you mean by 'array of pointers'? Write a program in C to calculate the difference of the corresponding elements of two arrays of integers of same size.

Ans. Array of Pointers: Array of pointers is an array which stores pointers or addresses of memory locations instead of values. For example,

```
int *a[10];
char *s[100];
```

Program:

```
#include <stdio.h>
#include <conio.h>
#define N 5
 void main( )
{ int a[N], b[N], c[N], i;
printf("\n Enter %d elements for array A:", N);
for(i = 0; i < N; i++)
scanf("%d", &a[i]);
printf("\n Enter %d elements for array B:", N);
for(i = 0; i < N; i++)
scanf("%d", &b[i]);
for(i = 0; i < N; i++)
c[i] = a[i] – b[i];
printf("\n Difference between array A and B is:");
for(i = 0; i < N; i++)
printf("\n%d", c[i]);       }
```

Q2. (a) Write the usage of the following (with an example of each):
(i) #define
(ii) enum

Ans. (i) The #define directive defines a macro.

Syntax:#define <id>[(<id2>, ...)] <token string>

Example: #define N 5

(ii) enum defines a set of constants of type int.

Syntax: enum[<type_tag>] {<constant_name> [= <value>], ...} [var_list];

<type_tag> is an optional type tag that names the set.

<constant_name> is the name of a constant that can optionally be assigned the value of <value>.

Example: enum modes {LASTMODE = -1, BW40 = 0, C40, BW80, C80, MONO = 7};

/* "modes" is the type tag.
"LASTMODE", "BW40", "C40", etc. are the constant names.
The value of C40 is 1 (BW40 + 1); BW80 = 2 (C40 + 1), etc.*/

(b) Write a macro for the following :
(i) to find the smallest number among 3 given numbers.
(ii) to find the factorial of a given number N.

Ans. (i) #define min(x, y, z) ((x < y) ? ((x < z) ? x : z) : ((y < z) ? y : z))
(ii) #define fact(n) (n * (fact(n – 1)))

(c) What are the differences between structure and union? Give one illustrative example of usage of the union.
Refer to Page-50 – 51, Q.No.-5

Q3. (a) Write a program in C, using structures to generate a report for employees which displays the total salary, designation, department, address etc. Assumptions can be made wherever necessary.

Ans.
```
#include <stdio.h>
#include <conio.h>
struct emp
{ char name[20];
int sal;
char desig[20];
char dept[20];
char addr[50];
};
void main( )
{ struct emp e[50];
int i, tsal;
for(i = 0; i < 50; i++)
{ printf("Enter Details of Employee #d", i + 1);
printf("\nName:");
gets(e[i].name);
printf("\nSalary:");
scanf("%d", &e[i].sal);
printf("\nDesignation:");
gets(e[i].desig);
printf("\nDepartment:");
gets(e[i].dept);
printf("\nAddress:");
gets(e[i].addr);
} clrscr( );
printf("\n\t\tList of Employees");
for(i = 0; i < 50; i++)
{ tsal = e[i].sal * 1.46;
printf("\n%d\t%s\t%d\t%s\t%s\t%s", i + 1, e[i].name, tsal, e[i].desig, e[i].dept,
e[i].addr);
}
```

```
}
```

(b) Write a program to read formatted data from the file.

Ans.
```
#include <stdio.h>
#include <conio.h>
void main( )
{ FILE *fp;
int n;
while(!eof(fp))
{ fscanf(fp, "%2d", &n);
printf("\n%d", n);
} }
```

(c) Give a brief note on null pointer assignment. Write a program in 'C' to illustrate this concept.

Ans. A null pointer is conceptually different from an uninitialized pointer. A null pointer is known not to point to any object; an uninitialized pointer might point anywhere. According to the C language definition, a constant 0 in a pointer context is converted into a null pointer at compile time. That is, in an initialization, assignment or comparison when one side is a variable or expression of pointer type, the compiler can tell that a constant 0 on the other side requests a null pointer and generate the correctly-typed null pointer value. For example,

```
char *p = 0;
```

Q4. (a) Write a program which reads a file and counts the number of lines and words in the file, assuming that a line can contain at most 80 characters. Refer to Page No.-152 – 153, Q.No.-5(b)

(b) Give differences between :
(i) Sequential and Random Access files
(ii) Global variable and Local variable

Ans. (i) Sequential access is sometimes the only way of accessing the data, for example, if it is on a tape. It may also be the access method of choice, for example, if we simply want to process a sequence of data elements in order. File constructed in a manner in which records may be placed in a random order; also called *direct access file*. Each record in a random access file has associated with it a relative index number. Whenever a record is read from a random access file, a computer program must produce a relative index number for this record in order to locate the record in the file. This type of file design offers the following advantages:

(1) it provides rapid access to the desired information. In a decision-making environment where information is needed quickly, random access is a requisite

to rapid retrieval;
(2) it is efficient for retrieving a relatively few records at a time; and
(3) it provides a method of keeping files up to data as transactions or events occur.

(ii) Variables have either *global* or *local* scope. A global variable exists only once in a program and is visible in every function. Modifications to it in one function are permanent and visible to all functions. Global variables are useful for values that are relatively constant or that many functions in the program must access, such as a session id.

A local variable, however, has a limited scope; it exists only within the block that it is declared in. Once that block ends, the variable is destroyed and its values lost. A local variable of the same name declared elsewhere is a different variable. A local variable can even exist multiple times simultaneously, if its block is entered again before it's exited – i.e. a recursive function call. Each call of the function will have a distinct local variable.

(c) Write a program and flowchart to display the following pattern :

```
1
2   3
4   5   6
7   8   9   10
11  12  13  14  15
16  17  18  19  20  21
```

Ans. Program:

```
#include <stdio.h>
#include <conio.h>

void main( )
{
int i, j = 1, k = 1, n = 21;
clrscr( );
for(i = 1; j <= n; i++)
{
printf("\n");
for(k = 1; k <= i; j++, k++)
printf("%3d", j);
}
}
```

Flowchart:

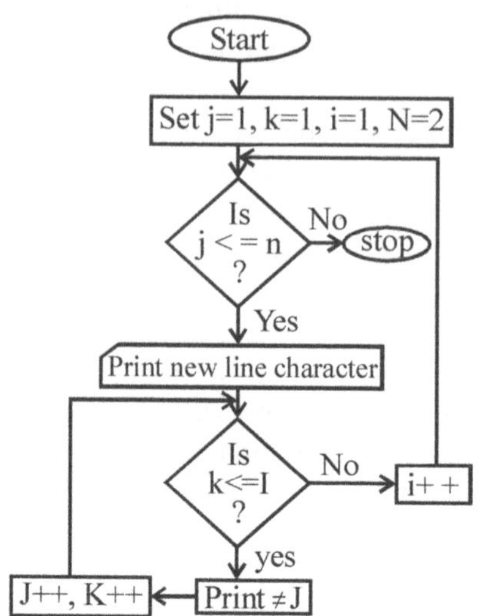

Q5. (a) Write a program in C to find the difference between two matrices of size (3×3).

Refer to Page No.-145 – 147, Q.No.-2(b)

(b) Write a program in C to sort a given list of numbers using bubble sort. Draw corresponding flowchart also.

Refer to Page No.-177 – 178, Q.No.-3(a)

(c) Explain meaning of following prototypes and mention return data type of each of them :

(i) int (*f) (char*);

(ii) int *f (char*);

(iii) double f (int a, int b, char c);

(iv) unsigned f ( );

Ans. (i) Declares a function pointer named f which will return integer type pointer and accepts one parameter of character pointer.

(ii) Declares a function named f which will return an integer pointer and accepts one parameter of character pointer.

(iii) Declares a function named f which will return a double type of value and accepts three parameters.

(iv) Declares a function named f which will return unsigned integer.

MCS-011 : Problem Solving and Programming
December, 2008

Note : (i) Question number 1 is **compulsory.**
(ii) Attempt any three questions from the rest.

Q1. (a) Design an algorithm, draw a corresponding flow chart and write a program in 'C', to find the factorial of a given number using recursion.
Refer to Page No.-142 – 143, Q.No.-1(c)
Flowchart:

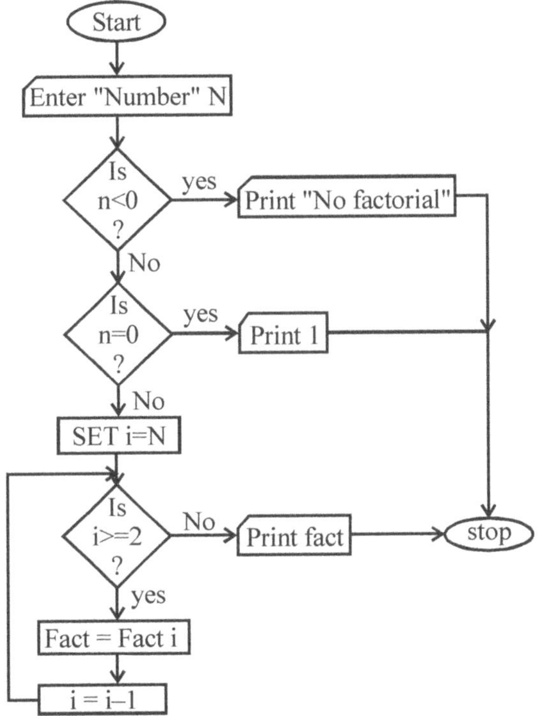

(b) Write a 'C' program to find whether a given five digits number is a palindrome.

Ans.
```
#include <stdio.h>
void main( )
{ int n;
int t, revn = 0;
printf("Enter an integer");
scanf("%d", &n);
t = n;
```

```
while(t)
{ revn = (revn * 10) + (t % 10);
t /= 10;
} if(t = = n)
printf("Palindrome");
else
printf("Not a Palindrome");
}
```

(c) Write a program in 'C' to find all Armstrong numbers in the range of 0 and 999.

Hint : An Armstrong number is an integer such that sum of the cubes of its digits is equal to the number itself, e.g. : 153 is Armstrong number.

Ans.
```
#include <stdio.h>
void main( )
{ int n, t, rem, asn;
for(n = 0; n <= 999; n++)
{ t = n; asn = 0;
while(t)
{ rem = t % 10;
asn = (rem * rem * rem) + asn;
t /= 10;
} if(t = = n)
printf("%d\n", t);
}       }
```

(d) When can two matrices of order m × n and p × q be multiplied ? Also write a program in 'C' to multiply two such matrices.

Refer to Page No.-175, Q.No.-1(d)

Q2. (a) Write a program in 'C' to generate a progress report for students which displays the total marks, average, and grades. The input for the system are marks secured in five courses (Assignment and Term end Examination). Pass (40%) in both the components are compulsory. Grades may be given accordingly. Assumptions can be made if necessary and specify them. Refer to Page No.-131 – 133, Q.No.-3(a)

(b) What is the difference between "&" and "& &"? Explain with an example. Refer to Page No.-181, Q.No.-4(b)

(c) Write a loop that calculate sum of the *n* elements of the series: 1 + 7 +13 + 19 + 25 +..........

Write the loop in 3 different ways

(i) using while loop

(ii) using do-while loop

Ans. (i) i= 1;

```
j = 1;
sum = 0;
while(j <= n)
{ sum += i;
i += 6; }
```

(ii) i = 1;

```
j = 1;
sum = 0;
do
{ sum += i;
i += 6; }
while(j <= n);
```

Q3. (a) Write a macro to find out whether the given character is lower case or not.

Ans. #define lcase(c) ((c >= 'a' && c <= 'z') ? 1 : 0)

(b) Write a program in 'C' to check whether the given year is leap or not. Also explain the logic of the program.

Ans.

```
#include <stdio.h>
void main( )
{ int year;
printf("Enter year:");
scanf("%d", &year);
if((year % 100 != 0 && year % 4 = = 0) || (year % 400 = = 0))
printf("Leap Year");
else
printf("Not a Leap Year");
}
```

Explanation: A year is a leap year if it is not a century year and divisible by 4 or divisible by 400 if it is a century year.

(c) Write a function definition to find the smallest among the given three numbers.

Ans.

```
int smallest(int a, int b, int c)
{ if(a < b)
if(a < c)
return a;
else
return c;
else if(b < c)
return b;
else
return c;
}
```

Q4. (a) Without using the 'strcpy' function, write a program to copy contents of string 2 to string 1, and find the length of the copied string using pointers.

Ans.
```
#include <stdio.h>
void main( )
{ char string1[100], string2[100] = "Hello", *s1, *s2;
int len = 0
s1 = string1;
s2 = string2;
while(s2)
}
*s1++ = *s2++;
len++;
} *s1 = '\0';
printf("%s", string1);
printf("%d", len);
}
```

(b) Write the usage of the following data types, with an example for each :

(i) enumerated data type **(ii) typedef**

Ans. (i) Refer to June-2008, Q.No.-2(a)(ii)

(ii) typedef is used to create user defined data types (or alias of existing data type). For example, typedef float currency;

Q5. (a) Design an algorithm and draw corresponding flow chart to convert a decimal number to its Hexadecimal equivalent.

Refer to Page No.-138 – 139, Q.No.-5(b)

(b) Explain the following storage class specifiers of a variables in terms of default value, lifetime, scope purpose and limitations (with an example)

(i) Auto **(ii) Register**

Ans.

	Auto	**Register**
Default value	Garbage value	0
Life Time	Block in which declared	Block in which declared
Scope	Local	Local
Purpose	For local temporary storage	For faster processing, generally used for loop counters
Limitations	Not available outside the block	**1.** Not available outside the block **2.** Generally used as counter of a loop

MCS-011 : Problem Solving and Programming
June, 2009

Note : (i) Question number 1 is **compulsory.**
(ii) Attempt any three questions from the rest.

Q1. (a) Develop an algorithm, draw the corresponding flow chart and write a program in 'C' to print the sum of the digits of a three digit number.

Ans. Step I:- Start
Step II:- Enter the 3-digits number
Step III:- Initial value, s=0
Step IV:- If n>0 then condition is true go to step V, otherwise go to step VI.
Step V:- $a = n\%10;$
$n = n/10;$
$s = s + a;$
Again go to step IV.
Step VI:- Print S
Step VII:- Stop

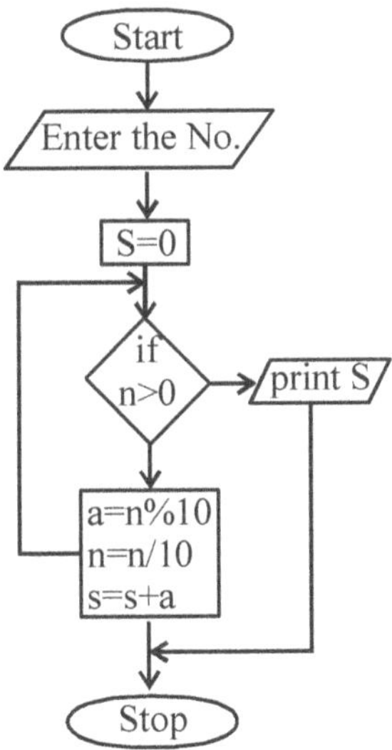

Program:
```
#include<stdio.h>
#include<conio.h>
void main()
{
```

```
int num,sum,k;
clrscr();
printf("enter the three digits number:-");
sum=0;
scanf("%d",&num);
while(num!=0)
{       k=num%10;
        sum=sum+k;
        num=num/10;
}
printf("sum of three digits=%d",sum);
getch();        }
```

(b) Write a program that does not use the inbuilt string function to perform the following :

(i) To compare two strings

Ans.
```
#include<string.h>
#include<stdio.h>
#include<conio.h>
void main()
{ int c=0,i,j;
char str1[10];
char str2[10];
clrscr();
printf("Enter the first string:-");
gets(str1);
printf("Enter the second string:-");
gets(str2);
for(i=0,j=0;(str2[i]!='\0'||str1[j]!='\0');i++,j++)
{       if(str1[i]!=str2[j])
        {       c++;        }       }
if(c==0)
        printf("string match");
else
        printf("string does not match");
getch();        }
```

(ii) To concatenate two strings

Ans.
```
#include<stdio.h>
#include<conio.h>
#include<string.h>
```

```
void main()
{       char str1[30],str2[30];
        int l1,l2,i;
        clrscr();
        printf("Enter the first string:-");
        gets(str1);
        printf("Enter the second string:-");
        gets(str2);
        l1=strlen(str1);
        l2=strlen(str2);
        for(i=0;i<=l2;i++)
        {       str1[l1+i]=str2[i];     }
        printf("concate  nation string=%s",str1);
        getch();        }
```

(c) Write 'C' programs to read a string and check whether it is palindrome or not.

Ans.
```
#include<stdio.h>
        #include<conio.h>
        #include<string.h>
void main()
{       char str1[50],str2[50];
        clrscr();
        printf("Enter the string:");
        gets(str1);
        strcpy(str2,str1);
        strrev(str1);
        if(strcmp(str2,str1) == 0)
        {       printf("The given string is a palindrome!!!");       }
        else
        {       printf("The given string is not a palindrome!!!");   }
        getch();        }
```

(d) Write the output of the following program :

```
main ( )
{ int x = 2, y = 3, S1, S2;
S1 = x + ( + + y);
S2 = + + x + y + +;
printf ("%d%d%d%d\n", S1, S2, x, y);        }
```

Ans.
```
#include<stdio.h>
#include<conio.h>
```

```
main( )
{       int x=2, y=3,s1,s2;
        s1=x+ (+ +y ) ;
        s2=++x+y++;
        printf ("%d%d%d%d\n",s1,s2,x,y);        }
/*Output:-
5634*/
```

(e) Differentiate between structure and union.

Refer to Chapter-2, Q.No.-5, Page-50

Q2. (a) Summarize the purpose of the format strings (like %s, %d, %c) that are commonly used within the printf function, with an example for each.

Refer to June-2006, Q.No.-2(a), Page-144

(b) Write a program in 'C' to print the following output 'n' rows. for example, if n = 3, the following should be output by the program :

```
            1
        1   2   1
    1   2   3   2   1
        1   2   1
            1
```

Ans.

```
#include<stdio.h>
#include<conio.h>
void main()
{       int n,i,j,k,t;
        clrscr();
        printf("Enter the number:-");
        scanf("%d",&n);
        for(i=1;i<=n;i++)
        {       for(j=1;j<=(n-i);j++)
                {       printf(" ");        }
                for(k=1;k<=i;k++)
                {       printf("%d",k);    }
                for(t=k-2;t>0;t—)
                {       printf("%d",t);    }
                printf("\n");               }
        for(i=1;i<n;i++)
        {       for(j=1;j<=i;j++)
                {       printf(" ");        }
                for(k=1;k<=(n-i);k++)
```

```
            {       printf("%d",k);         }
            for(t=k-2;t>0;t—)
            {       printf("%d",t);         }
            printf("\n");                   }
    getch();                                }
```

Q3. (a) Write a program in 'C' to copy one file to another. The program should read the filenames at command line.

Ans.

```
#include<stdio.h>
#include<conio.h>
#include<process.h>
void main()
{       FILE *fp1;
        FILE *fp2;
        int ch;
        if((fp1=fopen("f1.dat","r"))==NULL)
        {       printf("Error opening input file \n");
                exit(0);                }
        if((fp2=fopen("f2.dat","w"))==NULL)
        {       printf("Error opening input file \n");
                exit(0);                }
        while(!feof(fp1))
        {       ch=getc(fp1);
                putc(ch,fp2);           }
        fclose(fp1);
        fclose(fp2);
        getch();                        }
```

(b) Explain the meaning and usage of each of the following function prototypes :

(i) getch ( ) : getch() is a function which has its prototype defined in conio.h header file. It is basically used to take input a single character from keyboard. And this char is not displayed at the screen. It waits until it gets a input that's why it can be used as a screen stopper.

(ii) strcmp ( ) : Compares the C string *str1* to the C string *str2*. This function starts comparing the first character of each string. If they are equal to each other, it continues with the following pairs until the characters differ or until a terminating null-character is reached.

(iii) getchar ( )

Ans. getchar function is use to hold the output screen until any character is not entered by the user and this function is also use to input the character type data.

(iv) gets ( ) : gets function is a input function which is mainly use to input the string type of data **Ex:** gets(str1);

(v) puts ( ) : Puts is a output function same as printf function. Ex : puts("hello this is my first program");

Q4. (a) Write a program in 'C' in which a two-dimensional array is represented as an array of integer pointers to a set of single dimensional integer array.

Ans.
```
#include<stdio.h>
#include<conio.h>
void main()
{       int arr[10][10],arr1[100];
        int r,c,i,j,t;
        clrscr();
        printf("How many row in 10 element:-");
        scanf("%d",&r);
        printf("How many col in 10 element:-");
        scanf("%d",&c);
        printf("Enter the number in array:-");
        for(i=0;i<r;i++)
        {       for(j=0;j<c;j++)
                {       scanf("%d",&arr[i][j]);         }
        }
        printf("Output the number in two d array:-\n");
        for(i=0;i<r;i++)
        {       for(j=0;j<c;j++)
                {       printf("%d\t",arr[i][j]);       }
                printf("\n");                           }
        t=0;
        for(i=0;i<r;i++)
        {       for(j=0;j<c;j++)
                {       arr1[t]=arr[i][j];
                        t++;            }               }
        printf("Output the number in one d array:-\n");
        for(i=0;i<t;i++)
        {               printf("%d",arr1[i]);           }
        getch();                                        }
```

(b) Write a 'C' program to find the sum of the given series:
S = 1 – 2/2! + 3/3! – 4/4! --- n/n!

Ans.
```
#include<stdio.h>
#include<conio.h>
void main()
{       int n;
        float s,d,i,j,k,sign=-1;
        clrscr();
        printf("Enter the number:-");
        scanf("%d",&n);
        i=1;
        s=0;
        while(i<=n)
        {       sign=sign*-1;
                j=i;
                k=1;
                while(j>0)
                {       k=k*j;
                        j--;            }
                d=(sign*i)/k;
                s=s+d;
                i++;                    }
        printf("fact=%f",s);
        getch();                        }
```

Q5. (a) List and explain bitwise operators in 'C'.

Ans. The bitwise operators operate on numbers (always integers) as if they were sequences of binary bits. These operators will make the most sense, therefore, if we consider integers as represented in binary, octal, or hexadecimal (bases 2, 8, or 16), not decimal (base 10). Remember, you can use octal constants in C by prefixing them with an extra 0 (zero), and you can use hexadecimal constants by prefixing them with 0x (or 0X).

AND:- The & operator performs a bitwise AND on two integers. Each bit in the result is 1 only if both corresponding bits in the two input operands are 1. For example, 0x56 & 0x32 is 0x12, because (in binary):

```
  0 1 0 1 0 1 1 0
& 0 0 1 1 0 0 1 0
-----------------
  0 0 0 1 0 0 1 0
```

OR:- The | (vertical bar) operator performs a bitwise OR on two integers. Each bit in the result is 1 if either of the corresponding bits in the two input operands is 1. For example, 0x56 | 0x32 is 0x76, because:

```
  0 1 0 1 0 1 1 0
```

```
 | 0 0 1 1 0 0 1 0
 ----------------
   0 1 1 1 0 1 1 0
```

XOR:- The ^ (caret) operator performs a bitwise exclusive-OR on two integers. Each bit in the result is 1 if one, but not both, of the corresponding bits in the two input operands is 1. For example, 0x56 ^ 0x32 is 0x64:

```
   0 1 0 1 0 1 1 0
 ^ 0 0 1 1 0 0 1 0
 ----------------
   0 1 1 0 0 1 0 0
```

COMPLEMENT:- The ~ (tilde) operator performs a bitwise complement on its single integer operand. (The ~ operator is therefore a unary operator, like ! and the unary -, &, and * operators.) Complementing a number means to change all the 0 bits to 1 and all the 1s to 0s. For example, assuming 16-bit integers, ~0x56 is 0xffa9:

```
 ~ 0 0 0 0 0 0 0 0 0 1 0 1 0 1 1 0
 --------------------------------
   1 1 1 1 1 1 1 1 1 0 1 0 1 0 0 1
```

LEFT AND RIGHT SHIFT:- The << operator shifts its first operand left by a number of bits given by its second operand, filling in new 0 bits at the right. Similarly, the >> operator shifts its first operand right. If the first operand is unsigned, >> fills in 0 bits from the left, but if the first operand is signed, >> might fill in 1 bits if the high-order bit was already 1. (Uncertainty like this is one reason why it's usually a good idea to use all unsigned operands when working with the bitwise operators.) For example, 0x56 << 2 is 0x158:

```
     0 1 0 1 0 1 1 0 << 2
 --------------------
   0 1 0 1 0 1 1 0 0 0
```

And 0x56 >> 1 is 0x2b:

```
   0 1 0 1 0 1 1 0 >> 1
 ----------------
    0 1 0 1 0 1 1
```

(b) Write a program to count the number of characters, number of words and number of lines in a given file.

Ans.

```
#include<stdio.h>
#include<conio.h>
#include<ctype.h>
```

```
void main( )
{       char ch;
        int line=0, space=0, ct=0;
        clrscr( );
        printf("Enter the required no. of lines:\n");
        while((ch=getchar( ))!=EOF)
        {       if(ch==10)
                {       line++;         }
                if(isspace(ch))
                {       space++;        }
                ct++;                   }
        printf("\nNumber of Lines : %d", line+1);
        printf("\nNumber of Words: %d", space+1);
        printf("\nTotal Number of Characters: %d", ct);
        getch( );                       }
```

MCS-011 : Problem Solving and Programming
December, 2009

Note : (i) Question number 1 is **compulsory.**
(ii) Attempt any three questions from the rest.

Q1. (a) Develop an algorithm, and write a program to print the Fibonacci series upto a given number using recursion.
Refer To June-2008 Q 1. (b), Page-196

(b) What do you understand by function prototype? Write a program in 'C' to calculate the GCD of three numbers using the function prototype.
Ans. In programming, a declaration of a function to the compiler indicating what types of parameters are passed to it and what value is returned. The compiler can then report an error if a function within the program is not written to confirm to the prototype. Program in c to calculate the gcd of three numbers using the function prototype:-

```
        #include<stdio.h>
        #include<conio.h>
        void main()              {
        int x,y,z,remainder;
        clrscr();
        printf("Please enter the three numbers whose GCD you would like
to      find.\n");
        printf("Enter the first value x:-");
        scanf("%d",&x);
        printf("Enter the second value y:-");
        scanf("%d",&y);
        printf("Enter the three value z:-");
        scanf("%d",&z);
if(x== 0 || y== 0 || z==0)
{printf("Error: Division by 0. I'm afraid I can't do that, Dave.\n"); }
        if(x== 1 || y== 1 || z==1)
        {       printf("The GCD is 1.\n");      }
        if(x<y && x<z)
        {       if(y<z)
                {       remainder=z;
                        z=x;
                        x=remainder;            }       }
        else if(y<x && y<z)
        {       if(x<z)
                {       remainder=x;
```

```
                    x=z;
                    z=y;
                    y=remainder;    }       }
else
{       if(x<y)
        {       remainder=y;
                y=x;
                x=remainder;            }
        else
        {       remainder=x;
                x=y;
                y=remainder;            }       }
while(y!= 0)
{       remainder=x%y;
        x=y;
        y= remainder;                   }
while(x!= 0)
{       remainder=z%x;
        z=x;
        x= remainder;                   }
printf("The GCD is %d.\n",z);
getch();                                }
```

(c) List and explain any 5 reserved words of 'C' language.

Ans. The Reserved Word is also called the key word or special word. Keywords are building blocks for program statements. All reserved words must be written in lowercase. There are five reserved words of C language- int, char, break, case, struct.

(d) Differentiate between call by value and call by reference methods of parameters passing to a function giving an example of each.

Refer to December -2007, Q.No.-1.(b), Page No.- 186

(e) What will be the output of following 'C' programme?

```
main ()
{int i = 1, j = 1;
for (;;)
{ if (i > 5)
break;
else
j + = 1;
printf ("In %d", j)
```

i + = j;
}}

Ans.
```
#include<stdio.h>
#include<conio.h>
void main()
{ int i=1,j=1;
clrscr();
for(;;)
{ if(i>5)
break;
else
j+=j;
printf("In%d",j);
i+=j; }
getch(); }
```

Output:-

In2In4

Q2. (a) What do you mean by scope of a variable? Differentiate between Global and Local variables giving an example of each.

Ans. The scope of the variables can be broadly be classified as
Local Variables, Global Variables, and Local Variables:
The variables defined local to the block of the function would be accessible only within the block of the function and not outside the function. Such variables are called local variables. That is in other words the scope of the local variables is limited to the function in which these variables are declared.
Let us see this with a small example:

```
#include <iostream.h>
int global(int,int);
void main( )
{  int b;
   int s=5,u=6;
   b=global(s,u);
   cout<<"\n The Output is:"<<b;   }
        int global(int x,int y)
{       int z;
   z=x+y;
return(z);     }
```

In the above program the variables x, y, z are accessible only inside the function global( ) and their scope is limited only to the function global( ) and not outside the function. Thus the variables x, y, z are local to the function global. Similarly one would not be able to access variable b inside the function global as such. This is because variable b is local to function main.

Global Variables: Global variables are one which are visible in any part of the program code and can be used within all functions and outside all functions used in the program. The method of declaring global variables is to declare the variable outside the function or block.

```
#include <iostream.h>
int x,y,z;      //Global Variables
float a,b,c;    //Global Variables
void main( )
{ int s,u;      //Local Variables
  float w,q;        //Local Variables      }
```

(b) Explain the syntax of switch case statement in 'C' language. Also compare the performance of switch case with if else statement.

Refer to Chapter-2, Page-25 & 26

(c) Draw a flowchart and write a program in 'C' to convert a decimal number to its octal equivalent.

Ans.

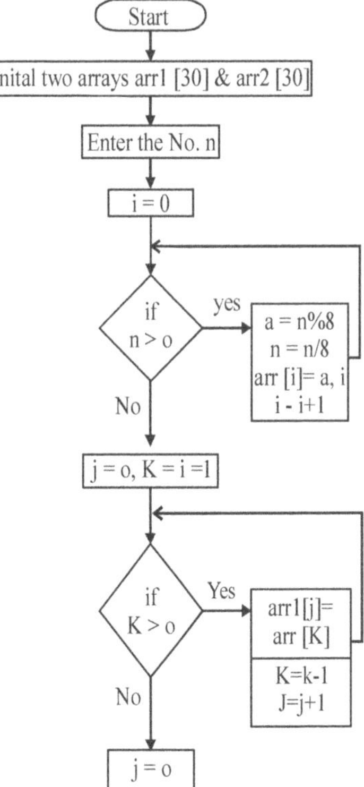

```
// Program to convert a decimal number to its octal equivalent.
#include<stdio.h>
#include<conio.h>
void main()
{
        int arr[30],arr1[30];
        int i,j,k,n,a;
        clrscr();
        printf("Enter the number:-");
        scanf("%d",&n);
        i=0;
        while(n>0)
        {
                a=n%8;
                n=n/8;
                arr[i]=a;
                i++;
        }
        for(j=0,k=i-1;k>=0;k—,j++)
        {
                arr1[j]=arr[k];
        }
        for(j=0;j<i;j++)
        {
                printf("%d",arr1[j]);
        }
        getch();
        }
```

Q3. (a) What are the precautions that must be taken care to use macros in 'C'? Define a macro to find the factorial of a given number n?

Ans. Refer to December-2005, Q.No.-4(a), Page-149

// Program to find the factorial of a given number using macro.

```
#include<stdio.h>
#include<conio.h>
#define fact(x) for(i=x-1;i>0;i—){x=x*i;}
int i;
int x;
void main()
```

```
{
        clrscr();
        fact(5);
        printf("%d",x);
        getch();
}
```

(b) Write a program in 'C' to find whether a given number is Armstrong number or not.

Refer to December-2008, Q. No.-1(c), Page-205

Q4. (a) Write program in 'C' for the multiplication of two square matrices.

Refer to December-2006, Q.No.-3 (b), Page-161

(b) What is pointer variable? How is a pointer variable declared? How is the address of a pointer variable determined? How pointer can be used to pass an entire array to a function in C? Explain with the help of an example.

Refer to Chapter-2, Page-40 to 45

Q5. (a) Explain fprintf ( ) and fscanf ( ) statements with an example of each.

Ans. fprintf() : writes a set of data values to a file

fscanf() : reads a set of data values from a file

The fprintf & fscanf functions: The fprintf and scanf functions are identical to printf and scanf functions except that they work on files. The first argument of these functions is a file pointer which specifies the file to be used. The general form of fprintf is fprintf(fp,"control string", list);

Where fp id a file pointer associated with a file that has been opened for writing. The control string is file output specifications list may include variable, constant and string.

fprintf(f1,%s%d%f",name,age,7.5);

Here name is an array variable of type char and age is an int variable

The general format of fscanf is fscanf(fp,"controlstring",list);

This statement would cause the reading of items in the control string.

(b) Write a program in 'C':

(i) To reverse a string

Ans. char * rev_string (char * str)

{

```
char temp;
int i , j;
for (i = 0 ; str[i]!= '\0' ; i++);

for(j = 0 ; j < i ; j++ , i—)
{
    temp = str[j];
    str[j] = str[i];
    str[i] = temp;
}
return str;
}
```

(ii) To copy str1 to str2 without the use of strcopy function.

Ans.

```
#include<stdio.h>
#include<conio.h>
#define m 100
void strcopy(char a[m], char b[m])
{
    int i;
for(i=0;i<m;i++)
{
b[i]=a[i];
}
return;
}

void main()
{
char a[m], b[m];
printf("Enter your array\t");
scanf("%s", a);
strcopy(a,b);
printf("Copied string\t%s", b);
getch();
}
```

MCS-011 : Problem Solving and Programming
June, 2010

Note : *Question Number 1 is* ***compulsory****. Attempt any* ***three*** *questions from the rest.*

Q1. (a) Write a program in C to search a record in an existing file and to update it.

Ans.
```
#include <stdio.h>
void main( )
{  struct record
   {  int rollno;
       char name [20];
    }rec;
   FILE *fp;
   int rn;
   fp=fopen("Rec.dat", "r+");
   if(fp==NULL)  exit(0);
     printf("\n Enter rollno you want to search:");
      scanf("%d", &rn);
   while(rec=fread(fp,(char *) &rec, sizeof (rec)))
   {  if(rec.rollno= =)rn)
      {  printf("\n Enter new name:");
          gets(rec.name);
           fwrite(fp,(char *) & rec, sizeof (rec));
        } exit (0);
        }
        fclose (fp);
        print f("\n Record not found");
}
```

(b) Explain the concept of array of pointers. Using pointers write a program to test whether the given string is a palindrome or not.

Refer to Page No.-198, Q.No.-1(d); and

```
#include<stdio.h>
void main ( )
{  char s[100];
   char *p1, *p2;
   int i, j;
   gets (s);
   for (i=0, s[i]; i++);
```

```
    i --.
    pl=s;
    p2 = & s[i];
    for (j=0, j<=i/2; j+f)
    {    if(*p1 ! = *p2)
         {   printf ("\n Not a palindrome");
             exit (0);
         }
         p1++;
         p2—;
    }
    printf("\n palindrome")'
}
```

(c) Differentiate between

(i) Various storage classes

Ans. Refer to Page No.-179, Q.No.-3(c)

(ii) Structure and union

Ans. Refer to Page No.-50, Q.No.-5

(d) Why C is called a middle level language? Give a flowchart to explain the program execution process. Explain each step in detail.

Ans. C is called a middle level language because it is a high level language and also supports low level programming features.

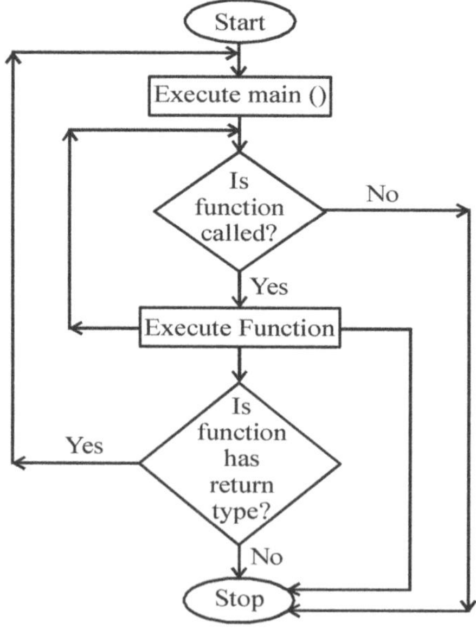

C program start by executing main(). The main() may call any other function if it does not call any function then the program will terminate after main() otherwise it will start executing the callee function which may call another function or itself, if a function having return type then the control will be transferred to caller function. The program may be terminated by other function also.

Q2. (a) Write a program to search an element in a given list of elements using linear search.

Ans.
```
#include <stdio.h>
void main ()
{   int a[10] = {1, 5, 2, 10, 6, 7, 5};
    int n=7;
    int elm;
    int i;
    print ("\n Enter element you want to search for");
    scanf("%d", & elm);
    for(i = 0; i < n; i ++)
    {  if(a[i] ==elm);
       {  printf("\n Found");
          exit (0);
       }
    }
    printf("\n Not Found");
    exit (0);
}
```

(b) Write a recursive program to calculate the factorial of a given number.

Ans. Refer to Page No.-186, Q.No.-1(c)

(c) Give an example to explain null pointer assignment.

Ans. Refer to Page No.-201, Q.No.-3(c)

Q3. (a) Write a program in C to find the multiplication of 2 matrices of size (3 x 3).

Ans.
```
#include <stdio.h>
void main()
{  int a[3][3] = {{1, 2, 3}, {4, 5, 6}, {7, 8, 9}};
   int b[3][3] = {{11, 12, 13}, {14, 15, 16}, {17, 18,19}};
   int c[3][3], i, j, k;
    for (i = 0; i < 3; i++)
```

```
for (j = 0; j < 3; j++)
{ c[i][j] = 0;
  for(k = 0; k < 3; k++)
     c[i][j] + = a[i][k] * b[k][j];
  for (i = 0; i < 3; i++)
  {     printf("\n");
    for(j = 0; j < 3; j++)
        printf("\t%.d", c[i][j]);
  }
}
```

(b) Write a macro for the following:
(i) to find largest number among 3 given numbers.
Ans. #define max(a, b, c) (a>b)?((a > c) ?a : c) : ((b > c) ? b : c)

(ii) to find cube of a given number.
Ans. #define cube(n) (n)*(n)*(n)

(c) Write a program in C, using structures to generate a report for students which displays Roll No. and Name of student, total marks obtained by the student. Assumptions can be made wherever necessary.
Ans.

```
#include <stdio.h>
struct student
{  int rollno;
   char name[20];
   int total;
};
void main()
{  struct student s[100];
   int n = 0; i;
   for (i = 0; i < 100; i++)
   { printf("\n Enter rollno:");
   scanf ("%d", & s[i].rollno);
   if (s[i].rollno ==0)
   { n = i;
     break;
   }
   printf("\n Enter name:");
   gets (s[i].name);
   printf("\n Enter total marks obtained:");
   scanf ("%d", & s[i].total);
```

```
}
printf("\n RollNo \t Name \t \t Total Marks");
for(i = 0; i < n; i++)
        printf("%d \t %20s \t %d", s[i].rollno, s[i].name,s[i].total);
}
```

Q4. (a) Write a program and flowchart to display the following pattern:

H
He
HeL
HeLL
HeLLO
HeLL
HeL
He
H

Ans.

```
#include <stdio.h>
void main()
{   char  s[6] = "Hello";
    int i, j;
    for (i = 0; i < 5; i++)
    {  printf("\n");
        for (j = 0; j < = i j++)
              printf ("%c", s[j]);
    }
    for (i = 3; i > 0; i—)
    {   printf("\n");
         for(j = 0; j < = i; j++)
              printf("%c", s[j]);
    }
}
```

Flowchart

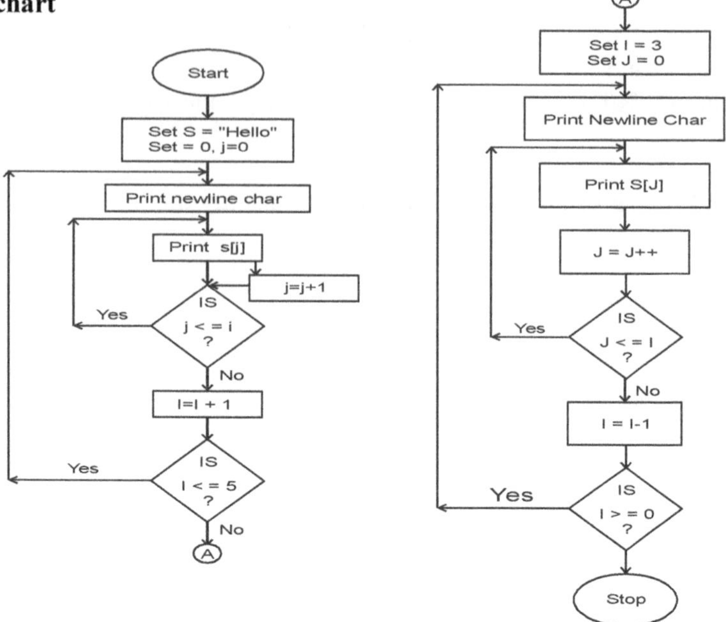

(b) Write a macro to demonstrate:
#define, #if, #else
preprocessor commands.

Ans. #define: Refer to Page No.-199, Q.No.-2(a)(i),
#if: Refer to Page No.-117, Q.No.-4(a)(i)&(ii)
#else: Refer to Page No.-117, Q.No.-4(a)(iii)

(c) Write a program in 'C' to find $1^2+3^2+5^2+7^2+9^2+......+N^2$

Ans.
```
#include <stdio.h>
void main()
{   int i,N;
    long sum = 0;
    scanf ("%d",&N);
   for (i = 1; i < = N; i = i+2)
        sum+ = i  * i;
   printf("\n sum = %td", sum);
}
```

Q5. (a) Write a program to append the contents of second file to the contents of first file.

Ans.
```
#include <stdio.h>
void main()
{   FILE  *f1, * f2;
    char e;
    f1 = fopen("abc,dat", "w+")
    f2 = fopen("xyz.dat", "r");
    while (c=fgetc(f2))
    { fputc (f1, c);
    }
    fclose(f1);
    fclose(f2);
}
```

(b) Explain the difference between a top-down approach and a bottom-up approach in programming.

Ans.

Top-down Approach	Bottom-down Approach
1. Design begins with largest component.	1. Design begins with smallest component.
2. It is based on General to specific features.	2. It is based on specific to General features.
3. Suitable for structured programming.	3. It is suitable for object oriented programming.

(c) What do you understand by a decision-control statement? Give an example of each.

Ans. Refer to Page No.-23-26

MCS-011 : Problem Solving and Programming
December, 2010

Note: *Question Number 1 is* ***compulsory****. Attempt any* ***three*** *questions from the rest.*

Q1. (a) Write an algorithm, in C to sort a given list of numbers in ascending order using bubble sort.

Ans. Refer to Page No.-177, Q.No.-3(a)

(b) What is a pointer? Give example. Write a program to swap the values using "pass by value" and "pass by reference" method.

Ans. Refer to Page No.-40, (Pointer definition) & Page No.-172, Q.No.-1(a)

(c) Explain file handling in C. What is EOF and its value? Write a program to copy one file to another.

Ans. File handling is the process through which we can store data permanently in files, manipulate it and retrieve it whenever it is required. C provides a set of library object & function for file handling. EOF is meant for End of File. It is a mark or flag in the file placed at the end of the file to denote the end of file is reached. If it is 1 then true otherwise 0.

Refer to Page No.-213, Q.No.-3(a)

(d) Explain (with example):-

(i) Unary Operators in C

Ans. Unary operator are the operators which takes only one operand to perform its operation. There are several unary operations available in C. Ex: ++, —, -, !, size of, etc.

(ii) Array

Ans. Refer to Page No.-35

(iii) Syntax and semantic errors.

Ans. Syntax errors: If the tokens of the language are not properly arranged as per specified grammatical rules (or syntax) then compiler will raise syntax error(s).

Semantic errors: If the tokens are not used accordingly to their semantics in the program then there will be semantic error or logical errors. These errors cannot be identified by the compiler they will be identified by testing activity (or process).

(iv) Sizeof operator

Ans. sizeof operator is used to return the size of the given data type or variable.
Ex:

sizeof (char) $\Rightarrow$ 1
sizeof (float) $\Rightarrow$ 4

Q2. (a) Write a program in C to display the following output:-

```
      1
    2 1 2
  3 2 1 2 3
4 3 2 1 2 3 4
  3 2 1 2 3
    2 1 2
      1
```

Ans.
```
#include <stdio.h>
void main()
{  int i, j;
   for (i = 1; i < 4; i++)
   {  printf("\n");
    for(j = 4; j x i; j—)
       print f (" ") ;
    for (; j >= i; j—)
       printf("%.d", j);
    for( j=2; j < = i; j++)
       printf("%.d", j);
   }
   for (i = 3; i > = 1; i—)
   {  printf("\n");
      for(j = 4; j > i; j—)
         printf(" ")
      for (; j > = i; j++)
         printf("%d", j);
      for(j=2; j<=i; j++)
         printf("%d", j);
   }
}
```

(b) Write a program to subtract 2 matrices of size 3x3.

Ans. Refer to Page No.-145, Q.No.-2(b)

(c) Explain function prototype with examples.

Ans. Refer to Page No.-218, Q.No.-1(b)

Q3. (a) What are various storage classes in C, give an example of each.

Ans. Refer to Page No.-179, Q.No.-3(c)

(b) Write loops that calculate the sum of given series:-
1+2+4+7+11+16+_ _ _ _ _ _ with:-

(i) do-while loop.

Ans.
```
sum = 1;
i = 1; j = 0;
  do {
        j++;
       sum +=j+i;
       i + =j;
      }while (j < = N);
```

(ii) for loop.

Ans.
```
for (sum = 1, i =1, j = 0; j < N;)
  {
   j++;
   sum + = j+i;
   i + = j;
}
```

(c) Using an example, give steps to calculate the average and worst case complexity of an algorithm.

Ans.
```
int a[N];
for (i =0; i<N-1; i++)                      ..... 1— N times
     for (j=I; j<N; j++)                    ..... 1— N times
          if (a[i] > a[j])
               swap (a[i] a[j])             ..... N(N-1)/2 times
```

$$\frac{\text{Worst Case Complexity}}{\frac{N(N-1)}{2} = (N^2)}$$

$$\frac{\text{Average Case Complexity}}{\frac{N(N-1)}{4} = (N^2)}$$

Q4. (a) Differentiate between:

(i) & and & &

Ans. & is a bitwise logical and operator while && is a logical and operator.

(ii) text and binary file

Ans. Text file store the data in ASCII character formal while binary file store the data in binary form.

(iii) pointer to function and function pointer.

Ans. Pointer to function is a pointer which points or addresses a function instead of variable. Function pointer is a variable or identifier used to map to pointer to function.

(iv) linker and loader.

Ans. Linker is a system software which is used to link the program with the library functions. It resolves the binding of the external function calls within the programs.

Loader is also a system software which resolve & reallocate the memory references in the program it helps in loading the program into the memory before execution.

(b) A C program contains the following declaration:-
int arr [3] [2]={ {1,2,}, {3,4}, {5,6} };
What is the meaning of the following:

(i) * (arr+2)

Ans. Points to the first element of third row i.e. arr[2][0].

(ii) * (* (arr)+1)+1)

Ans. Return 4 (i.e. arr[1][0] + 1)

(iii) * (* (arr)+2))

Ans. Return 5 (i.e. arr[2][0])

(iv) arr

Ans. Refer to the base address of the first element arr[0][0]

(v) (* (arr)+2)+1)

Ans. Refer 6 (i.e. arr[2][0] + 1)

(c) Write a program in C to concatenate 2 strings without using strcat ( ) function.

Ans. Refer to Page No.-210, Q.No.-1(b)(ii)

Q5. (a) Write a program in 'C' to implement binary search in a given list of numbers. Also give the average complexity of binary search.

Ans. Refer to Page No.-185, Q.No.-1(a)

The average complexity of binary search is O (log n).

(b) Using the concept of structures, write a program to display the salary, department, and other details of employees of an organisation. Make necessary assumptions wherever necessary.

Ans. Refer to Page No.-200, Q.No.-3(a)

(c) Explain dynamic memory allocation with examples.

Ans. Sometimes it is not possible to determine the requirement of size of memory at the time of program development. In this case, it is better to allocate the memory as per requirement of user or program during the execution of the program. This is accomplished by dynamic memory allocation feature of C. In this C provides 3 functions – malloc, alloc & calloc.

Ex.: char * s;

```
S = (char *) malloc (sizeof (char)*20);
```

MCS-011 : Problem Solving and Programming
June, 2011

Note : *Question Number 1 is* ***compulsory.*** *Answer* ***any three*** *questions from the rest.*

Q1. (a) What is an algorithm? Explain basic features of an algorithm.
Ans. Refer to Page No.-1 [Introduction to Algorithms]

(b) Write a C program to check whether a given string is a palindrome or not.
Ans. Refer to Page No.-107, Q.No.-1(c)

(c) Consider the following program segment in programming language C:

```
-------
sum = 0;
for (i = 1; i ≤ 10; i++)
sum + = i;
```

Write an equivalent program segment using
(i) do - while
Ans. Program code segment using do - while loop

```
sum=0;
i=1;
do
{
        sum=sum+i;
        i++;
} while(i<=10);
```

(ii) while
Ans. Program code segment using while loop

```
sum=0;
i=1;
while (i<=10)
{
        sum=sum+i,
        i++;
}
```

(d) What is a syntax - error? Give an example of syntax error in a C - program.
Ans. Refer to Page No.-232, Q.No.-1(d)(iii)

Example:

```
#include <stdio.h>
#include <conio.h>
void main( )
        {
        int a, b, c;
        printf("Enter 2 values");
        scanf("%d" "%d", &a, &b);          //Syntax error
        c = a + b;
printf("sum=" %d, &c);                     //Syntax error
getch( );
}
```

(e) Explain different arithmetical and logical operators available in C, with the help of examples.

Ans. Refer to Page No.-20 [Logical Operator]

Arithmetic operators:

+	Addition
-	Subtraction
×	Multiplication
%	Remainder/Mode
/	Divide

Example:

```
        #include <stdio.h>
        #include <conio.h>
        void main( )
        {
        int a, b, c, d;
        printf("\n Press 1 for addition");
        printf("\n Press 2 for multiplication");
        printf("\n Press 3 for division");
        printf("\n Enter your choice");
        scanf("%d", &d);
        switch(d)
        {
Case 1: printf("Enter 2 values");
        scanf("%d %d", &a, &b);
        c=a+b;
        printf("sum=%d", c);
        break;
Case 2: printf("\n Enter 2 values");
        scanf("%d %d", &a, &b);
```

```
        c=a*b;
        printf("Multiplication=%d", C);
        break;
Case 3: printf("Enter 2 values");
        scanf("%d %d", &a, &b);
        c=a/b
        printf("Division=%d", c);
        break;
default: printf("wrong choice");
        break;
        }
        getch( );
}
```

Output:

Press 1 for addition
Press 2 for multiplication
Press 3 for division
Enter your choice=1
Enter 2 values=2, 4
sum=6

(f) Explain the use of *malloc* function in C programming.

Ans. Malloc:

→ A block of memory may be allocated using the function malloc.

→ The malloc function reserve a block of memory of specified size & returns a pointer of type void. This means that we can assign it to any type of pointer. It takes the following form

Ptr=(cast_type*)malloc(byte_size);

Ptr is a pointer of type cast-type.

The malloc returns a pointer (of cast-type) to an area of memory with size byte-size. Example: x=(int*)malloc(100*size if (int));

On successful execution of this statement a memory space equivalent to "100 times the size of an int" bytes is reserved & the address of first byte of the memory allocated is assigned to the pointer x of type of int.

Similarly the statement, Cptr=(char*)malloc(10);

allocates 10 bytes of space for the pointer cptr of type char. This is illustrated as:

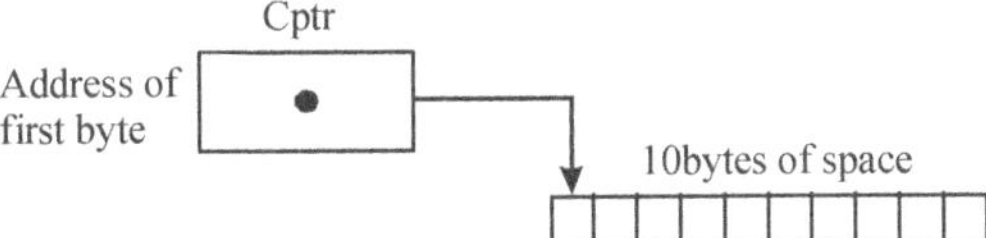

Example: /* write a program that uses a table of integers whose size will be specified interactively at rub-time.

```
#include <stdio.h>
#include <conio.h>
#include <stdlib.h>
#define NULL 0
main( )
{
int *p, *table;
int size;
printf("what is the size of table?");
scanf("%d", size);
printf("\n");
/*memory allocation*/
if(table= (int*)malloc(size * size of (int)))==NULL)
{
printf("No space available \n");
exit(1);
printf("\n Address of the first byte is %u", table);
/* Reading table values*/
printf("Input table values");
for (p=table; p<table+size; p++)
scanf("%d", &p);
/* Printing table values in reverse order*/
for(p=table+size-1; p>=table; p--)
printf("%d is stored at address %u/n", *p, p);
}
}
```

Output:

```
What is the size of the table?    5
Address of the first byte is      2262
Input table values                11    12    13    14    15
15 is stored at address 2270
14 is stored at address 2268
13 is stored at address 2266
12 is stored at address 2264
11 is stored at address 2262
```

Q2. (a) What is an array? Write a C program to add two matrices of 3 × 3 using arrays.

Ans. Refer to Page No.- 35 [Array Pointer and Arrays]

```
/*Program to add two matrices of 3×3 using array in c*/
#include <stdio.h>
#include <conio.h>
void main( )
{
int i, j;
int A[3][3];
int B[3][3];
int C[3][3]
printf("\n Enter elements of Matrix-A");
for(i=0; i < 4; i++)
{
for(j=0; j < 4; j++)
    {
scanf("%d", &A[i][j]);
    }
}
printf("\n Enter elements of Matrix-B");
for(i=0; i < 4; i++)
{
for(j=0; j < 4; j++)
    {
scanf("%d", &B[i][j]);
    }
}
printf("\n Addition of Matrix-A and Matrix-B")
for(i=0; i < 4; i++)
        {
        for(j=0; j < 4; j++)
        {
        c[i][j]=A[i][j] + B[i][j];
printf("\n Addition of Matrix-A & Matrix-B=%d", C[i][j]);
        }
}
        getch( );
        }
```

(b) What is the scope of a variable? Explain difference between global and local variable with example program.

Ans. Refer to Page No.-220, Q.No.-2(a)

Q3. (a) What is a string? Write a function in C for string concatenation without the use of inbuilt string function.

Ans. String:

→ String is collection of characters.
→ In other words, character Array is called string.
→ %s control string is used for string.
→ puts is used for printing the message on output screen i.e. puts(string_name)
→ gets is used to store the value/characters i.e. gets(string_name);
→ Declaration of string:

Syntax: Char string_name[size/Dimension];
Example: char name[10];
Now Refer to Page No.-210, Q.No.-1(b)(ii)

(b) What is a macro? Explain how a macro is defined in C. Also explain major differences between a macro and a function. Explain a situation when macro should be preferred over function with an example.

Ans. Refer to Page No.-149, Q.No.-4(a)

```
/* WAP to find maximum & minimum using macro*/
        #include <stdio.h>
        #include <conio.h>
        #define MIN 0
        #define MAX 10
        #define TRUE 1
        #define FALSE 0
        int main( )
        {
        int a;
        int okay=FALSE          /* The compiler sees this as int okay=0; */
printf("Input an integer between %d & %d", MIN, MAX);
scanf("%d", &a);
if(a>MAX)
        {
        printf("\n Too large");
        }
else if(a>MIN)
        {
        printf("\n Too small");
        }
        else
        {
```

```
        printf("Thanks");
        okay=TRUE;
        }
}
        return 0;
}
```

Q4. (a) What is a file in C programming ? Explain the use of fopen function in file handling. Explain different mode in which a file can be opened.

Ans. Refer to Page No.-54-57 [Files]

(b) What is a pointer ? Write a C program using pointer to print the name and price of the items sold in a retail shop on a specific date.

Ans. Refer to Page No.-38-42 [Pointer]

```
#include <stdio.h>
#include <conio.h>
        struct invent
        {
        Char *name[20];
        int dateofsold;
float price;
};
main( )
{
struct invent product[3], *ptr;
printf("INPUT");
for(ptr = product; ptr < product + 3; ptr++)
scanf("%s %d %f", ptr→name, &ptr→date, &ptr→price);
printf("OUTPUT \n");
ptr=product;
while(ptr < product + 3)
        {
printf("%s %d %10.2f \n", ptr→name, ptr→date, ptr→price);
ptr++;
}
}
```

Output:

```
        INPUT
        Washing machine     20/1/12     7500
        Iron                21/2/12      350
```

OUTPUT		
Washing machine	20/1/12	7500
Iron	21/2/12	350

Q5. (a) What is a structure? Explain how a structure is declared in C. Write a program in C using structure to store records of students in a class of 20 students.
Ans. Refer to Page No.-47-48 [Structures] & Page No.-228, Q.No.-3(c)

(b) Write a C program to demonstrate the use of switch - case statement.
Ans. Refer to Page No.-106, Q.No.-1(b)

(c) What is recursion ? Write a recursive C program to find the factorial of a given number.
Ans. Recursion:
→ The function that calls itself (inside function body) again & again is known as recursive function.
→ In recursion, the calling function & the called function are same.
→ Recursion is a powerful technique of solving a complicated problem in an easy way.
→ According to this technique a big problem can be solved by splitting it into smaller problems which are similar in nature to the original problem.
Now Refer to Page No.-142, Q.No.-1(c)

MCS-011 : Problem Solving and Programming
December, 2011

Note : *Question Number 1 is* ***compulsory.*** *Answer* ***any three*** *questions from the rest.*

Q1. (a) What are different basic data types in C? Explain the need of different numeric data types with example of each.

Ans. Refer to Page No.-16 [C data types]

Need of different numeric data types as follows:

(1) Integer types: Integers are whole numbers with range of values supported by a particular machine. Generally integer occupies one word of storage & since the word size of machine vary (typically 16 or 32 bits). The size of an integer that can be stored depend on the computer. If we use a 16 bit word length, the size of integer value is limited to range -32768 to +32767. A signed integer uses one bit for sign & 15 bits for the magnitude of the number.

In order to provide some control over the range of numbers & storage space, C has three classes of integer storage, namely short int, int, long int in both signed & unsigned forms.

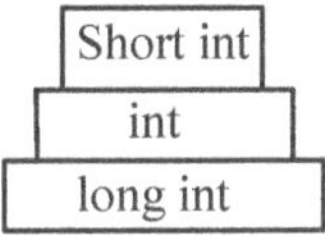

(2) Float Point types: Floating point or real numbers are stored in 32 bits with 6 digits of precision. Floating point numbers are defined in C by the keyword float. When the accuracy provided by the float number is not sufficient the type double can be used to define the number. A double data type number uses 64 bits giving a precision of 14 digits. There are known as double precision numbers. Remember that double type represents the same data type that float represents, but with a greater precision. To extend the precision further, we may use long double which uses 80 bits. The relationship among floating types is:

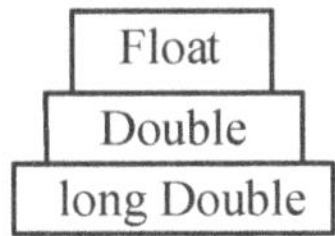

Example of integer type:

```
/* WAP to add two values input by user*/
#include <stdio.h>
#include <conio.h>
        void main( )
        {
```

```
int a, b, c;
printf ("\n Enter 2 values=");
scanf ("%d %d", &a, &b);
c=a+b;
printf ("\n sum=%d", c);
getch( );
}
```

Output:

Enter 2 values= 4, 6
sum=10
Enter 2 values= 4.2, 2.2
sum=6 (Note because integer data type is used so point values are neglected)

Examples: /* Write a Programme to calculate the area of circle using floating point*/

```
#include <stdio.h>
#include <conio.h>
void main( )
{
float r;
float pi=3.14;
float area;
printf("Enter radius in float=");
scanf("%f", &r);
area= pi*r*r;
printf("\n Area=%f", area);
getch( );
}
```

Output:

Enter radius in float=2.2
Area=15.1976

(b) Given the sizes of three different sides, write a C program to find whether a triangle can be formed or not.

Ans.

```
#include <stdio.h>
#include <conio.h>
void main( )
{ int s1, s2, s3;
printf("Enter three sides of a triangle");
scanf("%d%d%d", & s1, &s2, &s3);
if (s1+s2>s3 && s2+s3>s1 && s3+s1>s2)
printf("A triangle can be formed from these sides");
else
printf("A triangle cannot be formed from these sides.");
getch( );
}
```

(c) What are the logical operators in C? Explain how they can be used for constructing the logical expressions?

Ans. Refer to Page No.-20 [Logical Operator Example]

(d) What is an array? Write a C program using array to find largest and smallest number from a list of 100 given numbers.

Ans. Refer to Page No.-35 [Arrays] & Visit us at www.Gullybaba.com\mca\MCS-011

(e) Write a C program using *switch* to determine, whether the root of a quadratic equation is real or not.

Ans.
```
#include <stdio.h>
#include <conio.h>
#include <math.h>
void realRoots(double, double, double);          //Prototype Declaration
void imaginaryRoots(double, double, double);     //Prototype.
int main( )
{
/* Local variables*/
int option;
double a, b, c, d;
printf("Quadratic equation ax^2+bx+c=0 \n");
printf("* * * * * * * * * * * * * * * * * * * * * * * \n");
/*print list*/
printf("Real roots \n");
printf("Imaginary Roots \n");
printf("Repeated Roots \n");
printf("Exit \n");
/*Get option from user*/
scanf("%d", & option);
printf("* * * * * * * * * * * * \n");
/* Get a,b, & c from user */
printf("\n a=");
scanf("%lf", &a);
printf("b=");
scanf("%lf", &b);
printf("c=");
scanf("%lf", &c);
/*Calculate determinant*/
d=(b * b)-(4 * a * c);
/*use switch statement*/
switch(option)
{
/* If 1 was selected*/
Case'1':
        realRoots(a, b, sqrt(d))
```

```
        break;
/*If 2 was selected*/
Case '2':
imaginaryRoots(a,b,sqrt(-d));
break;
/*If 3 was selected*/
Case'3':
break;
Case'4':
break;
/*End of program*/
}
return 0;
}
/*Evaluate real roots/
void realRoots(double a, double b, double d)
{
/*calculate*/
double firstRoot=(–b/(2 * a)) + (d/(2 * a));
double secondRoot=(–b/(2 * a)) – (d/(2 * a));
/*print*/
printf("First Real Root:\t%lf\n", firstRoot);
printf("\n Second Real Root; \t%lf\n", secondRoot);
}
/*Evaluate imaginary roots*/
void imaginaryRoots(double a, double b, double d)
{
/*Calculate*/
double x=2 * a;
double first_term=(-b)/x;
double second_term=(d)/x;
/*print*/
if(second_term>=0)
{
printf("\n First Imaginary Root:\t%lf+%lf\n",first_term, second_term);
printf("\n Second Imaginary Root:\t%lf -%lf \n", first_term, second_term);
}
else
{
second_term=-(second_term);
printf("\n First Imaginary Root: \t%lf + % lf \n", first_term, second_term);
printf("\n Second Imaginary Root: \t%lf-%lf \n", first_term, second_term);
}
}
```

(f) Differentiate between call by value and call by reference using example program.

Ans. Refer to Page No.-186, Q.No.-1(b)

Q2. (a) Write a function subs(s, n) in C, which prints the first n-characters of the strings provided n is less than the length of the string.

Ans.
```
#include <stdio.h>
#include <conio.h>
void create( );
void main( )
{
char arr [10];
printf("Enter string");
gets(arr);
create(arr);
puts(arr);
getch( );
}
void create(char s)
{
if (s <strlen (arr))
{
puts(arr);
}
}
```

(b) Write a program in C to display the string "ARRAY" in the following format:

A
AR
ARR
ARRA
ARRAY

Ans.
```
#include <stdio.h>
#include <conio.h>
void main( )
        {
int i, j;
char arr[5]={'A', 'R', 'R', 'A', 'Y'};
clrscr( );
for(i=0; i<=4; i++)
{
for(j=1; j<=i-1; j++)
{
printf("%s", arr[i]);
}
```

```
printf("n");
}
getch( );
}
```

(c) What is union? How it is different from structure? Explain. How a union is declared in C? Also write a program in C to show use of union.
Ans. Refer to Page No.-48 [Union] & Page No.-50, Q.No.-5

Q3. (a) Explain the differences between static and auto variables, with example of each.
Ans. Refer to Page No.-17 [Storage Classes]

(b) Write a C program using pointer to reverse a given string.
Ans. Refer to Page No.-223, Q. No.-5(b)

(c) Explain the syntax of do-while statement. Also differentiate do-while from while statement.
Ans. Refer to Page No.-26 [Loop]

Q4. (a) What is recursion? Write a C program using recursion to print the Fibonacci series upto a given number.
Ans. Refer to Page No.-244, Q.No.-5(c) & Page No.-218, Q.No.-1(a)

(b) Write a C program using array to find the average price of apples and oranges, in ten cities in the country.

Ans.
```
#include <stdio.h>
#include <conio.h>
char apple[100];
char orange[100];
float temp;            /*temporary storage for prices entered*/
int num_count;         /* number to divide total by */
float total;           /* Total of prices entered*/
float average;         /* total divided by num_count*/
int main( )
{
printf("\n I will find the average of however many prices you enter. \n");
printf("Enter number now:");
/*Accept first input from user*/
fgets(input, sizeof(input), stdin);
temp=atof(input);
/*Initialize variables*/
num_count=0;
total=0.0;
average=0.0;
while(temp!=00.0)
```

```
{
++num_count;            /*increases with each price entered*/
total+= temp;           /* adds all prices entered to total*/
printf("Enter next number now:");
fgets(input, sizeof(input), stdin);
temp=atof(input);
        }
average=(total/num_count);
printf ("You entered % d prices. The average of those prices is % f \n", num_count,
average);
return 0;
}
```

Q5. (a) Write a C program to store string "This is my file" in a file.

Ans.

```
#include <stdio.h>
#include <conio.h>
#include <process.h>
#include <string.h>
void main( )
        {
        struct stud {
        char amrita[30];
        } s[30], st;
        int i;
        FILE *fp;
/*opening the file in write mode*/
        if((fp=fopen ("stud.dat", "w"))= =NULL)
                {
        printf("Error while creating a file \n");
                exit(0);
                }
/*reading an array of students*/
for (i = 0; i < 30; i++)
scanf("%s", s[i]);
/* write to a file*/
fwrite(s, sizeof(struct stud), 30, fp);
        fclose(fp);
        }
```

Output:

This program reads 30 records from the user, write records in the file.

(b) What is pointer to pointer? Explain need of pointer to pointer with an example. Also show how address of variable in this case is calculated/determined?

Ans. Pointer to pointer:

→ A pointer variable can be assigned the address of an ordinary variable & this variable itself could be another pointer. This means that a pointer can contain address of another pointer.

Example:

```
/* Program that declares a pointer to a pointer*/
#include <stdio.h>
#include <conio.h>
void main( )
        {
        int i=100;
        int *pi;
        int **pii;
        pi=&i;
        pii=&pi;
printf("Address of i=%u \n", &i);
printf("Address of i=%u \n", pi);
printf("Address of i=%u \n", *pii);
printf("Address of pi=%u \n", &pi);
printf("Address of pi=%u \n", pii);
printf("Address of pii=%u \n", &pii);
printf("value of i=%d \n",i);
printf("value of i=%d \n", *(&i));
printf("value of i=%d \n", *pi);
printf("value of i= %d", *pii);
}
```

Output:

```
Address of i=65524
Address of i=65524
Address of i=65524
Address of pi= 65522
Address of pi=65522
Address of pii=65520
Value of i=100
Value of i=100
Value of i=100
Value of i=100
```

MCS-011 : Problem Solving and Programming
June, 2012

Note : *Question Number 1* is **compulsory.** *Attempt* **any three** *questions from the rest.*

Q1. (a) It is said that 'C' is a middle level language. Mention those features of 'C' which enables this description. Give a short note on the 'compilation' process in 'C'.

Ans. Refer to Page No.-226, Q.No.-1(d)

Compiling a source code file in C++ is a four-step process. For example, if you have a C++ source code file named prog1.cpp and you execute the compile command g++ -Wall -ansi -o prog1 prog1.cpp

The compilation process looks like this:

(1) The C++ preprocessor copies the contents of the included header files into the source code file, generates macro code, and replaces symbolic constants defined using #define with their values.

(2) The expanded source code file produced by the C++ preprocessor is compiled into the assembly language for the platform.

(3) The assembler code generated by the compiler is assembled into the object code for the platform.

(4) The object code file generated by the assembler is linked together with the object code files for any library functions used to produce an executable file.

(b) Develop a flowchart and then write a program in 'C' to sort strings passed to the program through command line arguments. Also display the sorted strings.

Ans.

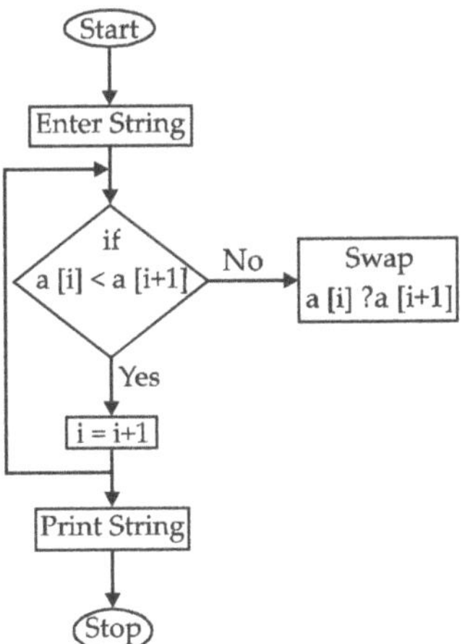

(c) Define 'pointers' in C. How is a Pointer variable declared? Give examples and explain Enumerate the utility of Pointer variables, with an example.

Ans. Refer to Page No.-40 [Pointer]

In C one can in fact declare variables to be pointers, that is variables which will hold the memory addresses of other variables.

The declaration

char *x;

declares x to be a pointer; x can now be assigned die address of a char-like variable. Similarly one can declare pointer variables to point to (i.e. hold the addresses of) ints, or longs, or floats or doubles, in short, of variables of any type, including user-defined types.

The statements

int *x, *y, z = 10;

long *p,q;

float *s;

double *t;

declare

(i) x and y to be pointer variables of type int. That is to say, x and y can hold the addresses of int like variables, such as z;

(ii) p is a pointer to longs. It can store the address of a long int, for instance of q;

(iii) s can store the addresses of float variables;

(iv) t is a pointer to double.

Utility of pointer variables are:

Pointers allow you to implement sharing without copying i.e. pass by reference v/s pass by copying. This allows a tremendous advantage when you are passing around big arrays as arguments to functions.

- Pointers allow modifications by a function that is not the creator of the memory i.e. function A can allocate the memory and function C can modify it, without using globals, which is a no-no for safe programming.
- Pointers allow us to use dynamic memory allocation.
- Pointers obviously give us the ability to implement complex data structures like linked lists, trees, etc
- Pointers allow ease of programming, especially when dealing with strings. This is due to the fact that a pointer increment will move by the size of the pointee i.e. easy coding to increment to the next memory location of an array, without worrying about how many bytes to move for each data type. I.e. a pointer to a char will move the pointer by a byte, pointer to an int, by the size of the int, etc NOTE that this is important because you do not have to worry about the size of the data types which can vary on different architectures.

• Pointers allow us to resize the data structure whenever needed. For example, if you have an array of size 10, it cannot be resized. But, an array created out of malloc and assigned to a pointer can be resized easily by creating a new memory area through malloc and copying the old contents over. This ability is very important in implementing sparse data structures also.

(d) Differentiate between:

(i) Function and sub routine

Ans. The 'Difference' Between Functions and Subroutines

Instead of the term 'subroutine', you're sure to come across the word 'function' many times as you deal with Perl and Perl resources. So let's have a look at the difference between 'function', 'subroutine', and 'operator'. The problem is that other programming languages use the terms ever so slightly differently.

Usually

In most programming languages, and in computer science in general, the following definitions apply:

• A function is something that takes a number of arguments (possibly zero), does something with term, and returns a value. A function can either be built into the programming language or it can be supplied by the user.

• An operator is a function that is usually represented by a symbol rather than a name and is almost always built into the programming language.

• A subroutine is some code provided by the user that performs an action and doesn't return a value. Unfortunately, languages like C have functions that can return nothing. These 'void functions' could be called subroutine – but they're not. That's life.

In Perl

Because some people who know other languages use the usual terms, Perl's definitions are a little confusing:

• If someone mentions a function in Perl, they almost certainly mean something built into Perl. However, they might be coming from C and mean a subroutine. The main reference documentation for Perl built-ins is called perlfunc. You can also find the complete list in Appendix C.

• An operator in Perl can have a name instead of a symbol, so it can look very much like a function. Hence, some people tend to use the terms interchangeably. Those built-ins that have symbols instead of names are documented in perlop, which also refers to 'named operators'. Perl itself peaks about the 'print operator', so we've used that terminology in this book. However, you're equally likely to hear Perl people talk about 'the print function'.

• Subroutines in Perl are akin to C's functions – they are sections of code that can take arguments, perform some operations with them, and may return a meaningful value, but don't have to.

(ii) Structure and Union with examples of each.
Ans. Refer to Page No.-47 [Structures & Union]

(e) Give the precedence chart for the operator in 'C'.
Ans. Refer to Page No.-187, Q.No.-1(d)

Q2. (a) Differentiate between an execution error and a syntax error. Give examples of execution and syntax errors.
Ans. Refer to Page No.-237, Q.No.-1(d)
Execution errors: While executing the function, S-PLUS encounters an error such as an undefined operation. One such example is plotting *x* against *y* with *x* and *y* having different lengths. S-PLUS stone the execution and we need to track where the error source originates. Most of the time, S-PLUS tells us Error in …
If the execution was aborted in a statement that is not the origin of the error, as when we try to plot only missing values, we need to find the source with tools referenced in the following item.
Example for syntax error

```
void main()
{
        printf("hello World ")   /* ; Statement missing  */
}
```

If you try to compile this programme in Turbo C/C++ compiler , it will shoot out the familiar error message
"Error : Statement ; missing in function main()" since because as per the C language grammar parser will look for a ; symbol as a terminator after or end of each executable statement in this case delimiter ; is missing and hence its termed as syntax error .
Example for runtime error

```
void main()
{
        int i  = 10;
        int j =  i / 0;
        printf("%d", j);
}
```

if you compile this programme sure it won't show you an error, but there is a serious error which the compiler could not identify >> " i / 0" this would generate a divide by 0 error and terminate the application without any consideration

(b) Write and explain the action of 'WHILE' statement. Develop a program to compute the average of every 3rd integer lying between 1 and 100.

Ans. The while Loop

When in a program a single statement or a certain group of statements are to be executed repeatedly depending upon certain test condition, then while statement is used.

The syntax is as follows:

```
While (test condition)
{
        Body _ of _ the _ loop;
}
```

Here, test condition is an expression that controls how long the loop keeps running. Body of the loop is a statement or group of statements enclosed in braces and are repeatedly executed till the value of test condition evaluates to true. As soon as the condition evaluates to false, the control jumps to the first statement following the while statement. If condition initially itself is false, the body of the loop will never be executed. While loop is sometimes called as entry-control loop, as it controls the execution of the body of the loop depending upon the value of the test condition.

```
# include <iostreem.h>
# include <canio.h>
void main ( )
{
        int i, sum = 0, count = 0, avg
        for (i = 1; i< = 100; i = i + 3)
        {
                count ++;
                sum = sum + i;
        }
        avg = sum/count;
        printf ("The average is % d", avg);
}
```

(c) Write a program in 'C' to copy the contents of one file to another file.

Ans. Refer to Page No.-232, Q.No.-1(c)

Q3. (a) Write a program in 'C' to compute the series:

$$(x)+(x+n)+\left(x+n^2\right)+\left(x+n^3\right)+....$$

for a total of m terms.

Where m, n and *x* are to be accepted by the user.

Ans.

```
# include <stdio.h>
void main ( )
```

```
{
        int x, m, n, i, j;
        int sum = 0, prod = 1;
        printf ("Enter no. of terms");
        scanf ("%d", &m);
        printf ("Enter first and second term of series");
        scanf ("%d %d", &x, &n);
        for (i = 1; i < m; i++)
        {
                for (j = 1; j <= i; j++)
                {
                        prod = prod * n;
                }
                Sum = sum + (x + prod);
        }
        printf ("The result of series is %d", x + sum);
}
```

(b) Differentiate between goto statement, break and continue.

Ans. The goto statement: The **goto** statement is used to alter the normal sequence of program instruction by transferring the control to some other portion of the program. The syntax is as follows:

goto label;

Here, **label** is an identifier that is used to label the statement to which control will be transferred. The targeted statement must be preceded by the unique label followed by colon.

Label : statement;

The break statement: Sometimes, it is required to jump out of a loop irrespective of the conditional test value. **Break** statement is used inside any loop to allow the control jump to the immediate statement following the loop. The syntax is as follows:

break;

When nested loops are used, then **break** jumps the control from the loop where it has been used. Break statement can be used inside any loop i.e., while, do-while, for and also in switch statement.

The continue statement: Unlike *break* statement, which is used to jump the control out of the loop, it is sometimes required to skip some part of the loop and to continue the execution with next loop iteration. ***Continue*** statement used inside the loop helps to bypass the section of a loop and passes the control to the beginning of the loop to continue the execution with the next loop iteration. The syntax is as follows:

continue;

(c) What is an assignment operator? Give example of its usage.

Ans. C provides an assignment operator for this purpose. The function of this operator is to assign the assignment operator for this purpose. The function of this operator is to assign the values or values in variables on right hand side of an expression to variables on the left hand side.

The syntax of the assignment expression is as follows:

Variable = constant / variable / expression;

The data type of the variable on left hand side should match the data type of constant/variable/expression on right hand side with a few exceptions where automatic type conversions are possible. Some examples of assignment statements are as follows:

```
b = a;        /* b is assigned the value of a */
b = 5;        /* b is assigned the value of 5 */
b = a+5;      /* b is assigned the value of expr a+5 * /
```

(d) What is a pointer to an array? Differentiate it from an array of pointers. Write a program using pointer to array to calculate the sum of n given numbers.

Ans. Refer to Page-35 [Array]

A pointer is a data spot that holds the location of another data spot. Meaning if P is a pointer its data is some hex code which is a location in memory. That location could be another pointer or actual data. So if Q is actual data (int), P could be a pointer to Q and by referencing P you traverse to the location Q to read the data stored in Q. In P is the location of Q, In Q is the data assigned. An array of pointers is an array that stores different pointers (each pointing to what-ever it is pointing). A pointer of an array is a Pointer that points to an array (meaning the it has the location of the array).

Arrays are designed so that the elements are stored in location one after the other so by having P++ (adding one to the base value of the pointer that points to the beginning of the array) You change it to hold the location of the next value of the array.

```
//Program to sum of n numbers
void main()
{
        int n=0,i,*p;
        clrscr();
        printf("enter the value of n");
        scanf("%d",&n);
        p=&n;
        for(i=0;i<=n;i++)
```

```
        {
                *p=*p+i;
        }
        printf("value of the sum is %d",*p);
        getch();
}
```

Q4. (a) Implement Binary search in 'C' language.

Ans. Refer to Page No.-236, Q.No.-5(a)

(b) With every use of a memory allocation function, what function must be used to release allocated memory which is no longer used? Give syntax also.

Ans. Free()

When you allocate memory with either malloc() or calloc(), it is taken from the dynamic memory pool that is available to your program. This pool is sometimes called the *heap,* and it is finite. When your program finishes using a particular block of dynamically allocated memory, you should deallocate, or free, the memory to make it available for future use. To free memory that was allocated dynamically, use free(). Its prototype is

void free(void *ptr);

The free() function releases the memory pointed to by ptr. This memory must have been allocated with malloc(), calloc(), or realloc(). If ptr is NULL, free() does nothing. Sample program below demonstrates the free() function.

(c) Write a recursive function in 'C' to count the number of nodes in a singly linked list.

Ans. Code for Program to find the number of nodes in the linked list using recursion in C Programming

```
#include <stdio.h>
#include <conio.h>
#include <alloc.h>
/* structure containing a data part and link part */
struct node
{
        int data ;
         struct node *link ;
} ;
        void append ( struct node **, int ) ;
        int length ( struct node * ) ;
        void main( )
```

```
{
        struct node *p ;
        p = NULL ; /* empty linked list */
        append ( &p, 1 ) ;
        append ( &p, 2 ) ;
        append ( &p, 3 ) ;
        append ( &p, 4 ) ;
        append ( &p, 5 ) ;
        clrscr( ) ;
        printf ( "Length of linked list = %d", length ( p ) ) ;
}
        /* adds a node at the end of a linked list */
        void append ( struct node **q, int num )
{
        struct node *temp ;
        temp = *q ;
        if ( *q == NULL ) /* if the list is empty, create first node */
        {
                *q = malloc ( sizeof ( struct node ) ) ;
                 temp = *q ;
        }
        else
        {
                 /* go to last node */
                while ( temp -> link != NULL )
                temp = temp -> link ;
                 /* add node at the end */
                temp -> link = malloc ( sizeof ( struct node ) ) ;
                temp = temp -> link ;
        }
        /* assign data to the last node */
        temp -> data = num ;
        temp -> link = NULL ;
}
        /* counts the number of nodes in a linked list */
        int length ( struct node *q )
        {
                staticint l ;
                /* if list is empty or if NULL is encountered */
                if ( q == NULL )
                return ( 0 ) ;
                else
```

```
        {
                /* go to next node */
                l = 1 + length ( q -> link ) ;
                return ( l ) ;
        }
}
```

Q5. (a) How are arrays processed in 'C'? Illustrate with the help of 2-D arrays as examples,

Ans. Array usually process one element at a time. If you want to process all elements of an array, write a loop.

Now Refer to Page No.-214, Q.No.-4(a)

(b) Give syntax of gets ( ) and getch ( )? Also give examples of usage of scanf ( )and printf ( ).

Ans. Syntax for getch () in C:

variable_name = getch();

getch() accepts only single character from keyboard. The character entered through getch() is not displayed in the screen (monitor).

Syntax for gets() in C:

gets(variable_name);

gets() accepts any line of string including spaces from the standard Input device (keyboard). gets() stops reading character from keyboard only when the enter key is pressed.

The unformatted output statements in C are **putch, putchar** and **puts.**

Printf()

printf("*format-string*", *expression, ...*);

The *format-string* can contain regular characters which are simply printed out, and *format specifications* or *place-holders*. For each place-holder in the format-string there must be one matching expression. The expressions are converted to strings according to the instructions in the corresponding place-holder and are mixed with the regular text in the format-string. Then the whole string is output. Here's an example:

printf("%i + %i = %i\n", 2, 3, (2+3));

will produce the following output (by converting the three integer arguments to strings using default formatting):

2 + 3 = 5

Scanf()

scanf("*conversion-string*", *&variable, ...*);

The conversion-string can contain three types of directives:

Regular characters: This is text that must be matched character by character with the input. Such entries are rarely used for interactive programs, but can be handy when working with formatted input files.

White-space characters: A blank, tab, or other white-space character will match any amount (including none) of any white-space. (So a single space will match any string of white-space, including newlines.) Note that it is legal for this to match no input at all (if there isn't a blank or tab, it is ok).

Conversion Specifiers: Similar to printf conversion specifiers but just different enough to cause many errors. They all begin with a per cent and end with a letter indicating the type of conversion. In between can be some special conversion controls, including the *length*. Unlike printf, failing to use the exact type and length for the conversion will result in unpredictable errors. Since few compilers will check the conversion-string for argument mis-matches, the result is a runtime (logic) error that can be hard to find. These conversion specifiers match a string of characters in the input, convert to the specified type (and length), and store the result in the RAM address provided by the corresponding argument. (The most common error with scanf is **not** using the *address-of* operator in front of a variable name for the argument.)

(c) A program in 'C' language contains the following decleration:
Static int x[8]={1, 2, 3, 4, 5, 6, 7, 8};
What is the meaning of:
(i) x?

Ans. x is the name of array and it is used to store the memory address of very first element of array, i.e. x[0] = 1.

(ii) (x+2)?

Ans. (x + 2) will store the address of x[2], i.e. 3. As it is an integer array and will move to 4 bytes on adding 2 to base address.

(iii) *x?

Ans. *n is value at pointer which is used to tell the value stored at the first address of location.
O/P: 1

(iv) Explain the results. *(x+2)?

Ans. O/P = 3
Value at address of x[2].

MCS-011 : Problem Solving and Programming
December, 2012

Note : *Question Number 1* is ***compulsory***. *Attempt* ***any three*** *questions from the rest.*

Q1. (a) Draw a flowchart and then develop an interactive 'C' program which finds whether a given integer number is prime or not. Make the use of a function subprogram.

Ans.

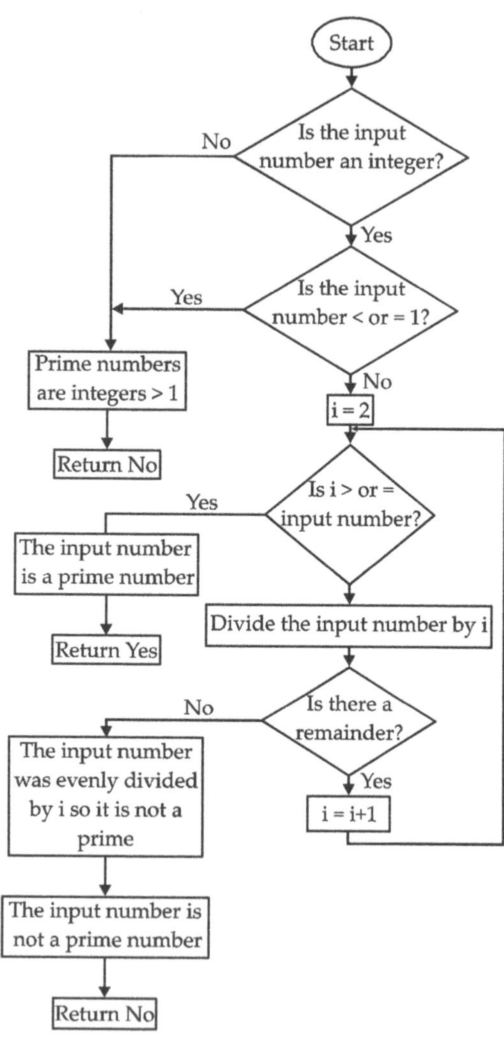

Program

```
#include<stdio.h>
int main()
{
	int num,i,count=0;
	printf("Enter a number: ");
	scanf("%d",&num);
	for(i=2;i<=num/2;i++)
	{
		if(num%i==0)
		{
			count++;
			break;
		}
	}
	if(count==0 && num!= 1)
	printf("%d is a prime number",num);
	else
	printf("%d is not a prime number",num);
	return 0;
}
```

(b) Differentiate between various storage classes in 'C'.

Ans. Refer to Page No.-179, Q.No.-3(c)

(c) Write down a recursive function in 'C' to calculate the factorial of a given number.

Ans. Refer to Page No.-186, Q.No.-1(c)

(d) Explain the concept of pointer to an array. Write a program in 'C' to copy the contents of an array to another array using pointers.

Ans. Refer to June-2012, Q.No.-3(d)

Copy Array Elements from one array to another

```
//a - Source Array ( elements will be copied from this array)
//b - Destination array ( elements copied into this array)
//- - - - - - - - - - - - - - - - - - - - - - - - - - - - - - - - - - - - - - - - -
#include<stdio.h>
#include<conio.h>
void main()
{
	int a[30],b[30],i,n;
```

```
        // Element of an array 'a' will be copied into array 'b'
        printf("n Enter no of elements :");
        scanf("%d",&n);
        /* Accepting values into Array a*/
        printf("n Enter the values :");
        for (i = 0 ; i < n ; i++)
        scanf("%d",&a[i]);
        /* Copying data from array 'a' to array 'b */
        for (i = 0 ;i < n ; i++)
        b[i]=a[i];
        /* printing of all elements of array */
        printf("the copied array is :");
        for(i=0;i < n;i++)
        printf("nb[%d]=%d",i,b[i]);266
        getch();
}
```

(e) Write a 'C' program that will enter a line of text, store it in an array and then display backwards. The length of the line should be undefined (being terminated by ENTER key), but less than 80 characters.

Ans.

```
# include <stdio.h>
/* Function to print reverse of the passed string */
void reverse(char *str)
{
        if(*str)
        {
                reverse(str+1);
                printf("%c", *str);
        }
}

        /* Driver program to test above function */
        int main()
{
        char a[] = "Geeks for Geeks";
        reverse(a);
        getchar();
        return 0;
}
```

Q2. (a) Explain null pointer assignment. Also give an example of use of null pointer.

Ans. Refer to Page No.-201, Q.No.-3(c)

(b) Write a macro for the following:
(i) to find square of a given number.
Ans. Same as Page No.-228, Q.No.-3(b)(ii)

(ii) to find smallest of 3 given number.
Ans. Refer to Page No.-199, Q.No.-2(b)(i)

(c) Write a program in 'C' to enter two 4×4 matrices and to display the product of these matrices. Explain and give suitable documentation.
Ans. // Program to multiply two matrices

```
#include<stdio.h>
int main()
{
        int a[5][5],b[5][5],c[5][5];
        int i,j,k,sum=0,m,n,o,p;
        printf("\nEnter the row and column of first matrix");
        scanf("%d %d",&m,&n);
        printf("\nEnter the row and column of second matrix");
        scanf("%d %d",&o,&p);
        if(n!=o)
        {
                printf("Matrix mutiplication is not possible");
                printf("\nColumn of first matrix must be same as row of
                second
                matrix");
        }
        else
        {
                printf("\nEnter the First matrix->");
                for(i=0;i<m;i++)
                for(j=0;j<n;j++)
                scanf("%d",&a[i][j]);
                printf("\nEnter the Second matrix->");
                for(i=0;i<o;i++)
                for(j=0;j<p;j++)
                scanf("%d",&b[i][j]);
                printf("\nThe First matrix is\n");
                for(i=0;i<m;i++)
                {
                        printf("\n");
```

```
                    for(j=0;j<n;j++)
                    {
                              printf("%d\t",a[i][j]);
                    }
          }
          printf("\nThe Second matrix is\n");
          for(i=0;i<o;i++)
          {
                    printf("\n");
                    for(j=0;j<p;j++)
                    {
                              printf("%d\t",b[i][j]);
                    }
          }
          for(i=0;i<m;i++)
          for(j=0;j<p;j++)
          c[i][j]=0;
          for(i=0;i<m;i++){//row of first matrix
          for(j=0;j<p;j++){//column of second matrix
          sum=0;
          for(k=0;k<n;k++)
          sum=sum+a[i][k]*b[k][j];
          c[i][j]=sum;
     }
     printf("\nThe multiplication of two matrix is\n");
     for(i=0;i<m;i++)
     {
          printf("\n");
          for(j=0;j<p;j++)
          {
                    printf("%d\t",c[i][j]);
          }
     }
     return 0;
}
```

Q3. (a) Write a program and flowchart to display the following:

```
    A
  B A B
C B A B C
  B A B
    A
```

Ans.
```
# include <stdio.h>
void main ( )
```

```
{
        int i, j, k;
        for (i = 1; i < 4; i++)
        for (j = 4; j < i; j—)
        printf (" ");
        for (k = 32; j > = i; j—, k++)
        printf ("%c", k);
}
        for (i = 3; i > = 1; i- -)
{
        printf ("\n");
        for (j = 4; j > i; j—)
        printf (" ");
        for (k = 32; j > = i; j++, k++)
        printf ("%d", k);
        for (j = 2; j < = i; j++)
        printf ("%d", j);
}
```

(b) Give the syntax of getch( ) and gets( ). Give examples also.
Ans. Refer to June-2012, Q.No.-5(b)

(c) Explain the action of do-while statement. With an example.
Ans. Refer to Page No.-30 [Do-while loop]

(d) What is the difference between a call by value and call by reference? Explain with examples.
Ans. Refer to Page No.-186, Q.No.-1(b)

Q4. (a) Write a C program to create a file and copy the contents of another given file into this newly created file.
Ans. Refer to Page No.-232, Q.No.-1(c)

(b) What is # ifdef? Give an example to explain use of # ifdef.
Ans. Refer to Page No.-19, Q.No.-19
#ifdef
#ifdef — Conditional reading of code.
Description
If a macro is defined then *#ifdef* can incorporate text into an orchestra upto the next *#end*. This is similar to, but independent of, the *macro system in the score language*.

Syntax

```
#ifdef NAME
....
#else
....
#end
```

#ifdef example

This example uses #ifdef to check for a identifier named DEBUG to determine if extra code should be included to display trace information in the results pane of the Command window:

```
#define DEBUG // Comment out if not debug version
#ifdef DEBUG
#define TRACE(m) ? m
#else
#define TRACE(m)
#endif
...
// Process names in list
if form.rowset.first( )
do
TRACE( form.rowset.fields[ "Last name" ].value ) // Display name as we go
// Do whatever
until not form.rowset.next( )
endif
```

(c) Differentiate between a structure and a union. Write a structure for a student and write a 'C' program to display the marks of the student for five subjects and also calculate the percentage of marks obtained.

Ans. Refer to Page No.-47 [Structures and Union] & Page No.-228, Q.No.-3(c).

Q5. (a) Give the syntax and examples of usage of scanf( ) and printf( ).

Ans. Refer to June-2012, Q.No.-5(b)

(b) Give 5 distinctive features of 'C' which states it to be a structured programming. What are the differences between a low level, a middle level and a high level language. Give examples.

Ans. The C language has the following characteristics:

• There is a small, fixed number of keywords, including a full set of flow of control primitives: for, if/else, while, switch, and do/while. There is basically one namespace, and user-defined names are not distinguished from keywords by any kind of sigil.

• There are a large number of arithmetical and logical operators, such as +, +=, ++, &, ~, etc.

- More than one assignment may be performed in a single statement.
- Function return values can be ignored when not needed.
- Typing is static, but weakly enforced: all data has a type, but implicit conversions can be performed; for instance, characters can be used as integers.

Low-Level

Of all of the categories, it's probably easiest to define what it means to be a low-level language. Machine code is low level because it runs directly on the processor. Low-level languages are appropriate for writing operating systems or firmware for micro-controllers. They can do just about *anything* with a little bit of work, but obviously you wouldn't want to write the next major web framework in one of them (I can see it now, "Assembly on Rails").

Characteristics

- Direct memory management
- Little-to-no abstraction from the hardware
- Register access
- Statements usually have an obvious correspondence with clock cycles
- Superb performance

Mid-Level

This is where things start getting vague. Most high-level languages are well defined, as are low-level languages, but mid-level languages tend to be a bit difficult to box. I really define the category by the size of application I would be willing to write using a given language. I would have no problem writing and maintaining a large desktop application in a mid-level language (such as Java), whereas to do so in a low-level language (like Assembly) would lead to unending pain.

Characteristics

- High level abstractions such as objects (or functionals)
- Static typing
- Extremely commonplace (mid-level languages are by far the most widely used)
- Virtual machines
- Garbage collection
- Easy to reason about program flow

High-Level

High-level languages are really interesting if you think about it. They are essentially mid-level languages which just take the concepts of abstraction and high-level constructs to the extreme. For example, Java is mostly object-oriented, but it still relies on primitives which are represented directly in memory. Ruby on the other hand is *completely* object-oriented. It has no primitives (outside of the runtime implementation) and everything can be treated as an object.

Characteristics

- Interpreted
- Dynamic constructs (open classes, message-style methods, etc)

- Poor performance
- Concise code
- Flexible syntax (good for internal DSLs)
- Hybrid paradigm (object-oriented *and* functional)
- Fanatic community

(c) Write a program to display the following patterns:

```
1 2 3 4 5
  2 3 4 5
    3 4 5
      4 5
        5
```

Ans.
```
# include <stdio.h>
void main ( )
{
        int i, j;
        for (i = 0; i < 5; i++)
        {
                for (j = 1; j < i; j++)
                {
                        printf (" ");
                }
                for (j = i + 1; j < = 5; j++)
                {
                        printf ("%d", j);
                }
                printf ("\n");
        }
}
```

(d) What is array of pointers to string? Declare an array of pointers to string having names of your five friends.

Ans. Refer to June-2008, Q.No.-1(d)

Declare an array of pointer to string having names of your five friends

char* names_of_days_of_friends[] =
{"Sumit", "Deepak", "Ritu", "Divya", "Neha"

Array of pointers to string C programming forum discussing all C derivatives, including C#, C++, Object-C, and even plain old vanilla C. These languages are low level languages, and used on projects such as device drivers, compilers, and even whole computer operating systems.

MCS-011 : Problem Solving and Programming
June, 2013

Note: *Question number 1 is **compulsory**. Attempt **any three** questions from the rest.*

Q1. (a) Explain type cast and size of operator in C language with example.

Ans. An operator is a symbol or string of C characters used as a function. Type Cast operator uses in convert one data type to another data types. Type casting may be two types:

- Implicit type cast
- Explicit type cast

Implicit type cast: In C, implicit type cast are automatically handled by compiler i.e. when two or more data types are getting execution then the final data-type will be that data type as it is declared, i.e it is not depend on conversion of data type.

It is clear understand by example as:

```
#include<stdio.h>
#include<conio.h>
void main()
{
 int i,j;
 float f;
 double d;
 i=d*f+f*j;
}
```

Explicit type cast: An explicit type cast is a cast that we should specify invoke with either the cast. The compiler does not automatically invoke to resolve the data type conversion.

Let's understand explicit with example:

```
/*A student marks of three subject as m1,m2,m3 and calculate Percentage(per)*/
#include<stdio.h>
#include<conio.h>
void main()
{
 int m1=70,m2=70,m3=100,total;
 float per;
 total=m1+m2+m3;
 per=total/300*100;6
 printf("%f",per);
}
```

The sizeof operator returns the size of its operand in bytes. The sizeof operator always precedes its operand. The operand may be an expression or it may be a cast.

Example:

Suppose i is an integer variable and c is a character type variable then
Printf("Size of integer : %d",sizeof(i));
Printf("Size of character : %c",sizeof(c));
Might generate the following output :
Size of integer : 2
Size of character : 1

(b) Write an algorithm to check whether the given number is prime or not.

Ans. step 1:start
step 2:input num
step 3:for(i=2 to num/2)do step 4
step 4: if(num%i==0)
output("the number is not prime")
else
output("thenumber is prime")
end if
end of step 3 loop
step 5:stop

(c) What is the difference between High level language and low level language? Why C is referred as middle level language?

Ans. High level languages allow much more abstraction than low level languages. This allows algorithms and functions to be written without requiring detailed knowledge of the hardware used in the computing platform. The compiler provides this interface transparently for the programmer.

Low level languages will require more involvement with the actual register and interrupt interfaces to the hardware. This can provide more control and efficiency for the program and can be good for applications which need high speed execution, but high level compilers are much better at optimising for speed now.

Examples of high level languages include C, C++, Java, etc.

Examples of low level languages include machine language specific to each processor and assembly language specific to each processor.

C is often called a middle-level computer language as it combines the elements of high-level languages with the functionalism of assembly language.

(d) How many bytes are assigned to store for following :
(i) Double
(ii) Unsigned char
(iii) Unsigned integer

Ans:

Type	**Size (bytes)**
Unsigned char	1 byte
Unsigned integer	4 bytes
double	8 bytes

(e) Write a program segment to generate the ' following pattern using *"for"* and *"while loop"*

```
*
* *
* * *
* * * *
```

Ans:

```
#include<stdio.h>
#include<conio.h>

int main()
{

    while(i>=5)      //for(int i=0; i<=5; i++)
    {           for(int j=0; j<i; j++)
            {
                printf(" * ");
            }
            printf("\n");
    }
    getch();
}
```

(f) Explain the concept of stepwise refinement technique.

Ans: Step-wise refinement is a technique for software development using a top-down, structured approach to solving a problem. It allows the developer to use a controlled method of developing an algorithm That will eventually solve a given problem.

The pseudo-code describes a general, non-specific way to solve the problem deferring the actual decisions until last minute. That way the developer can assign place-holders in the logic until they are actually needed. Then, each step involves the use of refining (adding the logic) a step in the development of the algorithm to make it more specific, doing so one step at at time. When everything has been refined you have a complete program; however, it takes multiple steps (step-wise refining) to get to that point where a complete, syntactically correct program emerges.

(g) Give the C expression for the following algebraic expression :

(i) ab^4c^2 — d/m-n

Ans.
```
main()
{
int a,b,c,d,m,n;
        float s;
        clrscr();
        printf("enter the values of  a,b,c,d,e,m,n ");
         scanf("%d%d%d%d %d %d %d ",&a,&b,&c,&d,&e,&m,&n);
         s= (a*(b*b*b*b)*(c*c)-(d/(m-n)));
       printf("the value of s=%f",s);
        getch();
}
```

(ii) ab — [(e + f)^9 /c]

Ans.
```
main()
{
int a,b,c,e,f;
        float s;
        clrscr();
        printf("enter the values of  a,b,c,e,f ");
         scanf("%d%d%d%d %d %d %d ",&a,&b,&c,&e,&f);
        s= ((a*b-
((e+f)*(e+f)*(e+f)*(e+f)*(e+f)*(e+f)*(e+f)*(e+f)*(e+f))/c);
       printf("the value of s=%f",s);
        getch();
}
```

(h) What is a logical error? Give an example of logical error in C.

Ans: In computer programming, a **logic error** is a bug in a program that causes it to operate incorrectly, but not to terminate abnormally. It is also called semantic errors. It is a type of runtime error that may simply produce the wrong output or may cause a program to crash while running.

```
int average(int a, int b)
{
   return a + b / 2;     /* should be (a + b) / 2 */
}
```

Q2. (a) What is a structure? How structures are passed as function arguments? Explain with an example.

Ans. Refer to Page No.-47-48 [Structures] & Page No.-228, Q.No.-3(c)

```
#include <stdio.h>
#include <stdlib.h>
#define EMPLOYEE_COUNT 4
struct ewage
{
      int ssn;
      int wage;
}

struct record
{
      int totalwage;
}

int compare(struct ewage s1, struct ewage s2, struct record *r);

int main (void)
{
   struct ewage e[EMPLOYEE_COUNT];
   struct record r[EMPLOYEE_COUNT];
   int i, j;
   for (i = 0; i < EMPLOYEE_COUNT; i ++)
   {
      for (j = i + 1; j < EMPLOYEE_COUNT; j ++)
 {
         int success = compare(e[i], e[j], &record[i]);
         if (success == 1)
                printf ("%d / %d | Record: %d \n", i, j, record[i]);
         else
                printf ("%d / %d | DOES NOT MATCH \n", i, j);
      }
   }
   system ("PAUSE");
   return 0;
}
int compare(struct ewage s1, struct ewage s2, struct record *r)
{
      if (s1.ssn == s2.ssn)
     {
            r->totalwage = s1.wage + s2.wage;
            return 1;
      }
      return 0;
}
```

(b) What is an array? How arrays are declared and initialized? Write a C program to add two matrices of 3 x 3 using arrays.

Ans. Refer to Page No.-240 Q.No.-2(a)

Q3. (a) Write a program to find out square and cube of given number using macros.

Ans.
```
#include<stdio.h>
#define SQUARE(A, B) (A * B)
#define CUBE (A, B,C) (A * B * C)
int main()
{
 int num1, num2, square, cube;
 printf("\nEnter the Two numbers\n");
 scanf("%d%d",&num1,&num2);
 square=SQUARE(num1,num2);
 cube=CUBE(num1,num2,num3);
 printf("\n\nSum of two numbers using Macros is:%d\n",square);
 printf("\n\nProduct of two numbers using macros is:%d\n",cube);
 return 0;
}
```

(b) What is # define preprocessor in C. How it is implemented and used in C?

Ans. Refer to Page No.-199, Q.No.-2(a)(i)

(c) What is a string ? Write a function in C to convert lower case letters to upper case letters in a given string without using strupp?

Ans. Refer to Page No.-242, Q.No.-3(a),
```
#include <stdio.h>
#include <conio.h>
main()
{
char ch[30];
char ch2[30];
printf("enter a string to convert\n")
gets(ch);
ch2=uppercase(ch);
printf("%c is uppercase of %c, ch2, ch);
getch();
}

uppercase(char s[30])
```

```
{
int i=0;
while (s[i]!='\0')
{
if(s[i]>96 &&s[i]<123)
s[i]=s[i]-32;
i++;
}
return (s[30]);
}
```

Q4. (a) What are address and indirection operators in C? How strings are declared through pointers? Write a program that test a string for a palindrome using pointer notation.

Ans. The indirection operator (*) accesses a value indirectly, through a pointer. The operand must be a pointer value. The result of the operation is the value addressed by the operand; that is, the value at the address to which its operand points. The type of the result is the type that the operand addresses.

The & (address) operator yields a pointer to its operand. The operand of the address-of operator can be either a function designator or an l-value that designates an object that is not a bit field and is not declared with the **register** storage-class specifier.

use a *character pointer* to keep track of a string.

```
char label[] = "Single";
char label2[10] = "Married";
char *labelPtr;
labelPtr = label;
```

Refer to Page No.-163, Q.No.-4(a)

(b) Give the types of file supported in C. Explain formulated Input/ Output functions as well as string Input/Output functions.

Ans. C programming language treats all the devices as files. C supports header files, Binary files, and text files.

The getchar() & putchar() functions

The **int getchar(void)** function reads the next available character from the screen and returns it as an integer. This function reads only single character at a time. You can use this method in the loop in case you want to read more than one characters from the screen.

The **int putchar(int c)** function puts the passed character on the screen and returns the same character. This function puts only single character at a time. You can use this method in the loop in case you want to display more than one character on the screen. Check the following example:

```
#include <stdio.h>
```

```
int main( )
{
  int c;

  printf( "Enter a value :");

  c = getchar( );
  printf( "\nYou entered: ");
  putchar( c );
 return 0;
}
```

The gets() & puts() functions

The **char *gets(char *s)** function reads a line from **stdin** into the buffer pointed to by **s** until either a terminating newline or EOF.

The **int puts(const char *s)** function writes the string s and a trailing newline to **stdout**.

```
#include <stdio.h>
int main( )
{
  char str[100];
  printf( "Enter a value :");
  gets( str );
  printf( "\nYou entered: ");
  puts( str );
  return 0;
}
```

The scanf() and printf() functions

The **int scanf(const char *format, ...)** function reads input from the standard input stream **stdin** and scans that input according to **format** provided.

The **int printf(const char *format, ...)** function writes output to the standard output stream **stdout** and produces output according to a format provided.

The **format** can be a simple constant string, but you can specify %s, %d, %c, %f, etc., to print or read strings, integer, character or float respectively. There are many other formatting options available which can be used based on requirements. For a complete detail you can refer to a man page for these function. For now let us proceed with a simple example which makes things clear:

```
include <stdio.h>
int main( )
```

```
{
  char str[100];
  int i;
  printf( "Enter a value :");
  scanf("%s %d", str, &i);
  printf( "\nYou entered: %s, %d ", str, i);
  return 0;
}
```

Q5. (a) Explain the use of following functions in C:
(i) Calloc function
Ans. Refer to Page No.-192, Q.No.-3(b)(4)

(ii) realloc function
Ans. Refer to Page No.-192, Q.No.-3(b)(5),

(iii) fseek ( )
Ans. fseek(): sets the file position of the stream to the given offset. The argument offset signifies the
number of bytes to seek from the given whence position.
Function prototype/syntax: int fseek(FILE *stream, long int offset, int whence)

(iv) f tell ( )
Ans. ftell(): returns the current file position of the given stream.
Function prototype/syntax: long int ftell(FILE *stream)

(v) str cpy ( )
Ans. strcpy( ) function copies contents of one string into another string.
Syntax for strcpy function is given below.
char * strcpy (char * destination, const char * source);
Example:
strcpy (str1, str2) – It copies contents of str2 into str1.
strcpy (str2, str1) – It copies contents of str1 into str2.

(b) Differentiate Sequential and Random Access files.
Ans. Refer to Page No.-201, Q.No.-4(b)(i)

(c) Explain briefly null pointer assignment. Write a program in C to illustrate this concept.
Ans. Refer to Page No.-201, Q.No.-3(c)

MCS-011 : Problem Solving a nd Programming
December, 2013

Note: *Question number 1 is* ***compulsory.*** *Attempt* ***any three*** *questions from the rest.*

Q 1. (a) Explain comma and conditional operator in C language with examples.

Ans. A comma expression contains two operands of any type separated by a comma and has left-to-right associativity. Two expressions separated by a comma are evaluated left to right. For example i and j are declared by the statements

int i , j;

The conditional operator is also known as ternary operator. It is called ternary operator because it takes three arguments. The conditional operator evaluates an expression returning a value if that expression is true and different one if the expression is evaluated as false. The general syntax of the conditional operator is:

Identifier = (test expression)? Expression1: Expression2;

(b) Write an algorithm to calculate the factorial of a given number.

Ans. Algorithm to calculate the factorial of a number

Step:1 Start

Step:2 Read a number n

Step:3 if(n<0)

write"factorial of negative numbers is not possible" and exit

(end of if statement)

Step:4 if(n=0)

write"factorial of 0=1" and exit

Step:5 fact=1

for(m=1;m<=n;m++)

{

fact= fact*m

}

Step:6 write"factorial".

Step:7 Stop

(c) Write a program to add 2 matrices A and B of order 3×3.

Ans. Refer to Page No.-240 Q.No.-2(a)

(d) Name different categories of constants in C language.

Ans. There are two Types of constant in C Language

(1) Primary Constant

Primary Constant have following sub categories

- Integer Constant
- Real constant
- Character constant

(2) Secondary Constant

Secondary Constant have following sub categories

- Array
- Pointer
- Structure
- Union
- Enum

(e) Write program segment to generate the following pattern using for loop and while loop.

1
1 2
1 2 3
1 2 3 4

Ans. Refer to Page No.-174 Q.No.-1(c)

(f) Explain the concept of Top Down Design Technique.

Ans. Also Called "stepwise Refinement".

Refer to June 2013 Q.No.-1(f)

(g) Give the C expression for following algebraic expression.

(i) $\dfrac{(a+b)^4 c^2 - d \times e}{m+n}$

Ans.

```
main()
{
int a,b,c,d,e,m,n;
        float s;
        clrscr();
        printf("enter the values of a,b,c,d,e,m,n ");
         scanf("%d%d%d%d %d %d %d ",&a,&b,&c,&d,&e,&m,&n);
         s= ((a+b)* (a+b)* (a+b)* (a+b))*(c*c)-(d*e)/(m+n));
        printf("the value of s=%f",s);
        getch();
}
```

(ii) $ab + (e-f)^4 / (c \times d)$

Ans.

```
main()
{
int a,b,c,d,e,f;
        float s;
        clrscr();
```

```
printf("enter the values of  a,b,c,d,e,f ");
scanf("%d%d%d%d %d %d %d ",&a,&b,&c,&d,&e,&e,&f);
s= ((a*b)+((e-f)* (e-f)*(e-f)*(e-f)))/(c*d));
printf("the value of s=%f",s);
getch();
}
```

(h) What is runtime error? Explain with an example.

Ans. Runtime error is also called execution error.

Refer to Page No.-256 Q.No.-2(a)

Q 2. (a) What is an union? Explain how a union is declared in C. Explain with an example how members of a union are accessed. Also, state the difference between an union and a structure.

Ans. Refer to Page No.-48 Q.No.-4 [Structures and Union]
Refer to Page-50, 51, Q.No.-5

(b) Explain syntax of Array declaration. write a C program in C to multiply two matrices of 3 × 3 using arrays.

Ans. Refer to Page No.-35[Array] & 79, Q.No.-7

Q 3. (a) Differentiate between macros and functions. Explain a situation when macro should be preferred over function.

No	Macro	Function
(1)	Macro is Preprocessed	Function is Compiled
(2)	No Type Checking	Type Checking is Done
(3)	Code Length increased	Code Length remains Same
(4)	Use of macro can lead to side effect	No side Effect
(5)	Speed of Execution is Faster	Speed of Execution is Slower
(6)	Before Compilation macro name is replaced by macro value	During function call, Transfer of Control take place
(7)	Useful where small code appears many time	Useful where large code appears many time
(8)	Generally Macros do not extend beyond one line	Function can be of any number of lines
(9)	Macro does not Check Compile Errors	Function Checks Compile Errors

Ans. The answer depends on the situation you are writing code for. The choice between using a macro and using a function is one of deciding between the tradeoff of faster program speed versus smaller program size. you should use macros to replace small, repeatable code sections, and you should use functions for larger coding tasks that might require several lines of code.

(b) Write a macro to the display string INDIA in following pattern:

I
IN
IND
INDI
INDIA
INDI
IND
IN
I

Ans. Refer to Page No.-229 Q.No.-4(a)

(c) What is a string? Write a function in C to find a string length without using strlen().

Ans. The string in C programming language is actually a one-dimensional array of characters which is terminated by a **null** character '\0'.

```
#include<stdio.h>
#include<conio.h>
void main(){
char *str;
int count = 0,i;
clrscr();
printf("\nEnter the String: ");
gets(str);
for(i=0;str[i]!='\0';i++){
count++;
}
printf("\nThe length of the string is %d.",count);
getch();
}
```

Q 4. (a) What are array of pointers? How they are declared and initialised? Using pointers write a program to read and display list to names of students.

Ans. Refer to page no.259 Q.No.3(d).

Consider some examples:

```
int data1, data2, *ptr1, *ptr2, *save;
    data1 = 100; data2 = 200;
    ptr1 = &data1; ptr2 = &data2;
```

Program to read and display list to names of students

```
#include <stdio.h>
#include <conio.h>
#include <math.h>
#include <alloc.h>
void main()
{
char *a[10],dum[10],s;
int i,k,j,n;
clrscr();
printf("enter the no of std....");
scanf("%d",&n);
printf("enter the name of students ");
for(k=0;k<n;k++)
scanf("%s",a[k]);
for(i=1;i<n;i++)
{
for(j=1;j<n-i;j++)
{if(strcmp(a[j-1],a[j])>0)
  {strcpy(*dum,*a[j-1]);
   strcpy(*a[j-1],*a[j]);
   strcpy(*a[j],*dum);
 }
 } }
 for(i=0;i<n;i++)
 printf("%s",a[i]);
 getch();
 }
```

(b) What is the purpose of using header files in C. Explain functions that are used in C for reading and writing of characters. Also, explain string input and output function in C.

Ans. A header file is a file with extension **.h** which contains C function declarations and macro definitions and to be shared between several source files.

Header files serve two purposes.

System header files declare the interfaces to parts of the operating system. You include them in your program to supply the definitions and declarations you need to invoke system calls and libraries.

Your own header files contain declarations for interfaces between the source files of your program. Each time you have a group of related declarations and macro definitions all or most of which are needed in several different source files, it is a good idea to create a header file for them.
Refer to june 2013 Question no 4(b).

Q 5. (a) Explain shift operators with examples.

Ans. The bitwise shift operators are as follows:

- Right shift (>>)
- Left shift (<<)

Both operands of the shift operators must be of integral types.

Examples of shift operators:

```
#include <iostream>
using namespace std;

int main() {
   cout  << "5 times 2 is " << (5 << 1) << endl
       << "20 divided by 4 is " << (20 >> 2) << endl;
}
```

(b) Explain Random and Sequential Access Files.

Ans. Refer to Page No.-201, Q.No.-4(b)(i)

(c) Explain the use of following functions in C:

(i) malloc( )

Ans. Refer to Page No.-192, Q.No.-3(b)(3)

(ii) fopen( )

Ans. Refer to Page No.-55 opening a file, Q.No.-8

(iii) fgets( )

Ans. fgets() is used to read a line of data from an external source. The C library function ***fgets()** reads a line from the specified stream and stores it into the string pointed to by **str**. It stops when either **(n-1)** characters are read, the newline character is read, or the end-of-file is reached, whichever comes first.

Following is the declaration for fgets() function.

char *fgets(char *str, int n, FILE *stream)

(iv) strcat( )

Ans. The C library function **strcat()** appends the string pointed to by **src** to the end of the string pointed to by **dest**. The strcat function concatenates or appends src to dest. All characters from src are copied including the terminating null character. Following is the declaration for strcat() function.

char *strcat(char *dest, const char *src)

(v) fptuc( )

Ans. fputs - put a string on a stream. The C library function fputs() writes a string to the specified stream up to but not including the null character.Following is the declaration for fputs() function.

int fputs(const char *str, FILE *stream)

(vi) fclose( )

Ans. The *fclose*() function shall cause the stream pointed to by *stream* to be flushed and the associated file to be closed. The C library function **fclose()** closes the stream. All buffers are flushed.

Following is the declaration for fclose() function.

int fclose(FILE *stream)

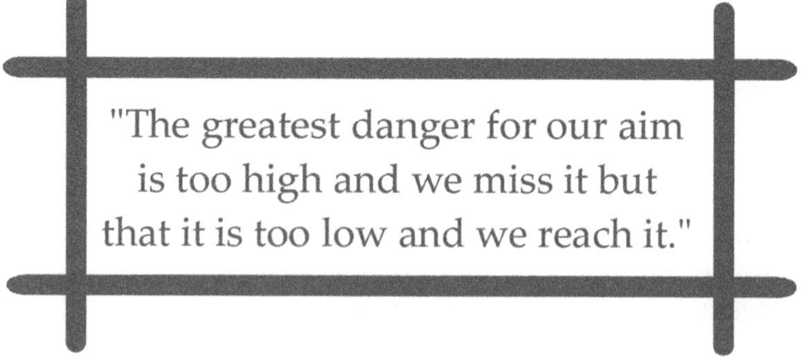

MCS-011 : Problem Solving and Programming
June, 2014

Note: *Question number 1 is* **compulsory.** *Answer* **any three** *questions from the rest.*

Q1. (a) Write an algorithm and draw corresponding flowchart to calculate the factorial of a given number.

(b) Using recursion, generate 'n' terms of fibonacci series (n > 0).

(c) Using file handling, create a file, insert some characters and count them.

(d) Using pointers concept, reverse a given string.

Q2. (a)Write a program to find the string length without using strlen () function.

(b) Write a program using C to calculate the Net salary if the basic, TA, DA, allowances and deductions are given, using structures concept.

Q3. (a) What is the use of continue statement? Explain with an example.

(b) Explain any four string functions with example for each.

(c) How will you write a function with no arguments and with return value? Give an example.

Q4. (a) Write a program to swap two values, using cell-by-value method.

(b) Write a program in C to multiply two matrices A and B.

Q5. (a) Write a macro to display the string COBOL in the following pattern.

```
C
C O
C O B
C O B O
C O B O L
```

(b) Define a macro to find maximum among of 3 given numbers using # ifdef, # else.

MCS-011 : Problem Solving and Programming
December, 2014

Note: *Question number 1 is* ***compulsory.*** *Answer* ***any three*** *questions from the rest.*

Q1. (a) Design an algorithm and draw a corresponding flow chart and write a C program to divide two numbers.

(b) What are the rules for naming variables in C?

(c) Write a program to search in an already created file "xyz.dat" which contains students' data and update it.
Hint: Use file handling concept.

(d) Write a program to calculate the first smallest divisor of a number using break statement.

(e) Write a program in C to swap the values of two variables using pointers concept.

Q2. (a) Write a program that initialises 3 names in an array of strings and displays them.

(b) What is call by value? Give example.

(c) Explain recursion program with a suitable example.

Q3. (a) Write a program to print first 10 even numbers using goto statement.

(b) Explain Function Prototypes with an example for each.

(c) Write a program to perform the comparison of two strings (use string function).

Q4. (a) Write a program in C to sort list of n integers, using any of the sorting algorithms.

(b) Write a program to test whether the given string is a palindrome or not.

Q5. (a) Write a macro to demonstrate #define, #if, #else preprocessor commands.

(b) Write a C program using fread() and fwrite() to create a file of records and then read and print the same file.

MCS-011 : Problem Solving and Programming
June, 2015

Note: *Question number 1 is* **compulsory.** *Answer* **any three** *questions from the rest.*

Q1. (a) Explain the different storage classes in 'C' programming language.

(b) What is the difference between "while-do" and "do-while" loop?

(c) Design a flowchart and then write a program in 'C' to convert a given complete string to upper case.

(d) What do you mean by "array of pointers"? Write a program in 'C' to calculate the sum of the corresponding elements of two arrays of integers of same size.

(e) List and explain the precedence of Arithmetic, Logical and Relational operators in 'C'.

Q2. (a) What is the difference between '&' and '&&' in 'C'? Explain with an example.

(b) Write a loop that calculates the sum of n elements of the following series:
1 + 4 + 7 + 10 + 13 .....
Use the loop during programming in the following two different ways:
(i) Using while loop
(ii) Using do-while loop

(c) What do you mean by scope of a variable? Differentiate between global and local variables giving an example of each.

Q3. (a) Write a program in 'C', using structures to generate a report for n students which displays the Roll No., Class, Subjects, Marks, Total, Grade, etc. Assumptions can be made wherever necessary.

(b) Write a program in 'C' to print the following output 'n' rows. For example, if n = 3, the following should be output by the program:

```
    1
  1 2 1
1 2 3 2 1
  1 2 1
    1
```

Q4. (a) Explain the meaning and usage of each of the following function prototypes:

(i) getch( )

(ii) strcmp( )

(iii) getchar( )

(iv) gets( )

(v) puts( )

(b) Write a program to multiply 2 matrices of size 3 × 3.

Q5. (a) A 'C' program contains the following declaration:

int arr $[3]=\{\{3,1\},\{4,1\},\{3,2\}\}$;

What is the meaning of the following:

(i) * (arr + 1)

(ii) * (* (arr) + 2) + 1

(iii) * (*(arr) + 1)

(iv) arr

(v) (*(arr) + 1) + 1

(b) Write a recursive program in 'C' to check whether a given string is a palindrome or not.

(c) Explain the syntax of switch case statement in 'C' language. Also compare the performance of *switch case* with *if else* statement.

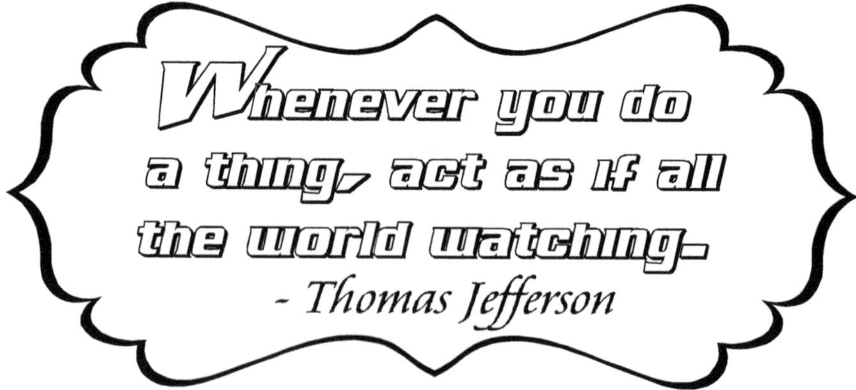

MCS-011 : Problem Solving and Programming
December, 2015

Note: *Question number 1 is* ***compulsory.*** *Answer* ***any three*** *questions from the rest.*

Q1. (a) Draw a flowchart and write a program in 'C' to implement binary search in a given list of numbers.

(b) Explain the concept of dynamic memory allocation with an example.

(c) Write a program in 'C' to find all Armstrong numbers in the range of 0 and 999.
Hint: An Armstrong number is an integer such that the sum of the cube of its digits is equal to the number itself, e.g. 153 is an Armstrong number.

(d) Explain the use of the following data types with an example for each:
(i) enumerated data type
(ii) type def

Q2. (a) Without using the 'strcpy' function write a program to copy the contents of string 2 to string 1, and find the length of the copied string using pointers.

(b) Explain the relational operators in 'C' with an example for each.

(c) What is type conversion? What are the different ways of type conversion? Explain with an example for each.

Q3. (a) Explain the use of the following statements with an example for each:
(i) Goto
(ii) Break
(iii) Exit
(iv) Continue

(b) Design an algorithm and draw a corresponding flowchart to convert a decimal number into an octal number equivalent.

Q4. (a) Write a program in 'C' to display the following output:

```
      1
    2 2 2
  3 3 3 3 3
4 4 4 4 4 4 4
  3 3 3 3 3
    2 2 2
      1
```

(b) Explain the following with examples:
(i) Unary operators in 'C'
(ii) Multidimensional Array
(iii) Syntax and Semantic errors
(iv) Size operator

Q5. (a) Write a program in 'C' to copy the content from one file to another file.

(b) What is pointer-to-pointer? Explain the need of pointer-to-pointer with an example. Also show how the address of variable in this case is calculated and determined.

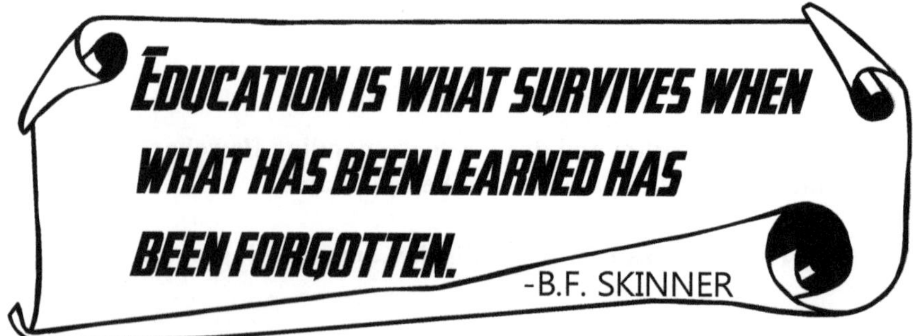

MCS-011 : Problem Solving and Programming
June, 2016

Note: *Question number 1 is* **compulsory.** *Attempt* **any three** *questions from the rest.*

Q1. (a) Explain how you will analyse the efficiency of an algorithm.

Ans. (a) Measuring the efficiency of algorithms: The topic of algorithms is a topic that is central to computer science. Measuring an algorithm's efficiency is important because your choice of an algorithm for a given application often has a great impact. Word processors, ATMs, video games and life support systems all depend on efficient algorithms.

The analysis of algorithms is the area of computer science that provides tools for contrasting the efficiency of different methods of solution. Notice the use of the term methods of solution rather than programs; it is important to emphasise that the analysis concerns itself primarily with significant differences in efficiency-differences that we can usually obtain only through superior methods of solution and rarely through clever tricks in coding.

Although the efficient use of both time and space is important, inexpensive memory has reduced the significance of space efficiency. Thus, we will focus primarily on time efficiency. One possible approach is to implement the two algorithms in C++ and run the programs. There are three difficulties with this approach:

(1) How are the algorithms coded? Does one algorithm run faster than another because of better programming? We should not compare implementations rather than the algorithms. Implementations are sensitive to factors such as programming style that cloud the issue.

(2) What computer should you use? The only fair way would be to use the same computer for both programs. But even then, the particular operations that one algorithm uses may be faster or slower than the other-and may be just the reverse on a different computer. In short, we should compare the efficiency of the algorithms independent of a particular computer.

(3) What data should the programs use? There is always a danger that we will select instances of the problem for which one of the algorithms runs uncharacteristically fast. For example, when comparing a sequential search and a binary search of a sorted array. If the test case happens to be that we are searching for an item that happens to be the smallest in the array, the sequential search will find the item more quickly than the binary search.

To overcome these difficulties, computer scientists employ mathematical techniques that analyse algorithms independently of specific implementations, computers or data. We begin this analysis by counting the number of significant operations in a particular solution.

As an example of calculating the time it takes to execute a piece of code, consider the nested for loops below:

```
for (i = 1; i <= N; ++i)
for (j = 1; j <= i; ++j)
for (k = 0; k < 5; ++k)
Task T;
```

If task T requires t time units, the innermost loop on K requires 5*t time units. We will discuss how to calculate the total time, which is: 5*t*N*(N+1)/2 time units.

This example derives an algorithm's time requirements as a function of problem size. The way to measure a problem's size depends on the application. The searches we have discussed depend on the size of the array we are searching. The most important thing to learn is how quickly the algorithm's time requirement grows as a function of the problem size. A statement such as: Algorithm A requires time proportional to f(N) enables us to compare algorithm A with another algorithm B which requires g(N) time units.

Algorithm A is said to be order f(N), which is denoted as O(f(N)); f(N) is called the algorithm's growth rate function. Because the notation uses the capital letter O to denote order, it is called Big O notation. If a problem of size N requires time that is directly proportional to N, the problem is O(N) – that is, order N. If the time requirement is directly proportional to N, the problem is $O(N^2)$, and so on.

(b) Design a flow chart and write an algorithm to calculate the factorial of a given number using recursion.

Ans. Refer to June-2006, Q.No.-1(c) & Refer to December-2008, Q.No.-1(a)

(c) Explain the concept of pointer to an array. Using this write an interactive program in "C" to find out the string length of a given string, as input.

Ans. Refer to Page No.-35 (Arrays Pointer and Arrays)

(d) Write a program in "C", using structures, to calculate the Gross income and Net income if the Attendance, Basic pay, Grade pay, Deductions and Allowances are given as input.

Ans. Refer to June-2008, Q.No.-3(c)(Same as)

Q2. (a) Write a program to read the full name from the keyboard and display its corresponding short name.

Ex: I/P: ANIL KUMAR GULATI

O/P: A K GULATI

Ans. Each program requires three important steps to do work. It is Input, Process and Output. It is the basic concept of almost all the programming language. It is also known as I-P-O cycle. The program requires some input from the user. Next, the program processes the input with programming language and finally shows the output.

Consider the simple C# code, in which you will enter your name and your name will be displayed with some text message in command prompt.

```
using System;
using System.Collections.Generic;
using System.Linq;
using System.Text;
namespace First_c_sharp_code
{
    class Program
    {
        static void Main(string[] args)
        {
            string name; //Variable for storing string value
            //Displaying message for entring value
            Console.WriteLine("Please Enter Your Good Name");
            //Accepting and holding values in name variable
            name = Console.ReadLine();
            //Displaying Output
            Console.WriteLine("Welcome {0} in your first csharp program", name);
            //Holding console screen
            Console.ReadLine();
        }
    }
}
```

```
Please Enter Your Good Name
Steven Clark
Welcome Steven Clark in your first csharp program
_
```

However, classes and objects are not mentioned in initial level, so you can find Main(string[] agrs) method to writing code.

Explanation:

```
using System;
using System.Collections.Generic;
using System.Linq;
using System.Text;
```

It is used for including C# class library. C# has huge collection of classes and objects. If you want to use those classes then you will have to include their library name in your program.

string name; //Variable for storing string value
It is a string variable that stores value input by user. A variable is a symbolic name of special data types that is used to store value in memory temporarily. Here, name is variable of string data types.
Console.WriteLine("Please Enter Your Good Name");
It is used for displaying message on console.
name = Console.ReadLine();
Storing value in the name variable.
Console.WriteLine("Welcome {0} in your first csharp program", name);
Again used for displaying message on the console. A new thing in this line is {0}. It is pronounced as place holder that is used for displaying variable value. In the above line, {0} print the value of name.
In C#, Console.WriteLine() and Console.ReadLine() are the very important method.
Console.WriteLine() : It is used for displaying message on the console.
Console.ReadLine() : It is used for accepting user input.

(b) Write a program to display the string "UNIX" in the following format:
U
UN
UNI
UNIX
UNIX
UNI
UN
U

Ans. Write a program to display the string "UNIX" in the following format.
U
UN
UNI
UNIX
UNIX
UNI
UN
U

```
/* Program to display the string in the above shown format*/
# include <stdio.h>
main()
{
int x, y;
static char string[ ] = "UNIX";
```

```
printf("\n");
for( x=0; x<4; x++)
{
y = x + 1;
/* reserves 4 character of space on to the monitor and minus sign is for left justified*/
printf("%-4.*s \n", y, string);
/* and for every loop the * is replaced by value of y */
/* y value starts with 1 and for every time it is incremented by 1 until it reaches to 4*/
}
for( x=3; x>=0; x- -)
{
y = x + 1;
        printf("%-4.*s \n", y, string);
/* y value starts with 4 and for every time it is decrements by 1 until it reaches to 1*/
}
}
```

OUTPUT

```
U
UN
UNI
UNIX
UNIX
UNI
UN
U
```

Q3. (a) What is the use of "continue" statement and explain it with the help of an example?

Ans. Continue statement The continue statement causes the program to skip the rest of the loop in the current iteration as if the end of the statement block had been reached, causing it to jump to the start of the following iteration. For example, we are going to skip the number 5 in our countdown:

Program: 10

```
// continue loop example
#include <iostream.h>
using namespace std;
int main ()
{
```

```
for (int n=10; n>0; n—) {
if (n==5) continue;
cout << n << ", ";
}
cout << "FIRE!\n";
return 0;
}
```

Output:

10, 9, 8, 7, 6, 4, 3, 2, 1, FIRE!

(b) Explain any four string functions with an example for each.

Ans. Following are some of the useful string handling functions supported by C.

strlen()
strcpy()
strncpy()
strcat()

These functions are defined in string.h header file. Hence we need to include this header file whenever we use these string handling functions in our program. All these functions take either character pointer or character arrays as arguments.

(1) strlen()

strlen() function returns the length of the string. strlen() function returns integer value.

Example:

1. char *str = "Learn C Online";
2. int strLength;
3. strLength = strlen(str); //strLength contains the length of the string i.e. 14

(2) strcpy()

strcpy() function is used to copy one string to another. The Destination_String should be a variable and Source_String can either be a string constant or a variable.

Syntax:

strcpy(Destination_String,Source_String);

Example:

1. char *Destination_String;
2. char *Source_String = "Learn C Online";
3. strcpy(Destination_String,Source_String);
4. printf("%s", Destination_String);

Output:

Learn C Online

(3) strncpy()

strncpy() is used to copy only the left most n characters from source to destination. The Destination_String should be a variable and Source_String can either be a string constant or a variable.

Syntax:

strncpy(Destination_String, Source_String,no_of_characters);

strcat()

strcat() is used to concatenate two strings.

The Destination_String should be a variable and Source_String can either be a string constant or a variable.

Syntax:

strcat(Destination_String, Source_String);

Example:

1. char *Destination_String =”Learn “;
2. char *Source_String = “C Online”;
3. strcat(Destination_String, Source_String);
4. puts(Destination_String);

Output:

Learn C Online

(c) How will you write a function with no arguments and with return value? Also, write an example function–definition for this.

Ans. Code for Functions with no arguments and no return values in C Programming:

```
/* Function declaration */
void printline (void);
voidvalue (void);
  main()
  {
     printline();
     value();
     printline();
  }
  /*      Function1: printline( )        */
void printline(void)   /* contains no arguments */
  {
     int i ;
     for(i=1; i <= 35; i++)
        printf(“%c”,’-’);
     printf(“\n”);
  }
```

```
 /*      Function2: value( )          */
voidvalue(void)      /* contains no arguments */
 {
    int   year, period;
    float  inrate, sum, principal;
    printf("Principal amount?");
    scanf("%f", &principal);
    printf("Interest rate?   ");
    scanf("%f", &inrate);
    printf("Period?          ");
    scanf("%d", &period);
    sum = principal;
    year = 1;
    while(year <= period)
    {
       sum = sum *(1+inrate);
       year = year +1;
    }
    printf("\n%8.2f %5.2f %5d %12.2f\n",
          principal,inrate,period,sum);
 }
```

Output

```
Principal amount?     5000
Interest rate?        0.12
Period?               5
5000.00  0.12         5      8811.71
```

Q4. (a) Write a program to swap two values of variables, using pointers.

Ans. Refer to Page No.-172, Q.No.-1(a)

(b) Write a program, using structures of read and display data for 10 students.

Hint: Assumptions can be made wherever necessary.

Ans. In this program, a structure(student) is created which contains name, roll and marks as its data member. Then, an array of structure of 10 elements is created. Then, data(name, roll and marks) for 10 elements is asked to user and stored in array of structure. Finally, the data entered by user is displayed.

Source Code to Store Information of 10 students Using Structure

```
#include <stdio.h>
struct student{
    char name[50];
   int roll;
   float marks;
```

```
};
int main(){
    struct student s[10];
    int i;
    printf("Enter information of students:\n");
    for(i=0;i<10;++i)
    {
        s[i].roll=i+1;
        printf("\nFor roll number %d\n",s[i].roll);
        printf("Enter name: ");
        scanf("%s",s[i].name);
        printf("Enter marks: ");
        scanf("%f",&s[i].marks);
        printf("\n");
    }
    printf("Displaying information of students:\n\n");
    for(i=0;i<10;++i)
    {
     printf("\nInformation for roll number %d:\n",i+1);
     printf("Name: ");
     puts(s[i].name);
     printf("Marks: %.1f",s[i].marks);
    }
   return 0;
}
```

Output

```
Enter information of students:
For roll number 1
Enter name: Tom
Enter marks: 98
For roll number 2
Enter name: Jerry
Enter marks: 89
.
.
.
Displaying information of students:
Information for roll number 1:
Name: Tom
Marks: 98
.
.
.
```

Q5. (a) Write a macro to display the string "COBOL" in the following format:

C
CO
COB
COBO
COBOL
COBOL
COBO
COB
CO
C

Ans.

C
CO
COB
COBO
COBOL
COBOL
COBO
COB
CO
C

```
/* Program to display the string as given in the problem*/
# include<stdio.h>
# define LOOP for(x=0; x<5; x++) \
{ y=x+1; \
printf("%-5.*s\n", y, string); } \
for(x=4; x>=0; x—) \
{ y=x+1; \
printf("%-5.*s \n", y, string); }
main()
{
int x, y;
static char string[ ] = "COBOL";
printf("\n");
LOOP;
}
```

When the above program is executed the reference to macro (loop) is replaced by the set of statements contained within the macro definition.

OUTPUT

C
CO
COB
COBO
COBOL
COBOL
COBO
COB
CO
C

Recollect that CALL BY VALUE Vs CALL BY REFERENCE given in the previous uint. By CALL BY VALUE, the swapping was not taking place, because the visibility of the variables was restricted to with in the function in the case of local variables. You can resolve this by using a macro. Here is **swap** in action when using a macro:

```
#define swap(x, y) {int tmp = x; x = y; y = tmp; }
```

Now we have swapping code that works. Why does this work? It is because the CPP just simply replaces text. Wherever swap is called, the CPP will replace the macro call with the macro meaning, (defined text).

Caution in using macros

You should be very careful in using Macros. In particular the textual substitution means that arithmetic expressions are liable to be corrupted by the order of evaluation rules (precedence rules). Here is an example of a macro, which won't work.

```
#define DOUBLE(n) n + n
```

Now if we have a statement,

```
z = DOUBLE(p) * q;
```

This will be expanded to

```
z = p + p * q;
```

And since * has a higher priority than +, the compiler will treat it as.

```
z = p + (p * q);
```

The problem can be solved using a more robust definition of DOUBLE

```
#define DOUBLE(n) (n + n)
```

Here, the braces around the definition force the expression to be evaluated before any surrounding operators are applied. This should make the macro more reliable.

(b) Write a program to multiply two matrices of size M × N and N × P respectively.

Ans. Refer to June-2005, Q.No.-1(d)(Same as)

MCS-011 : Problem Solving and Programming
December, 2016

Note: *Question number 1 is* ***compulsory.*** *Attempt* ***any three*** *questions from the rest.*

Q1. (a) Give the structure of a C program. Develop an algorithm, a flow chart and a program to add "n" numbers and find their average.
Ans. Refer to Page No.-6, Q.No.-4 & Page No.-13, Q.No.-5

(b) Write a C program to illustrate how the marks of 10 students are read in an array and then used to find the maximum marks obtained by a student in the class.
Ans. Refer to December-2006, Q.No.-3(a)(same as)

(c) Using pointers, write a C program to find out the position and address of the first occurrence of any character given as input in a string.
Ans. Refer to Page No.- 87, Q.No.-15(same as)

(d) Write a program, using files, to copy the contents of one file to another with a different file name.
Ans. Refer to Page No.- 76, Q.No.-4

Q2. (a) Write a program to initialize 3 names in an array of strings and display them.
Ans. Refer to December-2006, Q.No.-5(b)(ii)

(b) What is Call By Value? Give an example.
Ans. We have always created new variables for arguments in the function and then passed the values of actual arguments to them. Such function calls are called **"call by value".**

Example:

Write a program to multiply the two given numbers

```
#include <stdio.h>
main()
{
int x, y, z;
int mul(int, int);
printf ("Enter two numbers: \n");
scanf ("%d %d",&x,&y);
z= mul(x, y); /* function call by value */
```

```
printf ("\n The product of the two numbers is: %d", z);
/* Function to multiply two numbers */
int mul(int a, int b)
{
int c;
c =a*b;
return(c); }
```

OUTPUT

Enter two numbers:
23 2
The product of two numbers is: 46

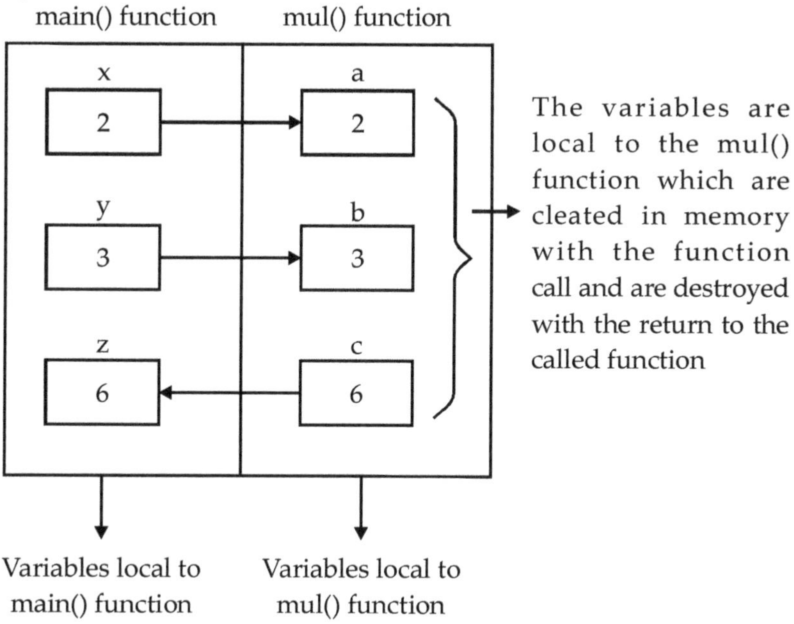

main() function mul() function

x	a
2 →	2
y	b
3 →	3
z	c
6	← 6

The variables are local to the mul() function which are cleated in memory with the function call and are destroyed with the return to the called function

Variables local to main() function

Variables local to mul() function

(c) Explain function prototypes with an example for each.

Ans. Function Prototypes require that every function which is to be accessed should be declared in the calling function. The function declaration, that will be discussed earlier, will be included for every function in its calling function.

Example:

```
/*Program to calculate the square of a given integer using the function prototype*/
#include <stdio.h>
main ( )
{
```

```
int n , sq ;
int square (int ); /* function prototype */
printf ("Enter a number to calculate square value");
scanf("%d",&n);
sq = square(n); /* function call with parameter passing */
printf ("\nSsquare of the number is: %d", sq);
}
/* square function */
int square (int no) /*passing of argument */
{
int result; /* local variable to function square */
result = no*no;
return (result); /* returns an integer value */
}
```

OUTPUT

Enter a number to calculate square value: 5
Square of the number is: 25

Q3. (a) Write a program to print the first 10 even numbers using "goto" statement.

Ans. The goto statement is used to alter the normal sequence of program instructions by transferring the control to some other portion of the program. The syntax is as follows:

goto label;

Here, label is an identifier that is used to label the statement to which control will be transferred. The targeted statement must be preceded by the unique label followed by colon.

label: statement;

Although goto statement is used to alter the normal sequence of program execution but its usage in the program should be avoided. The most common applications are:

(i) To branch around statements under certain conditions in place of use of if-else statement,

(ii) To jump to the end of the loop under certain conditions bypassing the rest of statements inside the loop in place of continue statement,

(iii) To jump out of the loop avoiding the use of break statement.

goto can never be used to jump into the loop from outside and it should be preferably used for forward jump.

Situations may arise, however, in which the goto statement can be useful. To the possible extent, the use of the goto statement should generally be avoided.

Example:

Write a program to print first 10 even numbers

```
/* Program to print 10 even numbers */
#include <stdio.h>
main()
{
int i=2;
while(1)
{
printf("%d ",i);
i=i+2;
if (i>=20)
goto outside;
}
outside : printf("over");
}
```

OUTPUT

2 4 6 8 10 12 14 16 18 20 over

(b) Write a program to read two strings and append the second string to the first string, using arrays.

Ans. Refer to December-2005, Q.No.-3(b)(ii)

Q4. (a) Write a program to swap the values using the Pass by Value and Pass by Reference methods, separately.

Ans. Refer to June-2007, Q.No.-1(a)

(b) Write a program to test whether the given string is a palindrome or not.

Ans. Refer to June-2005, Q.No.-1(c)

Q5. (a) What is a macro? Write a macro to demonstrate #define, #if, #else preprocessor commands.

Ans. Refer to June-2011, Q.No.-3(b) & Page No.-94, Q.No.-20

(b) Write a program using fread() and fwrite() to create a file of records and then read and print the same file.

Ans. A block can be a record, a set of records or an array. These functions are also defined in standard library and are described below:

- fread( )
- fwrite( )

These two functions allow reading and writing of blocks of data. Their syntax is:

int fread(void *buf, int num_bytes, int count, FILE *fp);

int fwrite(void *buf, int num_bytes, int count, FILE *fp);

In case of fread(), buf is the pointer to a memory area that receives the data from the file and in fwrite(), it is the pointer to the information to be written to the file. num_bytes specifies the number of bytes to be read or written. These functions are quite helpful in case of binary files. Generally, these functions are used to read or write array of records from or to a file. The use of the above functions is shown in the following program.

Example:

Write a program using fread( ) and fwrite() to create a file of records and then read and print the same file.

```
/* Program to illustrate the fread() and fwrite() functions*/
#include<stdio.h>
#include<conio.h>
#include<process.h>
#include<string.h>
void main()
{
struct stud
{
char name[30];
int age;
int roll_no;
}s[30],st;
int i;
FILE *fp;
/*opening the file in write mode*/
if((fp=fopen("sud.dat","w"))== NULL)
{ printf("Error while creating a file\n");
exit(0); }
/* reading an array of students */
for(i=0;i<30;i++)
scanf("%s %d %d",s[i].name,s[i].age,s[i].roll_no);
/* writing to a file*/
fwrite(s,sizeof(struct stud),30,fp);
fclose(fp);
/* opening a file in read mode */
fp=fopen("stud.dat","r");
/* reading from a file and writing on the screen */
```

```
while(!feof(fp))
{
fread(&st,sizeof(struct stud),1,fp);
fprintf("%s %d %d",st.name,st.age,st.roll_no);
}
fclose(fp); }
```

OUTPUT

This program reads 30 records (name, age and roll_number) from the user, writes one record at a time to a file. The file is closed and then reopened in read mode; the records are again read from the file and written on to the screen.

MCS-011 : Problem Solving and Programming
June, 2017

Note: *Question number 1 is* ***compulsory****. Attempt* ***any three*** *questions from the rest.*

Q1. (a) Design an algorithm and draw a corresponding flow chart to convert a decimal number to its binary equivalent.

Ans. Refer to June-2005, Q.No.-4(b)

(b) Write a C program (use a switch statement for selection) to add or subtract 2 matrices having order
3 × 3, depending upon the choice made by the user.

Ans. Refer to June-2006, Q.No.-2(b)

(c) Write and explain the following types of functions with the help of an example program for each:

(i) Function with no arguments and no return value.

Ans. With no arguments and with return value

Suppose if a function does not receive any data from calling function but does send some value to the calling function, then it falls in this category.

Example

Write a program to find the sum of the first ten natural numbers.

```
/*Program to find sum of first ten natural numbers*/
#include<stdio.h>
int cal_sum()
 {
int i, s=0;
for (i=0; i<=10; i++)
s=s + i;
return(s);                /*function returning sum of first ten natural
numbers*/
}
main()
 {
int sum;
sum = cal_sum();
printf("Sum of first ten natural numbers is % d\n", sum);
}
```

OUTPUT

Sum of first ten natural numbers is 55

(ii) Function with arguments and no return value.

Ans. With Arguments and have no return value

If a function includes arguments but does not return anything, it falls in this category. One way communication takes place between the calling and the called function.

Before proceeding further, first we discuss the type of arguments or parameters here. There are two types of arguments:

- Actual arguments
- Formal arguments

Let us take an example to make this concept clear:

Example

Write a program to calculate sum of any three given numbers.

```
#include <stdio.h>
main()
{
int al, a2, a3;
void sum(int,int,int);
printf("Enter three numbers:");
scanf("%d%d%d",&al,&a2,&a3);
sum (al,a2,a3);  /* Type 3 function */
}
/*function to calculate sum of three numbers*/
void sum(int f1,int f2,int f3)
{
int s;
s = f1 + f2  +f3;
printf("\nThe sum of the three numbers is %d\n",s);
}
```

OUTPUT

Enter three numbers: 23 34 45

The sum of the three numbers is 102

Here f1, f2, f3 are formal arguments and a1, a2, a3 are actual arguments. Thus we see in the function declaration, the arguments are formal arguments, but when values are passed to the function during function call, they are actual arguments.

Note: The actual and formal arguments should match in type, order and number.

(d) Using pointers, write a C program to swap the values of two variables.

Ans. Refer to June-2007, Q.No.-1(a)

(e) Mention the rules for using the Big-O notation.
Ans. Refer to June-2005, Q.No.-5(a)

Q2. (a) Without using the inbuilt string functions like strcat ( ) and strlen ( ), write C programs for the following:
(i) To concatenate 2 strings
(ii) To find the length of any given string
Ans. Refer to June-2005, Q.No.-3(b)

(b) Define the term 'variable'. What are the rules to be followed to name a variable in "C"? Write the syntax to declare a variable and also mention how to assign values to it (initialize them).
Ans. Refer to June-2005, Q.No.-5(b)

Q3. (a) Write a program in "C", using structures, to find the sum of the Assignment and Term End Exam marks (for IGNOU MCA or BCA first semester courses) for 5 students.
Ans.
```
#include<stdio.h>
struct student
{
unsigned long int ENROL;
char NAME[15];
int
MCS011, MCS11V, MCS012, MCS12V, MCS013, MCS13V, MCS014, MCS14V, MCS015, MCS15V, MCS016, MCS16V, MCSL017, MCSL17V;
}STUD[12]={
{102038400,"GANESH",55,15,78,16,45,18,56,14,75,16,64,17,75,12},
{102038401,"MAHESH",80,14,56,14,51,11,61,18,56,14,49,16,78,14},
{102038402,"SURESH",51,12,75,13,16,14,18,14,71,14,19,14,51,11},
{102038403,"KALPESH",78,10,79,14,74,14,54,12,15,11,61,14,64,13},
{102038404,"RAHUL",74,17,65,15,45,13,41,11,55,14,56,12,54,10},
{102038405,"SUBBU",19,13,64,12,68,10,67,14,45,11,64,14,65,12},
{102038406,"RAKESH",55,11,78,19,45,17,56,14,75,11,64,12,75,13},
{102038407,"ATUL",55,10,78,12,45,11,56,14,75,13,64,11,75,12},
{102038408,"DHARMESH",55,16,78,17,45,11,56,14,75,14,64,12,75,14},
{102038409,"AJAY",55,13,78,14,45,11,56,12,75,15,64,14,75,15},
{102038410,"ABDUL",55,15,78,17,45,11,56,12,75,15,64,14,75,16},
{102038411,"RASHMI,"55,17,78,15,45,11,56,12,75,14,64,12,75,15}
};
void main()
{
```

```
unsigned long int ENROL_NO;
void gen_result(unsigned long int);
clrscr();
printf("ENTER THE Enroll bwtn 102038399 to 8412 : ");
scanf("%ld",&ENROL_NO);
if(ENROL_NO>102038399 && ENROL_NO<102038412)
gen_result(ENROL_NO);
else
printf("\n YOU HAVE ENTERED WRONG ENROLMENT NO. !!");
getch();
}
void gen_result(unsigned long int ENROL)
{
char STATUS;
int M011,M012,M013,M014,M015,M016,M017;
M011=STUD[ENROL-102038400].MCS011+STUD[ENROL-
102038400].MCS11V;
M012=STUD[ENROL-102038400].MCS012+STUD[ENROL-
102038400].MCS12V;
M013=STUD[ENROL-102038400].MCS013+STUD[ENROL-
102038400].MCS13V;
M014=STUD[ENROL-102038400].MCS014+STUD[ENROL-
102038400].MCS14V;
M015=STUD[ENROL-102038400].MCS015+STUD[ENROL-
102038400].MCS15V;
M016=STUD[ENROL-102038400].MCS016+STUD[ENROL-
102038400].MCS16V;
M017=STUD[ENROL-102038400].MCSL017+STUD[ENROL-
102038400].MCSL17V;
printf("\n\t\tINDIRA GANDHI NATIONAL OPEN UNIVERSITY");
printf("\n\t\t\t(ASSIGNMENT – 2015-2016)");
printf("\n\n\tENROLMENT NO.\t: %ld",ENROL);
printf("n\tNAME\t\t:%s",STUD[ENROL-102038400].NAME);
printf("\n\tPROGRAMME CODE\t:MCA");
printf("\n\t__________________________________________"),
printf("\n\tCOURSE\t\tASSIGN\t\tVIVA\t\tTOTAL");
printf("\n\tCODE\t\t(80%)\t\t(20%)\t\t(100%)\tSTATUS");
printf("\n\t__________________________________________");
if(M011<40)STATUS='N'; else STATUS='S';
printf("\n\tMCS011\t\t%d\t\t%d\t\t%d\t%cC",STUD[ENROL-
102038400].MCS011,STUD[ENROL-102038400].MCS11V,M011,STATUS);
```

```
if(M012<40) STATUS='N'; else STATUS='S';
printf("\n\n\tMCS012\t\t%d\t\t%d\t\t%d\t%cC",STUD[ENROL-102038400].MCS012,STUD[ENROL-102038400].MCS12V,M012,STATUS);
if(M013<40)STATUS='N'; else STATUS='S';
printf("\n\n\tMCS013\t\t%d\t\t%d\t\t%d\t%cC",STUD[ENROL-102038400].MCS013,STUD[ENROL-102038400].MCS13V,M013,STATUS);
if(M014<40)STATUS='N'; else STATUS='S';
printf("\n\n\tMCS014\t\t%d\t\t%d\t\t%d\t%cC",STUD[ENROL-102038400].MCS014,STUD[ENROL-102038400].MCS14V,M014,STATUS);
if(M015<40)STATUS='N'; else STATUS='S';
printf("\n\n\tMCS015\t\t%d\t\t%d\t\t%d\t%cC",STUD[ENROL-102038400].MCS015,STUD[ENROL-102038400].MCS15V,M015,STATUS);
if(M016<40)STATUS='N'; else STATUS='S';
printf("\n\n\tMCS016\t\t%d\t\t%d\t\t%d\t%cC",STUD[ENROL-102038400].MCS016,STUD[ENROL-102038400].MCS16V,M016,STATUS);
if(M017<40)STATUS='N'; else STATUS='S';
printf("\n\n\tMCSL017\t\t%d\t\t%d\t\t%d\t%cC",STUD[ENROL-102038400].MCSL017,STUD[ENROL102038400].MCSL17V,M017,STATUS);
printf("\n\t_____________________________________________");
printf("\n\t\tSC :-SUCCESSFUL COMPLETED\tNC :- NOT COMPLETED");
}
```

(b) Explain the concept of "file handling" in C programming. Explain the use of fopen ( ) and fclose ( ) functions associated with it. Also mention various modes in which a file can be allowed to open with an example for each.

Ans. Refer to December-2010, Q.No.-1(c)

Open A File Using The Function fopen()

Once file pointer variables has been declared, the next step is to open a file. The fopen() function opens a stream for use and links a file with that stream. This function returns a file pointer, described in the previous section. The syntax is as follows:

FILE*fopen(char *filename, *mode);

where mode is string, containing the desired open status. The filename must be a string of characters that provide a valid file name for the operating system and may include a path specification. The legal mode strings are shown below in the table:

Legal values to the fopen() mode parameter

MODE	MEANING
"r" / "rt"	opens a text file for read only access
"w" / "wt"	creates a text file for write only access
"a" / "at"	text file for appending to a file
"r+t"	open a text file for read and write access
"w+t"	creates a text file for read and write access,
"a+t"	opens or creates a text file and read access
"rb"	opens a binary file for read only access
"wb"	create a binary file for write only access
"ab"	binary file for appending to a file
"r+b"	opens a binary or read and write access
"w+b"	creates a binary or read and write access,
"a+b"	open or binary file and read access

The following code fragment explains how to open a file for reading.

Code Fragment

```
#include<stdio.h>
main()
  {
   FILE *fp;
   if ((fp=fopen("file1.dat","r"))==NULL)
   {
   printf("FILE DOES NOT EXIST\n");
   exit(0);
   }
  }
```

The value returned by the *fopen()* function is a file pointer. If any error occurs while opening the file, the value of this pointer is *NULL*, a constant declared in <stdio.h>. Always check for this possibility as shown in the above example.

Close A File Using The Function Fclose()

When the processing of the file is finished, the file should be closed using the fclose() function, whose syntax is:

int fclose(FILE *fptr);

This function flushes any unwritten data for stream, discards any unread buffered input, frees any automatically allocated buffer, and then closes the stream. The return value is 0 if the file is closed successfully or a constant *EOF*, an end-of file marker, if an error occurred. This constant is also defined in <stdio.h>. If the function fclose() is not called explicitly, the operating system normally will close the file when the program execution terminates. The following code fragment explains how to close a file.

Code Fragment

```
#include <stdio.h>
main ( )
{
FILE *fp;
if ((fp=fopen("file1.dat", "r"))==NULL)
  {
   printf("FILE DOES NOT EXIST\n");
   exit(0);
  }
/* close the file */
fclose(fp);
}
```

Once the file is closed, it cannot be used further. If required it can be opened in same or another mode.

Q4. (a) Explain different arithmetic, logical and relational operators in C, with the help of examples.

Ans. Refer to June-2011, Q.No.-1(e)

Relational operators:

These operators are used to distinguish between two values depending on their relations. These operators provide the relationship between the two expressions. Is the relation is true then it returns a value 1 otherwise o for false relation. The relational operators together with their conditions and meaning are described in table:

Table Relational Operators in C

Relational Operator	Condition	Meaning
==	x==y	x is equal to y
!=	x!=y	x is not equal to y
<	x<y	x is less than y
<=	x<=y	x is less than or equal to y
>	x>y	x is greater than y
>=	x>=y	x is greater or equal to y

Relational operators usually appear in statements which are inquiring about the truth of some particular relationship between variables. Normally, the relational operators in C are the operators in the expressions that appear between the parentheses.

For example,
(i) if (thisNum<minimumSoFar) minimumSoFar = thisNum
(ii) if (job == Teacher) salary == minimum Wage
(iii) if (numberOfLegs !=8) thisBug = insect
(iv) if (degreeOfPolynomial<2) polynomial = linear

Let us see a simple C program containing the If statement (will be introduced in detail in the next unit). It displays the relationship between two numbers read from the keyboard.

Example:

```
/*Program to find relationship between two numbers*/
#include<stdio.h>
main( )
{
int a, b;
printf ("Please enter two integers: ");
scanf("%d%d", &a, &b);
if(a<=b)
printf ("%d<=%d\n",a,b);
else
printf("%d>%d\n",a,b);
}
```

OUTPUT

Please enter two integers: 12 17
12<=17

We can change the values assigned to a and b and check the result.

(b) Write and explain the use of the following in C programming, with an example for each:

(i) Break statement

Ans. It is required to jump out of a loop irrespective of the conditional test value. Break statement is used inside any loop to allow the control jump to the immediate statement following the loop. The syntax is as follows:

break;

When nested loops are used, then break jumps the control from the loop where it has been used. *Break* statement can be used inside any loop i.e., while, do-while, for and also in switch statement.

Let us consider a program to illustrate break statement.

Example

Write a program to calculate the first smallest divisor of a number.

```
/*Program to calculate smallest divisor of a number*/
#include<stdio.h>
```

```
main( )
{
int div,num,i;
printf("Enter any number:\n");
scanf("%d",,&num);
for(i=2;i<=num;++i)
   {
  if((num%i)==0)
         {
         printf("Smallest divisor for number %d is %d",num,i);
         break;
         }
   }
}
```

OUTPUT

Enter any number:

9

Smallest divisor for number 9 is 3

In the above program, we divide the input number with the integer starting from 2 onwards, and print the smallest divisor as soon as remainder comes out to be zero. Since we are only interested in first smallest divisor and not all divisors of a given number, so jump out of the *for* loop using break statement without further going for the next iteration of *for* loop.

Break is different from exit. Former jumps the control out of the loop while exit stops the execution of the entire program.

(ii) Continue statement

Ans. *Break* statement, which is used to jump the control out of the loop, it is sometimes required to skip some part of the loop and to continue the execution with next loop iteration. ***Continue*** statement used inside the loop helps to bypass the section of a loop and passes the control to the beginning of the loop to continue the execution with the next loop iteration. The syntax is as follows:

continue;

Let us see the program given below to know the working of the ***continue*** statement.

Example

Write a program to print first 20 natural numbers skipping the numbers divisible by 5.

/* Program to print first 20 natural numbers skipping the numbers divisible by 5*/

```
#include<stdio.h>
main( )
{
        int i;
        for (i=1;i<=20;++i)
        {
        if((i%5)==0)
              continue;
        printf("%d",i);
     }
}
```

OUTPUT

1 2 3 4 6 7 8 9 11 12 13 14 16 17 18 19

Here, the printf statement is bypassed each time when value stored in ***i*** is divisible by 5.

(iii) malloc( )

Ans. Refer to December-2007, Q.No.-3(b)

(iv) void

Ans.

```
#include <stdio.h>
int main (void)
{
  int i;
  for (i=1; i <= 5; i + +)
  {
        printf("%d " , i * i) ;
  }
  for(i=1; i <=5; i + +)
  {
      printf("%d ", i*i);
  }
  return 0;
}
```

We have to write the same loop twice. We may want to somehow put this code in a separate place and simply jump to this code when we want to use it. This would look like:

```
#include <stdio.h>
void Print Squares(void)
{
   int i;
```

```
    for(i=1; i <=5; i + +)
    {
      printf("%d ", i*i);
    }
}

int main(void)
{
        Print_Squares( );
        Print_Squares( );
return 0;
}
```

Q5. Explain the following with the help of suitable example for each:
(a) Automatic Variables

Ans. The variables local to a function are automatic i.e., declared within the function. The scope of lies within the function itself. The automatic defined in different functions, even if they have same name, are treated as different. It is the default storage class for variables declared in a function.

Points to remember:

- The auto is optional therefore there is no need to write it.
- All the formal arguments also have the auto storage class.
- The initialization of the auto-variables can be done:
- in declarations
- using assignment expression in a function
- If not initialized the unpredictable value is defined.
- The value is not retained after exit from the program.

Let us study these variables by a sample program given below:

Example

```
/* To print the value of automatic variables*/
#include<stdio.h>
main (int argc, char*argv[ ])
{
int  a, b;
double d;
printf("%d", argc);
a=10;
b=5;
d=(b * b)-(a/2);
printf("%d,%d,%f",a,b,d);
}
```

All the variables a, b, d, argc and argv [ ] have automatic storage class.

(b) Global Variables

Ans. Refer to December-2009, Q.No.-2(a)

(c) Static Variables

Ans. In case of single file programs static variables are defined within functions and individually have the same scope as automatic variable. But static variables retain their values throughout the execution of program within their previous values.

Points to remember:

• The specifier precedes the declaration. Static and the value cannot be accessed outside of their defining function.

• The static variables may have same name as that of external variables but the local variable take precedence in the function. Therefore external variables maintain their independence with locally defined auto and static variables.

• Initial value is expressed as the constant and not expression.

• Zeros are assigned to all variables whose declarations do not include explicit initial values. Hence they always have assigned values.

• Initialisation is done only is the first execution.

Let us study this sample program to print value of a static variable:

Example

```
/*Program to illustrate the use of static variable*/
#include<stdio.h>
main()
{
int call_static();
int i,j;
i=j=0;
j = call_static();
printf("%d\n",j);
j = call_static();
printf("%d\n"j);
j = call_static();
printf("%d\n",j);
}
int  call_static()
{
static int i=1;
int  j;
j = i;
```

```
i + +;
return(j);
}
```

OUTPUT

1
2
3

This is because ***i*** is a static variable and retains its previous value in next execution of function call_static( ). To remind you ***j*** is having auto storage class. Both functions main and call_static have the same local variable ***i*** and ***j*** but their values never get mixed.

(d) Register Variables

Ans. Three storage class specifications namely, Automatic, External and Static, there is a register storage class. Registers are special storage areas within a computer's CPU. All the arithmetic and logical operations are carried out with these registers.

For the same program, the execution time can be reduced if certain values can be stored in registers rather than memory. These programs are smaller in size (as few instructions are required) and few data transfers are required. The reduction is there in machine code and not in source code. They are declared by the proceeding declaration by register reserved word as follows:

register int m;

Points to remember:

- These variables are stored in registers of computers. If the registers are not available they are put in memory.
- Usually 2 or 3 register variable are there in the program.
- Scope is same as automatic variable, local to a function in which they are declared.
- Address operator '&' cannot be applied to a register variable.
- If the register is not available the variable is though to be like the automatic variable.
- Usually associated integer variable but with other types it is allowed having same size (short or unsigned).
- Can be formal arguments in functions.
- Pointers to register variables are not allowed.

These variables can be used for loop indices also to increase efficiency.

MCS-011 : Problem Solving and Programming
December, 2017

Note: *Question number 1 is* **compulsory.** *Answer any three questions from the rest.*

Q1. (a) Write an algorithm and draw corresponding flow chart to check whether the given number is prime or not.

Ans.

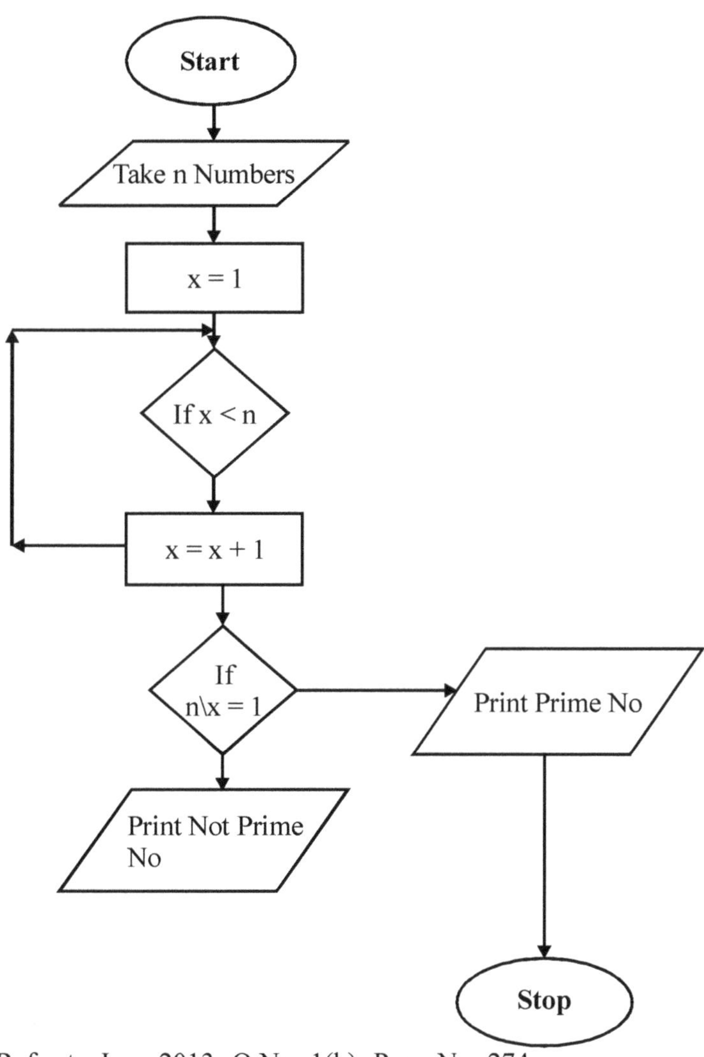

Now, Refer to June-2013, Q.No.-1(b), Page No.-274

(b) Write a program to search an element in a given list of elements using linear search.

Ans. Refer to June-2010, Q.No.-2(a), Page No.-227

(c) Differentiate between a macro and a function. To illustrate, write a macro and a function to swap values of 2 variables x and y.

Ans. Refer to December 2013, Q.No.-3(a), Page No.-284

The idea is that a variable defined in a block structure exists only inside the block structure. So, I can create a temporary variable without affecting the code.

Here is my solution:

```
#include <stdio.h>

#define swap(t, x, y) {t tmp = x; x = y; y = tmp;}
int main() {
 int x = 10, y = 2;
 swap(int, x, y);
 printf("%d %d", x, y);
 return 0;
}
```

c macros

(d) Write a program to read a file and count the number of lines in the file.

Note: Should not use an in-built function.

Ans. Refer to Chapter-2, Q.No.-8, Page No.-54

Q2. (a) What are Linker errors? Also explain Logical and Runtime errors.

Ans. Linker Errors

If a program contains syntax errors then the program does not compile, but it may happen that the program compiles successfully but we are unable to get the executable file, this happens when there are certain linker errors in the program. For example, the object code of certain standard library function is not present in the standard C library; the definition for this function is present in the header file that is why we do not get a compiler error. Such kinds of errors are called linker errors. The executable file would be created successfully only if these linker errors are corrected.

Logical and Runtime Errors

After the program is compiled and linked successfully we execute the program. Now there are three possibilities:

(1) The program executes and we get correct results,
(2) The program executes and we get wrong results, and
(3) The program does not execute completely and aborts in between.

The first case simply means that the program is correct. In the second case, we get wrong results; it means that there is some logical mistake in our program. This kind of error is known as logical error. This error is the most difficult to correct. This error is corrected by debugging. Debugging is the process of removing the errors from the program. This means manually checking the program step by step and verifying the results at each step. Debugging can be made easier by a tracer provided in Turbo C environment.

(b) Using structures, write a C program to calculate the Gross salary and Net salary, if Basic, Grade Pay, TA and DA are given. Deductions like Loans, Tax, LIC, etc. need to be considered, if any.
Note: Assumptions can be made wherever necessary and list them.
Ans. Same as June-2006, Q.No.-5(a), Page No.-151

Q3. (a) Explain *For* loop and *Do* loop control statements with an example for each.
Ans. Refer to Chapter-2, Page No.-28 and Page No.-30

(b) Explain any four string functions with an example for each.
Ans. Refer to June 2016, Q.No.-3 (b), Page No.-300

Q4. (a) Explain the categories of functions. Also illustrate a *"function with arguments and has no return value"*.
Ans. We categorise a function's invoking (calling) depending on arguments or parameters and their returning a value. In simple words we can divide a function's invoking into four types depending on whether parameters are passed to a function or not and whether a function returns some value or not. The various types of invoking functions are:
- With no arguments and with no return value.
- With no arguments and with return value
- With arguments and with no return value
- With arguments and with return value.

Function with Arguments and have no return value
If a function includes arguments but does not return anything, it falls in this category. One way communication takes place between the calling and the called function.

Before proceeding further, first we discuss the type of arguments or parameters here. There are two types of arguments:

- Actual arguments
- Formal arguments

Let us take an example to make this concept clear:

Write a program to calculate sum of any three given numbers.

```
#include <stdio.h>
main()
{
int a1, a2, a3;
void sum(int, int, int);
printf("Enter three numbers:");
scanf("%d%d%d",&a1,&a2,&a3);
sum(a1,a2,a3); /* Type 3 function */
}

/* function to calculate sum of three numbers */
void sum (int f1, int f2, int f3)
{
int s;
s=f1+f2+f3;
printf("/nThe sum of the three numbers is %d\n",s);
}
```

OUTPUT

Enter three numbers: 23 34 45

The sum of the three numbers is 102

Here f1, f2, f3 are *formal arguments* and a1, a2, a3 are *actual arguments.* Thus we see in the function declaration, the arguments are formal arguments, but when values are passed to the function during function call, they are actual arguments.

(b) What is Recursion? Write a program to find the factorial of a number.

Ans. Refer to June-2011, Q.No.-5(c), Page No.-244

Q5. (a) What are Unions? Give an example code segment to initiate a union and to access a member of a union.

Ans. Refer to Chapter-2, Q.No.-4, Page No.-48

(b) Write a program to test whether the given string is a number palindrome or not.

Ans. Refer to June-2010, Q.No.-1(b), Page No.-225

MCS-011 : Problem Solving and Programming
June, 2018

Note: *Question number 1 is* ***compulsory.*** *Answer any three questions from the rest.*

Q1. (a) Write an algorithm and draw the corresponding flowchart to calculate the factorial of a given number.

Ans. Refer to June-2005, Q.No.-1(a) (Pg. No.-105)

Following is an algorithm to calculate the factorial of the given number:

(1) Start
(2) Read the number n
(3) [Initialize]
  i ← 1 , fact ← 1
(4) Repeat steps 4 through 6 until i = n
(5) fact ← fact * i
(6) i ← i + 1
(7) Print fact
(8) Stop

(b) Write a program to find the maximum marks among the given marks of 10 students.

Ans. Program;

```
#include < stdio.h>
int main ( ) {
int a{10};
int i;
int greatest ;
printf ("Enter ten values:") ;
// Store 10 numbers in an array
for (i = 0 ; i < 10 ; i ++) {
scanf ("%d", &a[ i ]);
}
// Assume that a[0] is greatest
greatest = a [0] ;
for (i = 0 ; i < 10 ; i ++) {
if (a [ i ] > greatest) {
greatest = a [ i ] ;
```

```
}
}
print f ("
Greatest of ten numbers is %d", greatest);
return 0 ;
}
```

(c) Write a macro to display string "*Cobol*" in the following pattern:

C
C O
C O B
C O B O
C O B O L
C O B O L
C O B O
C O B
C O
C

Ans. /* Program to display the string as given in the problem */

```
# include<stdio.h>
# define        LOOP  for(x=0; x<5; x++)                      \
                {         y=x+1;                               \
                      printf("%-5.*s\n", y, string); }         \
                      for (x=4; x>=0; x- -)                    \
                      {          y=x+1;                        \
                      printf("%-5.*s\n",y, string; }           \
main ()
{
        int x, y;
        static char string [ ]="COBOL";
        printf ("\n");
        LOOP;
}
```

When the above program is executed the reference to macro (loop) is replaced by the set of statement contained within the macro definition.

OUTPUT

```
C
C O
C O B
C O B O
C O B O L
C O B O L
C O B O
C O B
C O
C
```

(d) Write a program to copy the file contents of file1 to another file, file2. Write the complete program using files concept of C programming.
Ans. Same as June-2005, Q.No.-2(b) (Pg. No.-114)

Q2. (a) Define a pointer. How is a pointer variable different from an array? Illustrate the pointers concept with the help of a program in C.
Ans. Refer to Chapter-2, Q.No.-1 and Q. No.-2 (Pg. No.-40, 42, 43)

(b) Write a program to calculate an air ticket fare after discount, given the following conditions:
If passenger is
(i) below 14 years then there is 50% discount on fare.
(ii) above 50 years, 20% discount.
(iii) above 14 and below 50 then 10% discount only.
Note: Assumptions can be made wherever necessary and list them.
Ans. /* Program to calculate an Air ticket fare after discount */

```
# include < stdio.h>
main ()
{
int age;
float fare;
printf("\n Enter the age of passenger:\n");
scanf ("%d",&age);
printf("\n Enter the Air ticket fare \n").
scanf("%f',&fare);
```

```
if (age < 14)
    fare = fare - 0.5 * fare;
else
    if (age <= 50)
    {
        fare = fare - 0.1 * fare;
    }
        else
    {
        fare = fare - 0.2 * fare;
    }
print f("\n Air ticket fare to be charged after discount is %.2f', fare);
}
```

OUTPUT

Enter the age of passenger

12

Enter the Air ticket fare

2000.00

Air ticket fare to be charged after discount is 1000.00

Q3. (a) Explain GOTO, BREAK and CONTINUE statements with an example for each.

Ans. The **goto** statement is used to alter the normal sequence of program instructions by transferring the control to some other portion of the program. The syntax is as follows:

goto label;

Here, label is an identifier that is used to label the statement to which control will be transferred. The targeted statement must be preceded by the unique label followed by colon.

label : statement;

Although goto statement is used to alter the normal sequence of program execution but its usage in the program should be avoided. The most common applications are:

but its usage in the program should be avoided. The most common applications are:

(i) To branch around statements under certain conditions in place of use of if- else statement,

(ii) To jump to the end of the loop under certain conditions bypassing the rest of statements inside the loop in place of continue statement,
(iii) To jump out of the loop avoiding the use of break statement.
goto can never be used to jump into the loop from outside and it should be preferably used for forward jump.
Situations may arise, however, in which the goto statement can be useful. To the possible extent, the use of the goto statement should generally be avoided.
Let us consider a program to illustrate goto and label statements.

Example:

Write a program to print first 10 even numbers

```
/* Program to print 10 even numbers */
#include <stdio.h>
main()
{
int i=2;
while(1)
   {
   printf("%d ",i);
   i=i+2;
   if (i>=20)
   goto outside;
   }
 outside : printf("over");
  }
```

OUTPUT

2 4 6 8 10 12 14 16 18 20 over

BREAK

Sometimes, it is required to jump out of a loop irrespective of the conditional test value. **Break** statement is used inside any loop to allow the control jump to the immediate statement following the loop. The syntax is as follows:

break;

When nested loops are used, then **break** jumps the control from the loop where it has been used. Break statement can be used inside any loop i.e., while, do-while, for and also in switch statement.
Let us consider a program to illustrate break statement.

Example

Write a program to calculate the first smallest divisor of a number.

```
/*Program to calculate smallest divisor of a number */
#include <stdio.h>
main( )
{
int div,num,i;
printf("Enter any number:\n");
scanf("%d",&num);
for (i=2;i<=num;++i)
{
if ((num % i) == 0)
{
printf("Smallest divisor for number %d is %d",num,i);
break;
}
}
}
```

OUTPUT

Enter any number:

9

Smallest divisor for number 9 is 3

In the above program, we divide the input number with the integer starting from 2 onwards, and print the smallest divisor as soon as remainder comes out to be zero. Since we are only interested in first smallest divisor and not all divisors of a given number, so jump out of the for loop using break statement without further going for the next iteration of for loop.

Break is different from exit. Former jumps the control out of the loop while exit stops the execution of the entire program.

Unlike break statement, which is used to jump the control out of the loop, it is sometimes required to skip some part of the loop and to continue the execution with next loop iteration. Continue statement used inside the loop helps to bypass the section of a loop and passes the control to the beginning of the loop to continue the execution with the next loop iteration. The syntax is as follows:

continue;

Let us see the program given below to know the working of the continue statement.

Example

Write a program to print first 20 natural numbers skipping the numbers divisible by 5.

```
/* Program to print first 20 natural numbers skipping the numbers divisible by 5 */
#include <stdio.h>
main( )
{
int i;
for (i=1;i<=20;++i)
{
if ((i % 5) == 0)
continue;
printf("%d ",i);
}
}
```

OUTPUT

1 2 3 4 6 7 8 9 11 112 13 14 16 17 18 19

Here, the printf statement is bypassed each time when value stored in ***i*** is divisible by 5.

(b) Write a program to find the string length without using strlen() function.

Ans. Refer to Chapter-5, Q.No.-25 (Pg. No.-98)

Q4. (a) Explain function call by reference. What are the advantages and disadvantages of it? Illustrate with the help of a code segment written in C.

Ans. Function call by reference in C. The call by reference method of passing arguments to afunction copies the address of an argument into the formal parameter. Inside the function, the address is used to access the actual argument used in the call. It means the changes made to the parameter affect the passed argument.

Advantages of passing by reference:

- References allow a function to change the value of the argument, which is sometimes useful. Otherwise, const references can be used to guarantee the function won't change the argument.

• Because a copy of the argument is not made, pass by reference is fast, even when used with large structs or classes.
• References can be used to return multiple values from a function (via out parameters).
• References must be initialized, so there's no worry about null values.
Disadvantages of passing by reference:
• Because a non-const reference cannot be initialized with an const l-value or an r-value (e.g. a literal or an expression), arguments to reference parameters must be normal variables.
• It can be hard to tell whether a parameter passed by non-const reference is meant to be input, output, or both. Judicious use of const and a naming suffix for out variables can help.
• It's impossible to tell from the function call whether the argument may change. An argument passed by value and passed by reference looks the same. We can only tell whether an argument is passed by value or reference by looking at the function declaration. This can lead to situations where the programmer does not realize a function will change the value of the argument.

Call by Reference/pointer/Address:

```
#include<stdio.h>
void interchange (int *num1, int *num2)
{
        int temp;
        temp = *num1;
        *num1 = *num2;
        *num2=temp;
}
int main () {
int num1 = 50, num2=70;
interchange (&num1, &num2);
printf("\nNumer 1 : %d", num1);
printf("\n Number 2 : %d" num2);
return (0);
}
```

(b) Write a program in C to take the marks of 4 courses (TEE and Assignments individually for each) and calculate the Total, Percentage and Grade.

Note: 40% is the pass marks for each component (TEE and Assignments) of a course.

Grade: A – Distinction – More than 75%
B – Very Good – 60% to 74.9%
C – Very Good – 50% to 59.9%
D – Average – 40% to 49.9%
E – Unsuccessful – Less than 40%

Ans.
```
#include < stdio. h>
void main ()
{
int n1, n2, n3, n4, m1, m2, m3, m4, p1, p2, p3, p4, q1, q2, q3, q4;
    Printf ("Enter the marks of course i");
    Scanf ("%d, %d, %d, %d", n1, n2, n3, n4);
    printf ("Enter the marks of course 2");
    Scanf ("%d %d %d %d", m1, m2, m3, m4);
    printf ("Enter the marks of course 3");
    Scanf ("%d %d %d %d", p1, p2, p3, p4);
    Printf (" Enter the marks of course 4");
     Scanf ("%d %d %d %d", q1 , q2, q3, q4");
float pe1 = (n1+ n2 + n3 +n4)/4;
float pe2 = (m1 +m2+ m3+ m4)/4;
float pe3 = (p1 +p2 +p3+p4)/4;
float pe4 = (q1+q2+q3+q4)/4;
Printf (" Percentage of every course", & pe1,&pe2,&pe3,&pe4);
{ if (pe1 > 75)
printf (" Distinction");
else if (pe1 > 60 && pe1< 74.9)
          printf ("very Good")
else if (pe1 > 50 && pe1< 59.9)
printf ("Good");
else if (pe1 > 40 && pe1< 49.9)
printf (" Average");
else if (pe1 < 40)
printf ("unsuccessful ");
}
{
{ if (pe2 > 75)
```

```
printf (" Distinction");
else if (pe2 > 60 && pe2< 74.9)
        printf ("very Good")
else if (pe2 > 50 && pe2< 59.9)
printf ("Good");
else if (pe2 > 40 && pe2< 49.9)
printf (" Average");
printf ("unsuccessful ");
}
{
{ if (pe3 > 75)
printf (" Distinction");
else if (pe3 > 60 && pe3 < 74.9)
        printf ("very Good")
else if (pe3 > 50 && pe3 < 59.9)
printf ("Good");
else if (pe3 > 40 && pe3 < 49.9)
printf (" Average");
printf ("unsuccessful ");
}
{
{ if (pe4 > 75)
printf (" Distinction");
else if (pe4 > 60 && pe4 < 74.9)
        printf ("very Good")
else if (pe4 > 50 && pe4< 59.9)
printf ("Good");
else if (pe4 > 40 && pe4 < 49.9)
printf (" Average");
printf ("unsuccessful ");
}
{
```

Q5. (a) Write a program in C language to multiply two matrices A and B of size 3 × 3.

Ans. Same as Chapter-5, Q.No.-2 (Pg. No.-74)

(b) Differentiate between sequential and random access files.

Ans. When we are talking about sequential or random access to data files we refer to the way data is written or read from a file on a computer system.

Sequential Access to a data file means that the computer system reads or writes information to the file sequentially, starting from the beginning of the file and proceeding step by step.

On the other hand, Random Access to a file means that the computer system can read or write information anywhere in the data file. This type of operation is also called "Direct Access" because the computer system knows where the data is stored (using Indexing) and hence goes "directly" and reads the data.

Sequential access has advantages when you access information in the same order all the time. Also is faster than random access.

On the other hand, random access file has the advantage that you can search through it and find the data you need more easily (using indexing for example). Random Access Memory (RAM) in computers works like that.

(c) Write short notes on the following:

(i) 3-dimensional arrays and their significance.

Ans. A multi-dimensional array is an array with more than one level/ dimension. For example, a 2D array, or two-dimensional array is an array of arrays, meaning it is amatrix of rows and columns (think of a table). A 3D array adds another dimension, turning it into an array of array of arrays.

Three Dimensional Array

```
// C Program to store and print 12 values entered by the user
# include <stdio.h>
int main ()
{
        int i, j, k, test [2] [3] [2];
        print f("Enter 12 values : \n");
        for (i = 0; i < 2; ++i) {
                for (j = 0; j < 3; ++j) {
                        scanf ("%d", &test [i] [j] [k]);
                }
```

```
        }
}
// printing values with proper index.
print f("\nDisplaying values:\n");
for (i = 0; i < 2; ++i) {
        for (j = 0; j < 3; ++j) {
                for (k = 0; k< 2; ++k) {
                printf ("test [%d][%d][%d] = %d\n", i, j, k, test [i][j][
                }
        }
}
return 0;
}
```

OUTPUT

```
Enter 12 values:
1 2 3 4 5 6 7  8 9 10 11 12
Displaying Values:
test [0] [0] [0] = 1
test [0] [0] [1] = 2
test [0] [1] [0] = 3
test [0] [1] [1] = 4
test [0] [2] [0] = 5
test [0] [2] [1] = 6
test [1] [0] [0] = 7
test [1] [0] [1] = 8
test [1] [1] [0] = 9
test [1] [1] [1] = 10
test [1] [2] [0] = 11
test [1] [2] [1] = 12
```

(ii) Ternary operator with an illustration.

Ans. The ternary operator is an operator that takes three arguments. The first argument is a comparison argument, the second is the result upon a true comparison, and the third is the result upon a false comparison. If it helps you can think of the operator as shortened way of writing an if-else statement.

C# includes a special type of decision making operator '?:' called the ternary operator.

Variable Syntax

Boolean Expression? First Statement: Second Statement ternary operator includes three parts. First part (before?) includes conditional expression that returns boolean value true or false. Second part (after ? and before :) contains a statement which will be returned if the conditional expression in the first part evalutes to true. The third part includes another statement which will be returned if the conditional expression returns false.

"Education is the most powerful weapon which you can use to change the world."

–Nelson Mandela

MCS-011 : Problem Solving and Programming
December, 2018

Note: *Question number 1 is* **compulsory.** *Answer any three questions from the rest.*

Q1. (a) Write an algorithm to find the highest marks. obtained by student(s) in "C programming" in a batch of 10 students. Also draw flow chart for this algorithm.
(c) Write a C program which takes a string as input and displays it length. (Do not use built-in strlen function).
(c) Write a program to swap the values of two variables using
(i) Pass by value method, and
(ii) Pass by reference method.
(d) What is the difference between a structure and a union? Write the syntax for declaration of a union, initialising the elements of union and also accessing its members in the program.

Q2. (a) Write a C program to copy the contents of a file into a newly created file (Use file handling concept).
(b) Write a C program using recursive function to find the factorial of a give number.

Q3. (a) Write a C program to add two matrices of size 3 × 3.
(b) What is a pointer? With the help of a program to find the square of a number, explain how a function returns a pointer.

Q4. (a) Write a macro to evaluate $f(x) = 2x^2 + 3x + 5$.
(b) Write a program to take two strings as input and append the second string to the first string using array.
(c) Explain the use of malloc(), calloc() and realloc() and write their syntax.

Q5. (a) Using structures, write a C program to calculate the Gross salary and Net salary, if Basic pay, Grade pay, TA and DA and other allowances and deductions are given as inputs.
(b) Explain the following with the help of a suitable example for each:
(i) if statement
(ii) nested if statement
(iii) switch statement
(iv) for loop

MCS-011 : Problem Solving and Programming
June, 2019

Note: *Question number 1 is* **compulsory.** *Answer any three questions from the rest.*

Q1. (a) Write an algorithm to find largest and smallest number among three numbers given as input. Also draw flowchart for this algorithm.

Ans. Step 1: Start

Step 2: Declare variables a,b and c.

Step 3: Read variables a,b and c.

Step 4: If a>b

    If a>c

        Display a is the largest number.

    Else

        Display c is the smallest number.

  Else

    If b>c

        Display b is the largest number.

    Else

        Display c is the smallest number.

Step 5: Stop

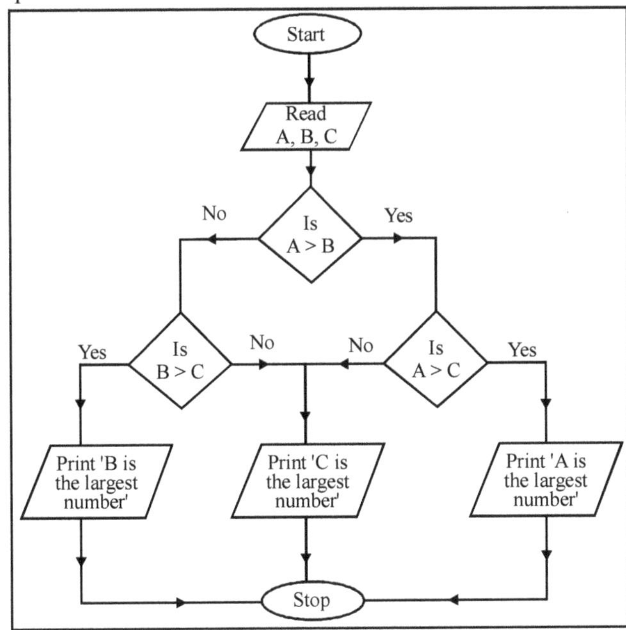

(b) Explain the use of break and continue statements with the help of a program.

Ans. Refer to June-2018, Q.No.-3(a) (Pg. No.-332)

(c) Write a program to generate the following pattern:

1

1 2

1 2 3

1 2 3 4

1 2 3 4 5

Ans. Refer to June-2007, Q.No.-1(c) (Pg. No.-174)

(d) Write a menu-driven program using switch statement to perform the following arithmetic operations on two variables:

(i) Add

(ii) Subtract

(iii) Multiplication

(iv) Division

Ans.
```
#include<stdio.h>
#include<conio.h>
void main()
{
  int a,b;
  int op;
  //clrscr();
  printf(" 1.Addition\n 2.Subtraction\n 3.Multiplication\n 4.Division\n");
  printf("Enter the values of a & b: ");
  scanf("%d %d",&a,&b);
  printf("Enter your Choice : ");
  scanf("%d",&op);
  switch(op)
  {
  case 1  :
    printf("Sum of %d and %d is : %d",a,b,a+b);
    break;
  case 2  :
    printf("Difference of %d and %d is : %d",a,b,a-b);
    break;
  case 3  :
    printf("Multiplication of %d and %d is : %d",a,b,a*b);
```

```
      break;
   case 4  :
      printf("Division of Two Numbers is %d : ",a/b);
      break;
   default :
      printf(" Enter Your Correct Choice.");
      break;
   }
   getch();
}
```

Q2. (a) Write a C program using array of pointers to strings to read name of your five friends and display them.

Ans.

```
#include <stdio.h>
#include <String.h>
int main()
{
//initializing the pointer string array
char *names[]={
"sumit",
"deepak",
"ritu",
"divya",
"neha"
};
char **ARRAY[5]={"SUMIT","DEEPAK","RITU","DIVYA","NEHA"};
int i,j,a;
printf("The names are:\n");
for(i=0 ;i<5 ;i++ )
printf("%s\n",names[i]);
//arranging names in alphabetically using selection sort
for(i=0 ;i<5 ;i++ ){
for(j=i+1 ;j<5 ;j++ ){
a=strcmp(names[i],names[j])
if(a>0){
temp=names[i];
names[i]=names[j];
names[j]=temp;
}
}
```

```
}
printf("The arranged names are:\n");
for(i=0 ;i<5 ;i++ )
printf("%s\n",names[i]);
return 0;
}
```

Output:-

```
The names are:
sumit
deepak
ritu
divya
neha
The arranged names are:
deepak
ritu
divya
neha
sumit
```

(b) Write a C program to calculate simple interest. If principal amount, rate of interest and duration are given as input.

$$\left(\textbf{Note : SI} = \frac{\textbf{P} \times \textbf{R} \times \textbf{T}}{\textbf{100}}\right)$$

Ans.

```
/**
C program to calculate simple interest
 **/
#include <stdio.h>
int main()
{
   float principle, time, rate, SI;
   /* Input principle, rate and time */
   printf("Enter principle (amount): ");
    scanf("%f", &principle);
   printf("Enter time: ");
    scanf("%f", &time);
   printf("Enter rate: ");
    scanf("%f", &rate);
   /* Calculate simple interest */
   SI = (principle * time * rate) / 100;
```

```
    /* Print the resultant value of SI */
    printf("Simple Interest = %f", SI);
    return 0;
}
```

Output
Enter principle (amount): 1200
Enter time: 2
Enter rate: 5.4
Simple Interest = 129.600006

Q3. (a) Write a C program to create two matrices A and B of size 3 × 3 and find A × B.

Ans. Same as Chapter-5, Q.No.-2 (Pg. No.-74)

(b) Explain the following with the help of an example for each:

(i) Static variable

Ans. Refer to June-2017, Q.No.-5(c) (Pg. No.-323)

(ii) Global variable

Ans. Refer to Dec-2009, Q.No.-2(a) (Pg. No.-220)

(iii) Register variable

Ans. Refer to June-2017, Q.No.-5(d) (Pg. No.-324)

(iv) Local variable

Ans. Refer to Dec-2009, Q.No.-2(a) (Pg. No.-220)

Q4. (a) Write a C program to create a macro to evaluate:

$$f(x) = 3x^3 + 2x^2 + x$$

Ans.

```
# include<stdio.h>
# define f(x) 3*x*x*x + 2*x*x + x
main()
{
int num;
printf("enter value x: ");
scanf("%d",&num);
printf("\nvalue of f(num) is %d", f(num));
}
```

(b) Write a C program which display the number of lines in a given file.

....

Ans. Refer to June-2009, Q.No.-5(b) (Pg. No.-216)

(c) Define recursion. With the help of a small C program segment and explain it.

Ans. Refer to June-2011, Q.No.-5(c) (Pg. No.-204)

Q5. (a) Explain the use of the following file functions:

(i) fseek ()

Ans. Refer to June-2013, Q.No.-5(iii) (Pg. No.-281)

(ii) rewind

Ans. The rewind function is used to move file pointer position to the beginning of the file. In a C program, we use rewind() as below.

rewind(fp);

(iii) ftell ()

Ans. Refer to June-2013, Q.No.-5(iv) (Pg. No.-281)

(iv) fwrite

Ans. The fwrite() function is used to write records (sequence of bytes) to the file. A record may be an array or a structure.

Syntax of fwrite() function

```
fwrite( ptr, int size, int n, FILE *fp );
```

The fwrite() function takes four arguments.

ptr : ptr is the reference of an array or a structure stored in memory.

size : size is the total number of bytes to be written.

n : n is number of times a record will be written.

FILE* : FILE* is a file where the records will be written in binary mode.

(b) Write a program to check whether a given string is a palindrone or not.

Ans. Refer to June-2005, Q.No.-1(c) (Pg. No.-107)

www.ingramcontent.com/pod-product-compliance
Ingram Content Group UK Ltd.
Pitfield, Milton Keynes, MK11 3LW, UK
UKHW021708190726
13853UKWH00001B/465

9 788189 086428